T0327067

Gary, the Most American
of All American Cities

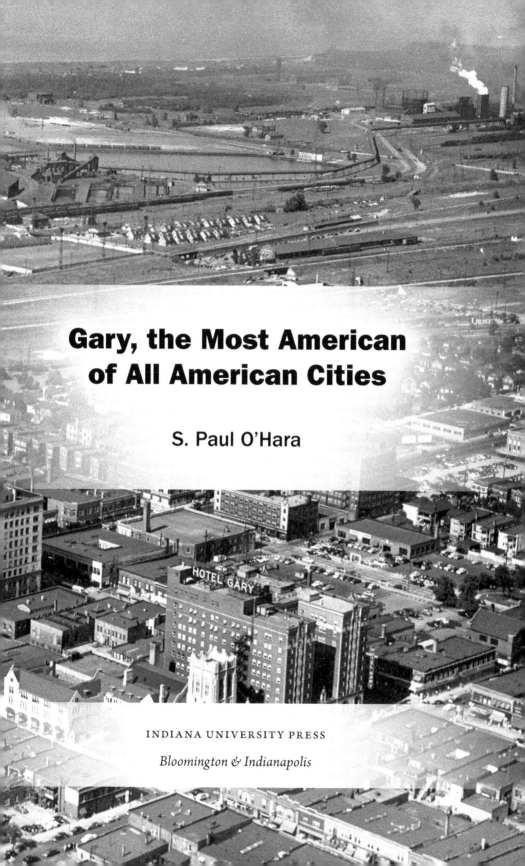

Gary, the Most American of All American Cities

S. Paul O'Hara

INDIANA UNIVERSITY PRESS

Bloomington & Indianapolis

This book is a publication of

Indiana University Press
601 North Morton Street
Bloomington, Indiana 47404-3797 USA

iupress.indiana.edu

Telephone orders 800-842-6796
Fax orders 812-855-7931
Orders by e-mail iuporder@indiana.edu

⊖ The paper used in this publication
meets the minimum requirements of the
American National Standard for Information Sciences—Permanence of Paper for
Printed Library Materials, ANSI Z39.48-
1992.

Manufactured in the United States of
America

Library of Congress Cataloging-in-Publi-
cation Data

O'Hara, S. Paul.
  Gary, the most American of all American
cities / S. Paul O'Hara.
    p. cm.
  Includes bibliographical references and
index.
  ISBN 978-0-253-35598-0 (cloth : alk.
paper) — ISBN 978-0-253-22288-6 (pbk.
: alk. paper) 1. Gary (Ind.)—History.
2. Steel industry and trade—Indiana—
Gary—History. 3. United States Steel
Corporation—History. 4. Industrialization—Social aspects—Indiana—Gary.
I. Title.
  F534.G2O43 2011
  977.2'99—dc22
                                    2010026584

1 2 3 4 5 16 15 14 13 12 11

We might venture that even more tragic than any classical or Shakespearean drama is the crisis of illumination when man realizes, much too late for any last minute panaceas, that he is unequal to the task of dealing with a universe of his own manufacture. Gloucester in King Lear blames the gods who kill us for sport, as wanton boys do flies. Shakespeare was even then at liberty to accuse the "gods." But whom dare we blame for Gary, Indiana?

PERRY MILLER

Gary is America. Every American city is Gary writ large or small.

GARRY JOEL AUGUST

CONTENTS

ACKNOWLEDGMENTS

I owe a great deal to the people who have helped me along the way in this project. The following is but a small sample of the most influential. This project started years ago as a dissertation, and as such I am particularly grateful for the guidance and patience of John Bodnar. I am indebted to many other members of the faculty of Indiana University, including but not exclusive to Dror Wahrman, Wendy Gamber, Eric Sandweiss, Claude Clegg, Steven Stowe, and Daniel James. I owe a special debt to James Madison, who started this project by offering a young graduate student a chance to guest lecture in his Indiana history class. My thanks to John Howe, Hyman Berman, and David Roediger, who all helped me find my way. More recently my colleagues at Xavier University have created both an intellectual and social environment for which I am thankful. Both they and the students in my classes have probably heard more about Gary, Indiana, over the years than they probably ever thought they wanted.

Several conferences have served as test forums for much of this material, and I would especially like to thank Leon Fink and the Newberry Seminar on Labor History as well as James Connolly and the Center for Middletown Studies, Small Cities Conference for their close readings and great suggestions. Along the way several other scholars have offered their advice and criticisms, including Jefferson Cowie, Joseph Heathcott, Robert Bruno, Marc Rodriguez, Joseph Bigott, James Lane, Steve McShane, and Andrew Cayton. During the research for this project, the expertise and assistance of archive staff proved an invaluable help. The staffs of the Chicago Historical Society, the Chicago Public Library, the Calumet Regional Archives, and the Indiana Historical Society know their material so well that they often pointed me in new directions and found great materials. The staff of Xavier's library also helped me track down a number of publications. My thanks go as well to my editor, Linda Oblack, and the staff of Indiana University Press.

This project incubated for a long time, so I owe a great deal to many scholars and friends. There are many names, but I mention a couple of the most influential. My thanks to Steven Sheehan, Lynn Pohl, Margaret Puskar-Pasewicz, Thomas Lappas, Nathan Wood, Elizabeth McMahon, Susan Ferentinos, Martin Minner, Francisco Barbosa, Sarah Keller, Richard Pizzi, Paul Unglaub, Christopher Weaver, and Timothy Borden. The largest debt is owed to Julia Cummings O'Hara, whose help cannot be done justice in such a small space as this. I also need to thank my sisters, Kris McCafferty and Jean Benson. Through what seemed like countless hours of playing school, they not only practiced their teaching but also made me into a student. All this is probably their fault. (Now may I go outside and play?) My parents, Steve and Katy O'Hara, have always been there with support, guidance, inspiration, and humor; this project was made possible by their efforts. It was my parents who taught me (largely by showing me) the importance of work and the pride and craftsmanship that goes into all labor. My thanks to Jerry for sharing my interests in big machinery and the details of how things work and for asking a lot of questions. His inquisitive nature and wide-eyed enthusiasm is infectious; it's a cool world when you see it as he sees it. Lastly, my thanks to Julie, who has made the years of research, writing, editing, discussing, and obsessing a grand adventure that I would not trade for all the steel in Gary.

Gary, the Most American of All American Cities

"Built as It Is on Shifting Sand"

An amazing feature of Gary, built as it is on shifting sands, is that it is actually so solid, so permanent, so strong. There is nothing suggestive of the shoddy or the temporary. Schools, libraries, clubs, commercial buildings, homes, churches, meeting places, all have the aspect as of having been built for permanence. The city has arisen so swiftly, so solidly, just because a great corporation ordered it! It is vastly more of an achievement than as if it had been ordered by an arbitrary monarch, with absolute control of a nation and of its resources.

ROBERT SHACKLETON, *THE BOOK OF CHICAGO,* 1920

The story of Gary, Indiana, has been told in many ways. When U.S. Steel finished building its newest steel production center in 1909, the corporation named the city after its chairman, Judge Elbert H. Gary. Because the company had seemingly conjured the city and its mill (or perhaps the mill and its city, because it is this very relationship that would determine much about Gary) out of thin air in only three years, the firing of the hearths in Gary prompted a celebration of the city's technological achievements, the continued march of progress, and the audaciousness of American industry. The business magazine *Survey* noted that "accustomed as Americans of this day are to rapid accomplishment, not one who visits the suddenly created town of Gary . . . fails to experience a new thrill of achievement." As the fanfare continued, boosters for the city proclaimed Gary the "city of the century," a moniker that soon graced all of the city's promotional literature and official letterhead. "This is not the age of magicians, we are told," concluded Elliott Flower of *Putnam's Magazine,* "and yet, judged by ordinary standards, the building of the city . . . must be regarded as something very close to magic." Likewise, the *Independent* proclaimed that "in Gary we see the so-called trust at its best. The old order is passing away. Man, the conqueror, and man, the liberator, takes on new dignity and glory as man, the creator."[1]

For its part U.S. Steel seemed to embrace its role in the momentous construction. It orchestrated the pageantry of the mill's opening including the arrival, amid blowing whistles, ringing bells, and firing cannons, of the first shipment of iron ore aboard the lake freighter *Elbert H. Gary.* Many within the crowd of thousands scrambled to collect pieces of iron ore as mementos. Likewise, in January 1909, Mary Louise Gleason, the daughter of Superintendent William Palmer Gleason, lit the first blast furnace. In addition to these opening ceremonies, the company also detailed every step of the construction with photographs. Images depict what the sand dunes of the Indiana shore looked like before construction began. Each new building was carefully documented and juxtaposed against empty spaces from a couple of years earlier. Urban amenities such as the sewer system and the streetcar also received photographic attention. But the bulk of the photography of Gary's construction was reserved for the building of the steel works. Here was industrial modernity at its finest. Huge structures, massive construction machines, rail lines, ship slips, blast furnaces, and towering smokestacks dominated the photography of early Gary. From a sandy wasteland, this was the tabula rasa upon which American capital was to write its greatest success.[2]

By the late twentieth century, however, mention of Gary would mean something quite different. For many, Gary was the city one saw (and passed through) to get to Chicago. It became part of the inconvenience and excitement of journeying into the Windy City. It offered the traveler heading west on the Indiana Toll Road the first confirmation of urbanism and served, with its smokestacks, industries, and decaying buildings, as a clear juxtaposition to the glittering wealth of Chicago's downtown. In his prologue to *Nature's Metropolis,* historian William Cronon describes just such a journey through the city. "The city announced itself to our noses before we ever saw it," Cronon says of his childhood trips to Chicago, "and we always pressed our faces against the windows to locate the sweet pungent odor that was Gary. (Gary and Chicago blend in my child's eye view as a single place, united in a child's mythic name: The City)."[3] Gary became something both attached to Chicago and a place to be passed through on the way to Chicago.

Such a view of the Indiana Toll Road as an entrance into Chicago or a quick path through the wasteland would have surprised midcentury residents of the steel city. Indeed, the Eisenhower years had been very good to U.S. Steel and its Indiana fiefdom. By midcentury the corporation was booming because of the postwar economy, and it had earned a reputation as a good corporate citizen. While the city of Gary earned a different reputation as a hotbed of gambling, numbers, and prostitution, such entertainments were available because of the profits and wages possible across the tracks in the Gary Works. The city had enough local pride and political willpower to delay the building of the toll road until compromises about its location could be reached. Yet once the highway was completed, its placement alongside the rail lines that physically divided the mill from the city confirmed long-standing spatial and social divisions within Gary. The key division has always been mill and town; the coming of the toll road only reinforced this.[4]

These three views of Gary (the triumph of capital consolidation, the social and spatial divisions of the mid–twentieth century, and the city's relationship to its metropolitan neighbor in the late twentieth century) represent the variety of ways that the story of Gary has been told. Gary, in the minds of the people telling these stories, was part of larger trends of industrialization and capital mobility. For others, the city was a fascinating site (or social laboratory) of diverse ethnic and racial patterns. For still others, Gary was first and foremost an industrial town. The U.S. Steel Gary Works produced steel; its smokestacks vented the kinds of pollutants that such work creates. The city developed quite literally in the shadow of these works. "Gary is a steel town," wrote James O'Gara during a visit in 1949. "When you have said that, you have just about covered the ground."[5]

But of course it doesn't. The story lines seeking to explain the steel city demonstrate both the variety of narratives that people could apply to the city and the meaning and implications of these narratives. For the builders of Gary, mapping urban space became an important part of their vision for the city. In order to impose order upon the new space, they clearly delineated the industrial and residential space with clear boundaries such as rail lines or rivers. Despite the intricate planning U.S. Steel put into Gary's construction, the company never claimed it was creating a utopian experiment. Rather, U.S. Steel always said that Gary was built upon economic and geographic terms, not utopian ideals. Thus the corporation could never be held responsible for the conditions of the town; there were no expectations for the company to meet.

Yet, because Gary was a brand-new space, outside observers chose to read limitless possibilities onto the city. Gary had no standing traditions of neighborhood, community, separation, or segregation. Gary was equally a blank slate for all these social categories. Residents and non-residents of Gary read and understood the process of applying meaning to the city very differently. For outside observers it was a chance to judge the success of Gary the experiment as well as an opportunity to disparage Gary the industrial center. And for some city residents, it was a chance to redraw the racial lines of the city and impose their own version of order. By the middle of the twentieth century, as American opinions toward industrialism and industrial spaces began to shift, so too did stories about and images of Gary. While an official narrative of technological advancement and massive scale still existed, it applied largely to the mills of the Gary Works and not to the city. When people spoke of Gary, they often described decline and decay. Yet the reasons for this decline, the fault for the decay, and the timing of the shift varied by storyteller.

This study traces the changing attitudes toward Gary from its conception through the period of deindustrialization. It is a tale told largely by outsiders because they were the ones with the power to create and impose such imagery, and they often plugged Gary into already established plotlines. A history of the way people spoke of Gary is a series of snapshots that frame the various ways Americans understood and felt about industrialism and industrial spaces. As the concerns and obsessions shifted throughout the twentieth century, so did the snapshots of Gary that the larger American public saw. Early in the century, the fear was that Gary was a hotbed of labor radicalism and frightening foreignness. By the 1920s and 1930s, Gary had become a city of bootlegging and organized crime. As postwar America's fears shifted from political corruption and liquor-law violations to the morality of public sexuality and youth, so too did the descriptions of Gary. In the throes of the civil rights movement and white flight, the dominant image of Gary was a city of crime and danger defined by its blackness. There was of course a relationship between the lived realities of Gary and its shifting national image. In the early decades, Gary's population did consist primarily of new immigrants and their children. The election of African American mayor Richard G. Hatcher in 1967 did trigger a crisis of racial politics in the city, and white flight to the surrounding communities did alter the city's racial composition. However, there were also connections implicit within these narratives that differed from the social lives of Gary residents. The assumptions of immigrant radicalism or black crime were less descriptions of Gary than symbols of national concerns. Whether it was the juxtaposition of immigrant radicalism and melting pot Americanization, vice and postwar domesticity, or black power and white flight suburbanization, Gary served as an exemplar of what Americans dreamed of as well as what they feared. It became, as some would argue, a "microcosm of all American cities." For Gary in the twentieth century, the story of the "city of the century" was more accurately the tale of two cities. Gary the mills, within the public imagination, was always a triumph of technology and American industrial might. Gary the city played a much more complicated role and often served as a counterpoint to the order of the mills. The newly created steel city quickly became a screen onto which Americans projected all of their hopes and fears about modernization and industrial society. Gary's industrial origins, its ethnic and racial makeup, and its place as a national metaphor defined any discussion of the city.

The narratives people read onto Gary demonstrate the changing expectations from modernity and industrialism at the turn of the twentieth century through deindustrialization in the late twentieth century. Despite the rhetoric that accompanied the opening of the mills and the early boosterism of some of its residents, Gary was the city of the century not solely because it represented the triumph of massive machinery and capital mobility. Rather, Gary should bear that moniker because it so strikingly symbolized major cultural shifts from nineteenth- to twentieth-century views on the relationship between industry, technology, and society. Unlike other attempts at building new model industrial spaces such as Pullman, Illinois, in which proper urban planning was supposed to be a panacea for social conflict, U.S. Steel's plans for Gary (in part developed in the shadow of the Pullman experience) were not intended to eliminate social conflict but simply to contain and withstand it in the name of the most efficient productivity possible. Yet failure to avoid social upheaval was still seen by many as a failure of vision. What Gary meant, what it symbolized, and thus what accounted for its failures or successes were largely in the eye of the beholder.

As early as 1912, only three years after the first firing of Gary's furnaces, Woodrow Wilson campaigned against industrial consolidation and anti-American monopoly by singling out Gary as an example of an industrial fiefdom outside the American tradition.[6] In response to deep criticisms in 1929 about the city's lack of culture and refinement, local rabbi Garry Joel August would rebut not only those criticisms but Wilson's as well by saying that "Gary is America. Every American city is Gary writ large and small."[7] In the late 1960s and early 1970s, the Hatcher administration would use the same language to both defend the city and claim Great Society funds. "They are not just our problems," Mayor Hatcher would say, "they're the country's, because they exist in some degree in every city."[8] This is almost exactly the same wording and sentiment that Mayor Thomas V. Barnes would use in 1987 when asking for federal help to address loss of jobs and rising violence. In 2002, when ABC News producers launched their multi-part documentary *In Search of America,* one of the places they came was Gary. Whether it was 1912 or 2002, here was the basic discussion of Gary. The debate over whether or not Gary represented America was a debate about just what did represent America. For every Wilsonian declaration of Gary's strangeness, there was a counterargument, like local papers argued in 1919, that Gary was the "most American of all American cities."

EVERY AMERICAN CITY IS GARY WRIT LARGE OR SMALL

There is little doubt that industrialization altered the American landscape. It completely transformed patterns of production and consumption, introduced new types of work and leisure, altered the physical appearance of cities, and subordinated older ways of life. Scholars have long noted the extensive physical and social nature of this transformation—centered especially in late nineteenth- and early twentieth-century America. Fewer, however, have explored its cultural manifestations, especially the way people understood the changes that were going on around them. This study examines the ways individuals from different classes and backgrounds understood industrial transformation. It focuses on the new industrial city of Gary, Indiana, as a crucible of American cultural responses to industrialization. Just as industrialization created wealth, class divisions, and segregated cities, it also generated a diverse set of images that explained the course of industrial and urban change as America entered the twentieth century.

There has been a long tradition of using Gary as a site for historical exploration. The steel works at Gary show up often in histories of U.S. Steel, and the mill is frequently part of larger examinations of industrial policy and history. Many scholars, such as Raymond Mohl and Neil Betten, have explored the history of ethnic and racial patterns within the city itself. So too has James B. Lane described the rich social history of the city.[9] Gary has also been a site for detailed studies of social forces and political history, whether that was religious experience, immigrant education, racial politics, or environmental advocacy.[10] At the same time Gary has served as an example within larger studies of urbanization. Within these works, including Graham Romeyn Taylor's work in 1915 and Sam Bass Warner in the 1970s, Gary serves as the typical industrial satellite city. Gary was, according to Warner, "a mill town set within a metropolitan region where workers could live and labor in their own community instead of commuting to work, [which] was a characteristic type of the era. All such satellites owed their appearance to the configuration of rail transportation and the scale of late nineteenth-century mechanized manufacture."[11] As such, U.S. Steel's construction in Gary was no different from Pullman in Illinois, Westinghouse in Pittsburgh, or Ford at River Rouge; it was part of larger urban and industrial trends. Community studies about Gary have told us a great deal about the people who lived in the city. Yet to study Gary as its own milieu is to miss its intimate relationship with both industrial Chicago and the nation. At the same time, to lump it together with other industrial satellites within urban history or to think about it as a site of contestation within labor history is to miss its cultural significance and symbolic importance. A cultural history of Gary within the public imagination offers a different perspective.

These debates about Gary came to demonstrate the ways in which concerns about industrialism could exist alongside triumphs of industrialism. Gary represented a new departure in urban thinking and industrial planning by reimagining the role of the urban periphery. Rather than the *banlieue* (or outskirts) of Baron Georges Haussmann's Paris, which served as a dumping ground of all that one cannot plan center stage (or center city), Gary was part of a new conception that valued the periphery greatly as an indispensable part of proper city functioning.[12] In other words, in modern industrialized urbanism, the periphery was not peripheral or tangential but rather central. Finally, the story of Gary challenged the way people thought about community, regionalism, and center and margins. The cultural grid of Gary existed locally in terms of separation of mill and town, regionally in terms of the industrial metropolis of Chicago and its periphery, and nationally in terms of the persistent question of whether Gary represented Americanism or some sort of perversion of Americanism.

The meaning of Gary, and thus the meaning of twentieth-century industrialism, was debated by placing narrative structures onto the city. The words people choose to use matters. As both Hayden White and Natalie Zemon Davis show, there are common narratives that people tend to repeat when they tell stories or write tales. By placing their story into an already established trope, they are immediately infusing it with meaning and associations. There are assumed connections, endings, and contexts because of this choice of narrative.[13] Especially within the culture of industrial modernity, when so much seemed new and unknowable, these narratives allowed people not only to categorize the newness but also to apply meaning in an attempt to understand the whole. In her study of Victorian London, Judith Walkowitz argues that the accounts of sexuality, prostitution, violence, and death that surrounded the Jack the Ripper killings were Londoners' way of distinguishing the city's districts and applying narrative grids to make sense of the city. Likewise Peter Fritzsche contends that Berlin at the turn of the century existed largely as a "word city." The descriptions, connections, and contexts provided by the city's newspapers gave residents a sense of what their city was and thus who they were. The vision of a place may start simply with new language and discursive categories, but ultimately those visions will drive perceptions and shape the reality of that place.[14]

In one sense, this study tries to duplicate for Gary what Walkowitz and Fritzsche have done respectively for Victorian London and modern Berlin; it is a study of narrative grids read onto urban spaces to create a word city. It also resembles the kind of cultural study of urban myth and reputation that Arlette Farge and Jacques Revel have written on pre-Revolution Paris, Amy Gilman Srebnick has studied in Jacksonian New York, or that Carl Smith and Timothy Spears have written for modern Chicago.[15] Yet, of course, there are important differences between such cities and Gary. So many of the studies of nineteenth- and twentieth-century metropolises, whether they be cultural studies of narrative or spatial turn analyses of material culture, stem from an assumption that the modern metropolis serves as a microcosm of the liberal state and the modern nation.[16] Different factions, groups, peoples, and interests clash within the social and cultural context of the city. The metropolis, then, becomes a privileged site for various economic, social, political, and cultural interactions.[17] Major cities serve as important sites of spectacle, symbolism, and national identity which knowledgeable residents could read and contest. Such an assumption of the metropolis as a national microcosm, however, really only applies to central cities.

As Maiken Umbach has argued, the struggle for power and identity in "second cities" such as Barcelona and Hamburg was quite different. While such cities thrived on the rise of bourgeois liberalism and industrialized urbanization, much of their autonomy and importance were eclipsed by the central metropolis. This categorization more closely fits Chicago, not only with the city's constant effort to define and refine its industrial and commercial spaces but also with the city's dual arrogance and inferiority inherent within its label as the "Second City." Within the industrial city in particular, spatial and social divisions between spaces of work and leisure, class and ethnicity, and danger and safety began to mark the urban landscape. The structural presence of mills and an industrial working class transformed these urban spaces, hence the middle-class fascination, as Carl Smith has shown, with urban disasters, disorder, and redemption.[18]

However, Gary was neither a capital city embodying the nation nor a second city fretting over its growth in size or its status. It was a planned industrial city on the periphery of Chicago. It was not a mill town that slowly transformed itself into an industrial center, nor was it a major industrial metropolis dominating its region such as Manchester or Chicago. Yet it was not the expolis of multiple spaces and far-ranging meaning that Los Angeles has come to symbolize.[19] Rather, Gary was both mill town and industrial periphery. Its physical spaces were built by and controlled by U.S. Steel, and its narrative grid was shaped by others.[20] Unlike Berlin or Chicago, Gary residents had little say about the construction or shape of this word city. This is not to say that residents of Gary had no agency as historical actors. Their options for resistance were to accept, tweak, reject, or reinvent these narratives. Yet this resistance came from within the paradigm; residents of Gary ultimately could not reinvent their city themselves. Instead, what emerged was a struggle between the image outsiders read onto Gary and the identity that residents tried to carve out from within this industrial paradigm.

While this study is largely about how people spoke of Gary, such descriptions were still very much rooted in the social structure. There were definite class origins to the ways in which people chose to view or understand the forces of modernization and to balance the issues of "progress" and "order." With capital mobility came the perceived need for order. Through their efforts to expand and find new markets and re-sources, capitalists wanted to redefine not only capital but also time and space. Yet as David Harvey points out, the only way capital can expand past time and space is to create permanent physical structures that are tied into the landscape. Thus the moment that capital created a structure, such as a factory, a sidewalk, a road, or a port, expansion tried to make that structure obsolete.[21]

At the same time, Americans came to frame their descriptions and comprehensions of culture and society in industrial terms. Across the class spectrum of Jacksonian America, people tended to look backward to evoke a preindustrial past. The struggle over culture and meaning in the twentieth century took a very different direction. All of the efforts to establish order and social control assumed the realities of industrializa-tion. Instead of evoking an ideal past, these movements tended to imagine an industrialized future. Even those who wished to reject the industrial vision were forced to critique the system from within the parameters of industrialism. As James Barrett points out, worker radicalism still used revolutionary language at the turn of the century, yet the revolutionary movements that European immigrants evoked were not the republican ideals of the American Revolution but the proletarian traditions of 1848.[22] Likewise, middle-class efforts in the Progressive Era did not seek to over-turn industrialism but rather to reform it through pragmatic efforts to make industrial society better.[23]

Political understandings of industrialism and order changed dramatically as workers were integrated into the New Deal state in the 1930s. The rhetoric of economic nationalism stressed the importance of industrial labor and industrial production to the stability and power of the nation, but it also recognized the place or workers and their industrial unions within the nation. As part of the newly emergent Congress of Industrial Organizations, the United Steelworkers of America at the Gary Works were very much a part of this cultural and political embrace of industrialism and the implicit rejection of more radical forms of both protest and order. By midcentury, however, the key definitions of progress, success, and citizenship had changed. As Lizabeth Cohen has pointed out, citizenship in the twentieth century was increasingly defined by consumerism. One's status was decided less by what one did at work than by what one owned at home. Instead of the steel mill, the key site for Americanism was the suburban home.[24] By the last decades of the century, the quest for order and fears of instability had less to do with industrialism than with the social divisions of race. However, as Thomas Sugrue and Robert Self have shown, structural changes in industrial production, highway construction, state investment and disinvestment, and capital mobility created the environment from which the "urban crisis" of the 1960s emerged. Far from a "natural" and inevitable death of American cities due to racial animosities, actions by industrialists and politicians created this new urban environment. However, by the 1980s, American cities, especially rusted industrial centers, seemed to many to be not only disordered but also perhaps uncontrollable and irredeemable.[25]

The paradox of industrial Gary is that it stands within and outside all of these narratives. It was the quintessential American mill town with all of the corresponding social forces of class, race, and gender. Yet it was also a unique space of planned construction where, because of the firm physical separation between Gary the steel mill and Gary the city, social forces functioned differently in both. While Gary did develop its own cultures and organic traditions, it lacked the free flow of culture, interaction, and development of a diverse metropolis such as Chicago. Indeed, industrial spaces were designed specifically to not be complex. Gary and similar industrial cities were constructed environments to serve the needs of industrial production and capitalism, just as mill towns had before and cities such as Los Angeles would later. The planning of Gary focused upon physical separations to guarantee production. Yet such peripheral spaces were not margins in the sense that they were disregarded. The planning and development of industrial spaces at the turn of the century suggests that industrialism, while placed upon the periphery of the metropolis, had moved to the center of the American consciousness. Only at the end of the twentieth century as they deindustrialized did these spaces become marginalized.

THE VERY EMBLEM OF THE INDUSTRIAL TWENTIETH CENTURY

Clifford Geertz once declared that culture, simply put, was the sum of the stories we tell ourselves about ourselves. The cultural history of Gary is, in many ways, the sum of stories we have told ourselves about Gary. It is the story of capitalism and industry (or the attitudes toward capitalism and industrialism) and the shifting terrain of these stories through the modernism, liberalism, and postmodernism of the twentieth century. Hayden White has told us how storytellers, in choosing their starting places and points of emphasis, are determining the narrative arc of their tale. People certainly did this with Gary.

If I am to take White's warnings seriously, however, I must realize that I too am choosing a narrative arc, for I too am an outsider who reads his idealized hopes onto Gary. White tells us that really the only recourse to these tropes is to be aware of our use of them, so let me try to be clear about mine. I am not from Gary or from the greater Chicagoland area. I feel much the same way when I visit Gary as the fictional narrator of Philip Roth's *I Married a Communist* does in passing through the city. "This was an America that I was not a native of and never would be and that I possessed as an American nonetheless," he says upon seeing Gary. "While I stared from the train window—took in what looked to me . . . the very emblem of the industrial twentieth century, and yet an immense archeological site."[26] I did, however, grow up in a working-class union family. I certainly thought of myself, especially in college and graduate school, as a child of the working class. I do then have a certain politicized worldview when it comes to industrial spaces and industrial workers. And I do, I assume, view Gary through these lenses.

As such I actively root for the city of Gary. I have great respect for the determination and stamina that it must take to produce steel—or for that matter to live in the shadow of a steel mill. I root for the Amalgamated Iron Workers in 1919 (even when I know things will not turn out well) and cheer the CIO in 1937. I think that much of the history of Gary's residents is a classic example of "weapons of the weak" and everyday forms of resistance. They took that which they were given and reshaped it into something that was their own. Although I think the residents have been largely powerless in shaping and controlling their own urban image, I find their recurring efforts to do so valiant and persistent, if not always successful. I am hopeful for the city's future and would very much like to see good jobs and economic stability return. If I were to have a hope for this study's impact upon Gary, it would be the uncovering of the constructed narratives about Gary. If we realize how we have chosen to speak about Gary, we can sever that connection and, perhaps, free the city from these burdens. After all, this is one of the great possibilities of a postmodern culture. Understanding social construction frees us to reinvent, reinterpret, and reshape. We need not be that which we once were.

That said, a study of the way people have talked about Gary does run the risk of repeating many of the persistent oversights about the city. On the one hand, it does privilege those people whose voices have always been privileged. It does reconfirm their cultural capital and runs the risk of denying cultural capital to others. Yet this study attempts to deny these privileged voices their power to create normative truth. One of the great benefits of the cultural turn, especially within the critical study of "whiteness" patterned by David Roediger, is the ability to unpack the constructed layers of privilege and reveal them for the exercises in power that they are.[27] Within this study, the privileged voices that create stories about Gary are critically scrutinized as voices of privilege. We need to realize how artificial even the categories of outsider and community have been. These categories were created by the participants themselves either to give themselves some distance from the city or to portray themselves as knowledgeable about the city. Thus criticisms come from "outsiders" and defenses come from members of the "community," yet at times the harshest criticisms came from former residents (especially former reporters for the local newspaper) and some of the fondest memories were written by people who had moved away. Each of these definitions was created to either imply or deny privilege. In this study, I repeat these categories but always with an understanding that they were constructed categories of discursive power.

Other oversights are harder to justify. For instance, readers will find little in these pages about the Latino population of Gary. Their industrial work, their social communities, their part in Gary's labor history, and their political struggles are missing from this study largely because it was missing from people's discussions of Gary. Within its national image and its regional context, Gary was rarely ever portrayed as anything other than European ethnic or black. Like much of U.S. political discourse of the twentieth century, stories of Gary were locked in a simple dichotomy of black and white. The social history of Latinos in Gary gets lost within this dichotomy. It is a history worth telling, but it does not happen here. Likewise, there is little labor or economic history here that places U.S. Steel or the CIO into a national or transnational perspective. It is not a history of work or of workers. I agree with Jefferson Cowie and Joseph Heathcott when they talk of the need to "strip industrial work of its broad-shouldered, social realist patina and see it for what it was: tough work that people did because it paid well and it was located in their communities." Which is not to say that workers did not have very real attachments to their sites of labor or that they did not build their identity around the realities and iconographies of steel work, yet we need to be careful not to read back our own smokestack nostalgia onto the workers of the past. There was deep meaning in the process of steel work and steel production, and while it may not have been the idealized class consciousness that we wish it to have been, its importance and its nuances should not be dismissed.[28]

In his review of new works on deindustrialization, Steven High remarks that so many tend to sideline the role of corporate capital. Despite the televised diatribes of Lou Dobbs and the frequent promises of political candidates concerning "outsourcing" of jobs, many historical works on deindustrialization view the debate over deindustrialization as a long process within which the companies are not really held accountable for their actions. Admittedly, that also happens here. This is not a history of U.S. Steel, nor does it really trace the rise and fall of industrial Gary, which is both complicated and fairly simple: there were once jobs, and then there were fewer jobs. It is a story of industrialism and post-industrialism that has little to do with either U.S. Steel or its workers. It is not even really a history of Gary, but rather a history of the idea of Gary. It is a story of how we have chosen to talk about and think about industrialism.[29]

AND THE FANCY COMES THAT THE CITY WOULD VANISH FROM SIGHT AS MAGICALLY AS IT AROSE

Of all the outside observers whose narratives and descriptions make up the cultural landscape of Gary, the one who best sets the tone for this study is Robert Shackleton. His extremely brief description of Gary for a 1920 travel guide, *The Book of Chicago,* encapsulates so many of the ways observers would come to see the steel city. On the one hand, he repeats much of the folklore of U.S. Steel's vision. This was a ragged wasteland, a "bit of savagery," from which a monument to modern industry arose. Such an accomplishment was made possible, he says, by the power, fore-sight, and personal will of the industrial barons of U.S. Steel. Although other industrial centers had proven to be locales of protest, poverty, and, in Shackleton's words, the "sad hopelessness of aspect of the working-men," he found no such problems in Gary. Instead, he saw a city that had "arisen so swiftly" for the purposes of industry and a "breezy manliness" and satisfaction among its residents. On display was the great triumph of industrial planning and modern urbanism; it was strong, it was modern, and it had all "the aspects of having been built for permanence."

Yet Shackleton remained concerned about the shifting sands upon which Gary was built. The city was not only "set up in a bit of savagery. The very terrain upon which the city stood was always shifting and "al-ways vastly threatening." Despite his praise for the city, Shackleton also imagined dark scenarios for the city's future. "And the fancy comes," he writes:

> that if the people were to be taken away for a little while, and the town left to itself, it would be blotted out; one feels that its houses would become hills and knolls of sand, that its streets, now thronged by day and brilliantly lighted by night, would become sand valleys, that scrub-oaks and pines would begin to grow here and that the city of Gary would vanish from sight as magically as it arose, with only a few mill chimneys standing up mysteri-ously to puzzle wondering travelers, until even those last signs of human life should rust and topple and disappear.[30]

Shackleton's alternating visions of light and darkness, success and im-
minent disaster serve as signposts for our journey through the cultural
history of Gary. His quotes serve as the opening vignettes to the different
sections of the study. The first section explores the ways in which industrialists and others first invented a need for a space such as Gary and then,
after Gary was built, explained its purpose. The second section focuses
on the shifting public debates about the meaning and social realities of
the city in the first half of the twentieth century. By the middle of the
century, the debate about Gary had changed from one of industrialism
to race and vice. The third section traces these story lines from the end
of World War II to deindustrialization at the end of the century. Shackleton's imagery also serves as a powerful reminder of Gary's basic narrative
paradox throughout the century: here was a city of steel, of permanence
and industrial strength, built upon a terrain of shifting sands.

PART ONE

Gary, the Magic City

CREATION MYTHS

A place was needed where the corporation could build great steel mills, and make homes for many thousands of steel workers and their families. In the selection of the site, and in the plans and arrangements for the new place, Elbert Gary showed such constant interest and gave such advice and exercised such leadership, that his business associates named the place in his honor. The intended greatest steel-making center was to be known as Gary.

ROBERT SHACKLETON, *THE BOOK OF CHICAGO*, 1920

ONE

"An Industrial Utopia"

THE SEARCH FOR INDUSTRIAL ORDER

The United States Steel Corporation had ensured that its process of converting large shipments of coal and iron ore into finished steel was fast, efficient, and seamless. Great care had gone into the planning of its newest production center in Gary, Indiana, so that no unnecessary movement, wasted energy, or pause in production would mar the creation of steel. The entire process started at the ore dock where, in an artificial canal 22 feet deep and 250 feet wide and lined with massive concrete retaining walls, the ore steamers from Duluth, Minnesota, would disgorge their content with the help of large unloading machines. Traveling conveyor bridges then moved the product into storage yards that were designed to hold enough supply to keep the mills running during the winter months when lake navigation was suspended. Moving through elevated storage bins via transfer cars and electric gates, the iron ore, along with limestone and coke, made its way into the massive blast furnaces, which baked the substance with high temperature gases. The blast furnace, which was continuously in operation, varied in temperature from the cool top with its newly added ingredients to the hot molten iron at its bottom. As the combination of ore, coke, and limestone heated, it descended in the furnace and slag floated to the top. This by-product was drawn off and either placed in the slag heap (which would eventually be used as lake fill for future expansion) or turned into pig metal. From taps in the bottom of the furnace the molten iron was removed and hauled away in 40-ton ladles. Each furnace at Gary had a capacity of 450 tons.

From there the molten iron was poured into several mixers before it traveled through Gary's open-hearth furnace. Here the mixture was subjected to the intense heat of burning gases passing over it. Much like the Bessemer process, the open hearth burned off the impurities of the metal and created the stronger product of steel. Once the metal met the standards of the grade the mill was producing that day, the molten steel was poured into ingot molds and allowed to cool into a solid state. From there the steel was moved into either one of the billet mills, where the ingots were rolled into smaller and more manageable sizes, or it moved into a rail mill where massive steel rails were rolled directly from the ingot without the necessity of reheating the steel. The rail mill at Gary was capable of making 4,000 tons of 80-pound rails in twenty-four hours.

Here was both the simplicity and awe-inspiring scale of the process of making steel in Gary. Starting from the shipping basin on the eastern side of the complex, the mixture of ingredients would flow westward from the blast furnace to the open-hearth furnace to the finishing mills. This process does not even take into account the massive power plant, the blower plant, and the complex system to trap, cleanse, and reuse the hot gases from the blast furnace. All quite efficient, all modernized and mechanized, and seemingly dehumanized. The above tour of the steel mills at Gary comes from *Scientific American*'s 1909 description of the newest steel center. The article makes no mention of the steelworkers involved in the process. Rather, it would seem that steel made itself. The magazine revels in the dehumanized passive voice: for instance, before the steel can be poured into the ingots, "the proper amount of ferro-manganese is added to the metal in each ladle and then they are picked up by 125-ton traveling cranes and carried to the platform, from which by opening a plug in the bottom the molten steel is poured." The only mention of human involvement by *Scientific American* is the operator of the transfer cars that bring the raw material into the blast furnace, yet even then "the operator merely starts the skip on its journey. Its journey up the incline and the halt at the charging platform above are purely automatic."[1]

The efficiency, integration, and technological innovation of the new Gary mill were fitting symbols for this new system of industry. With the completion of the transcontinental railroad in 1869, the size of potential markets and the scale of production grew rapidly. American industry began to reinvent itself in terms of centralization. This new system wove together massive production, rapid transportation, and expanding markets into a tightly locked network dominated by massive companies. It was an era of rapid growth and heavy industrialization. Much of this growth was made possible by the expansion of industrial technology and invention. For steel in particular, the development of the Bessemer process and the open hearth made production faster, cheaper, and larger in scale.

One of the industrialists leading this process in steel was Andrew Carnegie. For Carnegie there were three key principles to steel production. The first was an obsession with efficiency. With reduced costs, such as keeping the steel molten through constant production, came higher profits. Equally important was keeping the cost of labor low. Second, Carnegie readily encouraged cutthroat competition both in terms of price with his competitors and with production within his plants. These two concerns allowed Carnegie to survive the "price war" within steel in 1897. Third, and perhaps most important, Carnegie was always looking for expansion, in terms of steel production and its subsidiaries, including coal and iron mines and rail lines. By the turn of the century, Carnegie's company had come to dominate the American steel industry. The consolidation of Carnegie's steel empire with J. P. Morgan's banking interests, which created the U.S. Steel Corporation in 1901, only further consolidated this domination.

At its creation, U.S. Steel immediately became a major force in steel production. It contained over 200 companies and nearly 1,000 miles of railroad track, and it produced two-thirds of all American steel. Its value exceeded $1 billion, making it the first major American corporation in an era of rapid consolidation and corporate mergers. In addition, the corporation was an economic giant in Chicago. It controlled one-third of all the shipping tonnage on the Great Lakes and had a massive 330-acre steel plant in South Chicago. However, as the corporation began to examine ways to expand its production, it looked across the border at northwest Indiana. Not only did the Calumet Region promise nearly limitless land for expansion and growth, but relocation still placed the corporation on the major East Coast trunk lines and the Lake Michigan shipping lanes to the Mesabi iron range of Minnesota. To avoid the speculative boom that followed rumors of meatpacking relocation, U.S. Steel began secretly purchasing lakefront land in the Calumet Region to build its newest mill.[2]

When U.S. Steel arrived in Indiana in 1906, however, it was not the first industry in the region. Rather, the Calumet Region of northwestern Indiana already had a long and complicated history with industrialization. All of the trunk lines that terminated in Chicago ran through Lake

County, Indiana, making the space an attractive site for industrial expansion. The first large-scale industry of the region was the meatpacking plant of George Hammond. Having developed a system of refrigerating rail cars, Hammond was able to pack and send fresh meat from the Midwest to the urban markets of the East without the meat spoiling. This immediately made him a player in the meat market, yet Hammond was shut out of the Union Stockyards by the meatpacking trust that was emerging in Chicago. Hammond's response was to move across the state line into Indiana. In 1869 he opened the State Line Slaughterhouse in the city of Hammond, Indiana.

Over the next several decades, other industries, including the Inland Steel Company in East Chicago and Standard Oil in Whiting, would follow the same pattern of capital relocation. In 1890, as meatpackers in Chicago battled with the city over regulations, a rumor of an impending relocation led to an upsurge in land speculation throughout the county as people prepared for another major move. Despite these industrial relocations, however, the population of the region remained modest. In 1880, the county had a population of 15,000. By 1900, the number would be only 38,000. This, of course, would change with the arrival of U.S. Steel.

Despite its effort to move out of Chicago and transform seemingly empty space into a steel production center, U.S. Steel was cautious in limiting the expectations others may have had about the newest city of Gary. While the company was happy to have people talk about the display of industrial might and scientific planning, the official rhetoric about the city stressed that it was not a social experiment. Often plans for new industrial spaces such as Pullman, Illinois, brought expectations of utopian benevolence and social responsibility. (Workers, of course, felt quite differently about cities such as Pullman.) U.S. Steel felt no such obligation in designing Gary. This did not stop observers such as Henry Fuller of *Harper's Weekly* from declaring the newest site an industrial utopia. Here was a city not only made from scratch by a powerful corporation but also made to order. The construction of Gary was not simply capital relocation but an opportunity for vast expansion and efficient production. Unlike the rest of the Calumet Region, which had long been industrialized, Gary caught the attention of observers such as Henry Fuller because of its scale, its intricate planning, and its seemingly limitless possibilities. It was not just U.S. Steel's newest plant but also the corporation's opportunity to create industrial order. For many, the significance of Gary's construction was the evolution of utopian dreams that accompanied the spectacular industrial and urban growth of the Gilded Age.

"MONOTONOUSLY PATTERNED IN THE IMAGE OF COKETOWN": THE MEANING OF INDUSTRIAL UTOPIA

In its form as well as its meaning, Gary was a continuation of as well as a dramatic change from the utopian language and experiments of the early nineteenth century. Most of these utopian ideals emerged as the processes of market expansion and industrial modernization were just beginning. Thus some utopianists tried to reject industry and create a close-knit community, others tried to craft a more equitable form of industrialism, and still others embraced an industrial future but sought order through concrete planning. The question of utopia served as a critique of industry, modernization, and the sense of change and chaos. It was a fantasy of different options and different outcomes.

The earliest form of industrial utopianism was a rejection of both the metropolis and the market as well as a critique of modern social relations. In the United States, such communalist utopias often centered on religion and religious community. Thus there was the experimental community of Oneida which rejected not only the role of market individualism but also private property and Victorian marriage. The Pietists of Harmony, Indiana, removed themselves from the larger society in order to create a perfect and homogeneous community. When he took over the failing Harmony community and transformed it into New Harmony, Robert Owen embraced a different principle of utopian communities. Instead of rejecting machines, he tried to fix the inequalities of the market and create a different form of industrialism. What these utopias envisioned was not a pre-industrial religious community but rather a more fair and equal modern society, yet one still small in scale and communal in purpose.

Likewise, the designers of Lowell sought to combine republican community and industrial production within a pastoral setting. Many Americans of the early republic were enamored by the wealth and power that industrialization promised. But they were also concerned by what they saw as the dangerous, immoral, and nonrepublican conditions of English industrial cities, especially Manchester. American critics of such cities feared both industrial conditions, such as the permanent working class of Irish immigrants including men, women, and children, and the urban conditions of smoke, crowded housing, and vice districts. Instead of disordered industrial cities, American industrialists hoped to create republican centers of pre-industrial order within pastoral settings. Thus when planning their new industrial center of Lowell, the Boston Associates intentionally tried to infuse the city with republican virtues (including a rotating workforce of young women) and natural surroundings so as not to create industrial classes, poverty, pollution, and moral decay. By the 1840s, however, Lowell manufacturers had already begun to hire Irish laborers, including children, for lower wages.[3]

By the second half of the nineteenth century the ideologies of industrial modernity, which demanded massive scale and technological advancements, challenged the pastoral and communal assumptions of utopianism. Thus many utopianists such as Étienne Cabet did not envision small close-knit communities but rather used utopian planning to model a better future. Cabet's cities were to be large and modern, yet clean and ordered. By the end of the nineteenth century, this brand of broad utopianism would be the basic blueprint for experiments like Pullman, Illinois. Planned to manufacture luxury Pullman sleeping cars, the city of Pullman combined large-scale industrial production with reformist efforts toward the betterment of the workers who resided there. By controlling every aspect of the city, George Pullman attempted to eliminate industrial strife and social conflict through sanitation, education, and moral uplift. Yet it was this paternalistic control, combined with a series of wage cuts, which triggered a devastating strike in 1894. For a city which assumed that labor unrest could not occur within its planned environment, the strike shook the foundations of the experiment.

The creators of Gary, drawing on the lessons of Pullman and other utopian failures, made no such assumptions. Having witnessed Pullman's demise, their fundamental expectation in planning Gary was that industrial strife and social conflict were inevitable by-products of modernization. Moreover, the planners of U.S. Steel were clearly interested in learning from the Homestead strike of 1892. During that strike Andrew Carnegie and Henry Clay Frick turned their steel mill into a fortified stronghold by constructing a 12-foot-high fence around the plant, with rifle holes at useful intervals. As the failures of paternalism and order in

Pullman soured the experience of paternalistic planning for industrialists, many began to turn to the model offered by Carnegie and Homestead. A militarized factory came to represent order far more than a pastoral factory. The builders of such factories and their surrounding cities seemed not to be interested in the democratic community of middle-class reformers, the networks and interests of workers, or even the paternalism of planned industrialism. Rather, industrialism in the twentieth century was to be centered upon uninterrupted production and profits. The building of Gary came to represent both the culmination of the industrial utopia and its demise.

By 1922, Lewis Mumford would eulogize these efforts at utopia. Grand utopian schemes had failed precisely because they were so grand, disconnecting them, he would argue, from any social reality. Utopian thinkers had failed to catch Thomas More's playful pun in creating "utopia." It was a place caught in between outopia (nothingness) and eutopia (a good place): thus a utopia could never really exist. Efforts at reform had been "spotty and inconsecutive and incomplete." "It was not, let us remember, by any legislative device that the cities of the industrial age were monotonously patterned in the image of Coketown," he would say. "It was rather because everyone within these horrid centers accepted the same values and pursued the same ends." Far from a social ideal, industrial spaces "expressed the brutality and social disharmony of the community." Epitomizing the cultural pessimism of the 1920s as well as the shifting thought on utopias in the twentieth century, Mumford argued that utopias were not possible. Instead, we should borrow the methods of the utopianist thinker to "project an ideal community" but use it in a "practical way" to carve out smaller utopias where we could.[4]

"BELCHING FLAMES AND THE RISING SMOKE": THE SHOCK OF CHICAGO'S INDUSTRIALISM

If every utopian vision needs a dystopia to juxtapose itself against, then the utopianists who looked at Gary saw the lessons gleaned from the perceived chaos of industrial Chicago. Visitors to Chicago expressed a profound shock upon experiencing the sound, smell, and activity of the city. For some the experience might be one of horrors, but for others Chicago was a space of excitement, energy, and industrial might. The *Graphic*, for instance, was struck by the activity of Chicago steel production. "The clanking of the enormous cranes, the shouts of the industrial captains giving orders to the men, and the figures of workmen flitting to and from in the gloom, lighted up as they pass the area of light from the molten steel, are a poem and a painting combined, and give the observer a new and vivid idea of the dignity of labor and the complexity and importance of the great work going on before him."[5] When German sociologist Max Weber visited Chicago, he was both amazed and disturbed by the sight, especially by his experience with the Union Stockyards. For Weber, Chicago was a city of vast buildings, technological machinery, labor unrest, violent crime, and bewildering racial and ethnic diversity.

> As far as one can see from the tower of the firm of Armour & Son—nothing but cattle lowing, bleating, endless filth—in all directions, for the town goes on for miles and miles until it loses itself in the vastness of the suburbs— churches and chapels, storage elevators, smoking chimneys (every large hotel has its own elevator run on a steam engine) and houses of every kind. This is why the town is so far-flung; the areas of the city are distinguished from each other in degrees of cleanliness in accordance with the nationality of the residents. The devil has broken loose in the stockyards: a lost strike with great numbers of Italians and Negroes brought in as strikebreakers; shootings daily with dozens dead at both sides.... Close to our hotel, a cigar dealer was killed in broad daylight, a few steps away at dusk, three Negroes robbed a trolley car—all in all a unique flowering of culture! There is a swarming interaction of all peoples of the human race on every street.... The whole powerful city, more extensive than London—resembles, except for the better residential areas, a human being with his skin removed, and in which all the physiological process can be seen going on.[6]

For a social scientist such as Weber, this kind of chaos, excitement, and diversity made for a fascinating opportunity to view human interaction. Indeed, the University of Chicago made their surroundings a giant laboratory for scientific exploration.

As Timothy Spears has pointed out, the literature of Chicago embraced this notion of Chicago as a "shock city" of migrants' fears, hopes, successes, failures, conquests, and defeats. The literary Chicago of migrants allowed writers such as Hamlin Garland and Theodore Dreiser to imagine travelers in awe of their arrival, dumbstruck by the chaos, confused and tricked by the opportunists of the street, or, perhaps cunning themselves, adaptive and successful in the vast city of opportunity.[7]

Just as often, however, the literary descriptions of Chicago focused on its chaos and its filth. For the middle-class Laura in Frank Norris's story of the Chicago wheat market, a respectable and domestic life was nearly impossible in such a town. "She could not forgive its dirty streets," Norris writes, "the unspeakable squalor of some of its proper neighborhoods that sometimes developed, like cancerous growth, in the very heart of fine residential districts. The black murk that closed every vista of the business streets oppressed her, and the soot that stained linen and gloves each time she stirred was a never-ending distress."[8] "I have struck a city—a real city—and they call it Chicago," Rudyard Kipling wrote for his English audience. "It holds rather more than a million people with bodies, and stands on the same sort of soil as Calcutta. Having seen it, I urgently desire never to see it again. It is inhabited by savages. Its water is the water of the Hughli, and its air is dirt." Kipling was deeply unimpressed by all the places and the people that he had met in his travels across the United States. Yet he was particularly disgusted by Chicago. Kipling was disturbed by the stockyards, the poor quality of the air, and the sight of the canals, which he describes as "black as ink, and filled with untold abominations."[9]

As William Cronon has argued, many writers made a clear distinction between the city and the surrounding countryside. A major episode, then, in these tales was the moment that people left the country and entered the city. Often this transition was marked by the arrival of pollution and filth. "I shall never forget the feeling of dismay," Hamlin Garland writes, "with which . . . I perceived from the car window a huge smoke-cloud which embraced the whole eastern horizon." Garland's character Rose would have a similar encounter with Chicago pollution: "Terrors thickened. Smells assaulted her sensitive nostrils, incomprehensible and horrible odors. Everywhere men delved in dirt and murk and all unloveliness." So too did Charles Dudley Warner comment upon the frightening aspect of Chicago's environment: "the manufactories vomit dense clouds of bituminous coal smoke, which settle in a black mass." Cronon argues that this shock of transformation represents a changing of moral conditions for the characters. From the pastoral countryside, travelers of all ages and levels of innocence were entering into an urban environment of chaos.[10]

At the same time, visitors also commented upon the awe-inspiring technological advancements of the city. Literary Chicago was a divided place. It represented all of the greatest of possibilities of modernity, but it also demonstrated the deep threats that modernity may have caused. Declaring Chicago a "city of smoke," Italian traveler Giuseppe Giacosa described the deep tensions, divisions, and pollutions of the city. "During my stay of one week," Giacosa writes, "I did not see in Chicago anything but darkness: smoke, clouds, dirt, and an extraordinary number of sad and grieved persons." Indeed, for Giacosa, the striking images of Chicago were not just industrialization, modernization, and pollution but rather a more threatening reality. "The dominant characteristic of the exterior life of Chicago is violence," he concludes. "Everything leads you to extreme expressions: dimensions, movements, noises, rumors, window displays, spectacles, ostentation, misery, activity, and alcoholic degradation."[11]

For others, however, the noises, actions, smoke, and smells of industrial Chicago were proof that the city was a growing and profitable industrial center. "For miles around the sounds of industry, the belching flames and the rising smoke attract the eye and ear, arousing curiosity in old and young," bragged one such booster.[12] "Chicago, as it stands, has been accused of being a noisy city," pointed out the Committee on Industrial Locations in their pamphlet on *Chicago as an Industrial Center.* "Its smokestacks, its chimneys, and its babble of tongues have been criticized both at home and by those abroad." Yet, the committee pointed out, the presence of smoke was not a problem but rather a sign of growth. "It has been no disturbing factor that to the south of the University campus lies the smoke from one of the great steel mills of the world; that the chimneys from a mighty car-building plant spike the southern horizon; that the roar of traffic over some of the great railway systems of the world drifts by its very doors. Rather all these have been stimuli." All of which ensured not only the unique growth of Chicago but also its ideal industrial conditions. "With such an atmosphere at large," the committee self-servingly concluded, "there has been no room for the sharp lines of social demarcation that are found in so many of the older and more conservative centers of production." The committee acknowledged that unrest and social division might be part of Chicago's future. "Probably the time will come in Chicago as it has elsewhere in old civilizations," it speculated, "when social lines will dominate the industrial good fellowship which has been the city's *savoir faire*."[13]

"INDUSTRIAL UNREST IS A SOCIAL MALADY":
PLANNING FOR INDUSTRIAL ORDER

Despite the best efforts of boosters to sell the city as an economic engine of beneficial smoke and classless possibility, other critics saw in industrial expansion the possibility for chaos and upheaval. Between 1870 and 1901 (the year the committee published their promotional pamphlet), Chicago had developed deep social divisions and had been rocked by major labor unrest. One solution offered was industrial relocation. A tightly controlled (either through capitalist paternalism or police oversight) worker environment might prevent the kind of agitation and dangerous radicalism that middle- and upper-class citizens feared. While older generations of city leaders and boosters, such as William Ogden, made their fortunes in land speculation, the members of the new industrial elite were the creators of massive industrial plants, catalog firms, and department stores. Men such as Potter Palmer, Cyrus McCormick, Philip Armour, and Marshall Field were highly influential in shaping the city through economic concentration and capital mobility. This group also embraced the ideologies of modernization and put their faith in large-scale scientific advancement. Only by combining their considerable influence, they believed, could they strive for the kind of large reforms that would benefit not only their businesses but the larger city. Made up of the "right" kind of people with the "right" motivations, industrial clubs created a shared paternalism that tried to impose order upon the city.

One of the more prominent of these organizations was the Commercial Club. Created on December 27, 1877, the club included in its membership many of the leading merchants and industrialists of the city, including Field, Pullman, and McCormick. Following the violence of the Great Strike, members advocated the construction of permanent military bases and supported the building of the 16th Street Armory on Michigan Avenue in order to protect the homes of businessmen on Prairie Avenue.[14] By the mid-1880s and early 1890s, the club's interests expanded into plans to reshape the urban spaces and images of Chicago. Fearing that their city had been long derided as "murky, grimy, choky Chicago," club members tried to reimagine it as a cultured place of learning and high art.[15] At the forefront of this was the creation of the University of Chicago, but members of the Commercial Club also contributed their own projects;

Marshall Field, for instance, helped to create the Field Museum of Natural History.[16] Likewise, the World's Fair of 1893 created a unified vision of a modern, clean, and cultured future.

The Commercial Club was by no means the only such industrial organization. In 1889, the Sunset Club of Chicago emerged. Claiming its objective was "to foster rational good fellowship and tolerant discussion among business and professional men of all classes," the Sunset Club was not as elite as the Commercial Club. Thus its attention and language varied a bit from the latter. In its meetings, members discussed such issues as "Shall the World's Fair be open on Sunday," "Woman Suffrage," "The Eight Hour Day," "Drunkenness: its nature, causes, and cure," "How would you uplift the Masses," and "Immigration: its benefits and evils; what restrictions, if any, should be adopted." Through such meetings the members tried to make sense of modern conditions.

In a November 17, 1892, discussion by Z. S. Holbrook, the club tried to learn "the lessons of the Homestead troubles." This analysis ranged from outrage at the audacity of striker demands ("The strikers seemed to think they had as much a vested right in the property at Homestead as the Carnegie Company," Holbrook reported) to a desire for social uplift to prevent such violence from occurring in the future. "Industrial unrest is a social malady," he continued, "and has its origins in a genuine desire of the lower classes to better their conditions, but it unfortunately thrives upon the most depraved instincts and passions of men—the envy and hatred on the part of the unsuccessful and unfortunate for the successful and the well-to-do." But lest the club's plans for social uplift look like a classless utopia, Holbrook made it clear that workers should be taught the cold, hard rules of capital.

> By education, we mean that the laboring classes shall learn by heart these few eternal truths: . . . capital and labor are partners but capitalists and laborers are not—having chosen wages as its part, when wages are paid the obligations of capital cease except such as pertain to the domain of private conscience. The obligations of capital to share profits with labor are no greater than those of others to share their surplus with the needy.[17]

Indeed, if there were lessons to be learned from Homestead, it was that neither the laborers nor Carnegie understood the rules of capital. "When the Carnegie company prepared instead of a workshop, a factory in a free country for the employment of free men . . . they constructed a fort, an old-time castle to which were attached all modern agencies of destruction," concluded George Schilling in the same club discussion. "If they did that then I say they drew the sword, they issued the proclamation of war, and if they got the worst of it you ought to be satisfied."[18]

Organizations of the industrial elite, however, took various lessons from Homestead and understood the rules of capital very differently. In a speech before the Merchants Club of Chicago entitled "The Ethics of Corporate Management," Charles W. Eliot stated:

> The first duty of a corporation towards its employees is to provide those external conditions which will promote health, cheerfulness, and vigor in the working place. The efficiency of any large body of workmen is greatly promoted by healthy and cheerful surroundings. What is nowadays called welfare work is not a benevolence or a charity; it is simple economy, common sense, and common humanity.[19]

Herein lay the difference between these organizations and their understandings of capital. For less powerful groups such as the Sunset Club, the modern economy was a harsh taskmaster who could and would punish any violation, be that the actions of strikers or the arrogance of the Carnegie Steel Company. Yet for members of the Commercial Club or the Merchants Club, the fluid rules of capital allowed them to shape and reshape the city and the human relationships within it to fit their own needs. However, these needs became understood as "simple economy."

In response to the labor unrest of Homestead and Haymarket and the coming of age of modern industrial paternalism, several new industrialist groups emerged during the 1890s. One such organization was the Industrial Club of Chicago, which was dedicated to "those engaged in the industrial life of the city" and striving to "advance the public and industrial interests of the community." Like similar organizations, the Industrial Club tackled social issues such as "the condition of unrest in the community," but it was far more explicit in making the interests of the "public" and "industrial interests" the same thing.[20] In 1896, an even more influential group organized. The Merchants Club pushed more actively for its own vision of what the streets and culture of Chicago should look like. Just as other organizations had done, the Merchants Club held symposiums and discussions on industrial and social issues such as the "needs of a great city," "improvement of the south shore," "the lake front park," the "Great Lakes as a factor in transportation facilities," and perhaps most important "labor unrest in relation to modern industrial and commercial progress."[21] As always, these merchants and industrialists sought ways to ensure order and prevent unrest.

Perhaps the most important, and certainly the most acclaimed, attempt at this new kind of industrialism was the model city of Pullman, Illinois. Located just south of Chicago, Pullman promised to maintain all of the important modern amenities of the metropolis. The factory for Pullman railcars would still have access to all the major trunk lines and other benefits of the location. Yet Pullman would also be far enough away from Chicago to eliminate the social and moral dangers of the city, especially the vice districts of the Levee and the autonomy of neighborhoods such as the Back of the Yards. Instead, Pullman was to be a model city with a modern layout of educational facilities, "proper" sanitation, green spaces, and uplifting entertainment, all of which were controlled by George Pullman.[22] As such, Pullman represented both the culmination of pastoral reform and its combination with capital relocation. It was not enough that the residents of Pullman have clean water, open parks, and libraries, thus creating an environment for morality and order. Rather, the Pullman Company actively exercised power over the lives and homes of the workers and families to ensure their versions of morality and order.[23]

Pullman's removal of industrial spaces from the city allowed merchants, capitalists, and the other urban elite to reconceptualize Chicago as well. While the Pullman Company may have been keeping their workers away from the influences of the city, many boosters saw in Pullman the removal of dangerous elements, which would lead to a safer and more modern Chicago. As part of the effort to improve the national and international image of the city, Chicago hosted the 1893 Columbian Exposition and World's Fair. The fair became legendary for its audacious scale, its cleanliness and sanitation, its technological advancements, and its vision of a modern and orderly future. Instead of simple buildings, architect Daniel Burnham offered his vision of the perfect modern city. Impeccably clean with modern plumbing, drinkable water, allusions to classical civilizations, and not a smokestack to be seen, the White City became the central image of the exposition. It became the literal manifestation of the desire to create safe and clean spaces dedicated to middle- and upper-class entertainment.[24]

Of course, the White City did not stand alone. Burnham's creation only made sense in contrast to the dark industrialism of south Chicago, a comparison many visitors were eager to make for themselves. In addition, one of the most popular trips at the fair was the short train ride to Pullman, where modern and ordered industrialism existed economically close yet properly distanced from the White City. Such was the modern delineation and separation of urban spaces by class and use. Relocation of industry, the development of an industrial periphery, and the creation of spaces of leisure and amusement were part of an active agenda by the emerging industrial elite of Chicago not only to shape their city but to protect their place within the industrialized economy and modernized culture. The concerted efforts to plan the industrial periphery around the city and to create integrated, efficient, and enormous plants marked the growth of cities such as Pullman. At the same time, lessons learned from Pullman and Homestead reshaped how industrialists constructed the physical structure as well as the public expectations of new cities such as Gary. In its origins, then, Gary was part mill town, part model city, and part industrial periphery. U.S. Steel wanted the space to be a center of large-scale steel production, yet others read onto the site the possibility of efficient planning and industrial utopia. Gary existed on the periphery of industrial Chicago yet also offered an organized alternative to the perceived chaos of the metropolis. Gary was part of a pattern of capital relocation and industrialization in the Calumet Region, yet its size, planning, and implied meaning separated this city from the previous industrialization in the Calumet Region.

CONCLUSION: "INTO THE MODERN CITY OF
AMERICA—INTO THE MODEL CITY OF THE WORLD"

Like Weber, Kipling, and numerous other visitors before him, William Stead looked at Chicago and saw the same sort of violence, chaos, filth, growth, and human interaction. Yet, for the British reformer, Chicago was not an example of physiological science but rather a breakdown of moral reform and moral responsibility. In his 1894 call for social reform, *If Christ Came to Chicago*, Stead identified the dangerous elements of industrial

Chicago and suggested the kind of changes that might make Chicago a more Christian city. In his final chapter, Stead offered a vision of a utopian future for Chicago. In Stead's future, moral reforms and Christian charities had combined with massive structural changes to create an ideal city. It was the paving and cleaning of streets, the digging of subway and pneumatic tunnels, and the opening of massive waterways capable of bringing in cross-Atlantic steamers that made Chicago in the twentieth century a city free of moral vices and class conflict. It was not moral purity and social reform alone but rather the structural transformation of the city that would create a better future and transform the dangerous elements of vice and immorality.[25]

Although different in their approach, both Weber and Stead were taking part in a broader reevaluation of industrial cities. When people looked at the industrializing cities of the late nineteenth century, many saw a dark and dystopian wasteland of belching smoke, abject poverty, and constant danger; a space dominated by what William Blake would call the "dark Satanic mills." Yet, as Tristram Hunt has shown, Victorian cities were also vibrant sites for discussions on the meaning of industrialism. Not only were they critiqued as Dickensian cesspools, but industrial cities were also the center of hopeful visions of an industrial future. Far from writing off industrial centers and urban environments, the Victorians strove to reform, reclaim, and redeem their cities. Instead of being pessimistic or fatalistic, Victorians, Hunt argues, saw great utopian potential in cities. Indeed, it was Blake himself who promised a new Jerusalem on the site of satanic mills.[26] Stead's journey to Chicago and his plea for comprehensive reform tied the city into this larger culture of Victorian urbanism. As the editor of the *Pall Mall Gazette,* Stead had already made a name for himself as a reformer of London's streets. In 1885, he wrote and published the "Maiden Tribute of Modern Babylon," an exposé of the city's vice districts and white slavery. His conviction and prison sentence for buying a young girl in order to expose the practice had turned him into a martyr to reforming causes and an internationally renowned advocate. This was the reputation he brought to Chicago.[27]

While the steel city of Gary arose on its outer periphery, the city of Chicago continued to reinvent itself and its urban spaces. The triumphant arch at the gates of the Union Stockyards and the grand plans for the White City of the 1893 World's Fair were just the beginning of Daniel

Burnham's vision.[28] A comprehensive revision of Chicago's entire urban structure including all of its parks, streets, rail lines, and neighborhoods, Burnham's Plan of Chicago promised to be "Chicago's equivalent of Baron Haussmann's plan created and completed for the city of Paris."[29] For supporters, the plan was the perfect combination of modern technological audacity, industrial expansion and power, European-style culture and sophistication, and paternalistic control over the modern city's inherent chaos and unrest. Even with the audacious scale of Burnham's plan, the promotional language used to explain it made it seem as if it were an inevitable part of modern progress. As the Merchants Club, one of the champions of Burnham's plan, would say, "The Plan of Chicago began when the first cave man felled a tree across a stream." It was only simple human nature to try and improve transportation, economic growth, and living conditions. Yet this progress still relied on the active participation of leading citizens. "It was our sense of responsibility as Merchants Club men that finally brought action."[30] Such a plan not only provided for improved transportation that would attract wealth, but it also promised to calm the industrial unrest of the 1890s. "A city to be a good labor market," argued Archie H. Jones in favor of the plan, "must provide for the health and pleasure of the great body of workers." In order to do this, the Chicago Plan not only included grand sweeping boulevards but also a series of open green spaces to "beget calm parks and feelings."[31]

So vital, many believed, to the industrial health of the city was the plan that in 1907 the Merchants Club and the Commercial Club merged into the Commercial Club of Chicago to push for the plan's implementation.[32] In its presentation of the plan, the new Commercial Club praised not only the visionary scope of Burnham's ideas but also the important contributions and positions of its own members. "The Plan has been called a dream," the club concluded. "It is a dream; but a dream of business men for whose disinterested effort there can be no other reward than the satisfaction of a good citizenship. It is a dream not of whether Chicago will grow, but how it shall grow in its moral, intellectual, and physical attributes into the modern city of America—into the model city of the world."[33]

"The physical and moral deterioration of the human race under bad conditions of city life is one of the great problems of the age," concluded Alderman Bernard Snow:

That city life is producing a physically and morally deficient type is apparent, especially in old cities where the process had gone on longer. Our problem is to check this tendency here before we have a fixed type of physical and moral inferiority. . . . Proper housing, proper sanitation, air and sunlight, are the birthright of humanity, and when we permit them to be denied we must accept responsibility for the inevitable result.

But like so many others, Snow believed that the plan was not only about social reform and sanitation but that "dirt, grime, and sordid conditions are not a part of industrial and commercial success." Instead, he argued, "they are rather evidence of the failure to grasp the fundamental truth that men who are happy, whose lives are cast in pleasant places, who are clean of body and clean of mind, are the men who do things best." Others too picked up on the idea of urban spaces, sanitation, and a civic body. Charles Wacker concluded, "The old Romans used to say something like this: 'a healthy body brings about a healthy mind.' And that is perhaps truer in regard to the community than to the individual." Added Karl Bitter: "You are proposing in your plan of Chicago to provide conditions wherein your public body may grow more freely, cleanly, and healthily. Success to your efforts for the sake of morals."[34]

By the late nineteenth century, industrialists had come to embrace the ideologies of modernization which, as they conceived it, relied upon rapid expansion, technological and scientific advancement, and sheer size. These were the great possibilities and energies of Weber's Chicago. Yet at the same time industrialists feared the social chaos and unrest of Stead's Chicago. The only way to maintain order, they came to believe, was to create order through structural planning, clearly defined lines of separation, and the elimination of chaos. By planning for, creating, and maintaining control in the structures of the industrial city, industrial capitalists hoped to synchronize industrial expansion with industrial order. It was this process that helped lead to the construction of Gary, Indiana, as a concentrated space of industrial production on Chicago's eastern edge. It was this same process that allowed observers such as Henry Fuller to declare the city an industrial utopia. Yet U.S. Steel was more interested in industrial order than industrial utopia. As such, the construction of Gary emerged out of several traditions. Gary was an industrial extension of Chicago's periphery, yet it also offered organized planning juxtaposed against Chicago's chaos. It was a site of industrial relocation in the Calumet Region following in an established tradition of industrial relocation. Yet the city also had a larger scale than the other cities of the region. At the same time, the planning of Gary suggested an application of the lessons learned in Pullman and Homestead. It could be a model city that claimed not to be a model city. In different ways to different people, Gary offered models of industrial order.

TWO

"Making a City to Order"

U.S. STEEL AND THE BUILDING
OF AN INDUSTRIAL CENTER

"In approaching consideration of the model village," Eugene Buffing-ton, president of the Indiana Steel Company, wrote of Gary in 1909, "our thought naturally gravitates toward problems associated with the complex social relations found in present-day urban life." "Who can doubt," he continued, "that the future of our nation will be worked out, for weal or for woe, in the rapidly increasingly centres of concentrated population?" Because of its controlled construction, a "model village" could serve as a social laboratory for all of the anxieties confronting the modern metropolis.[1] Buffington's commentary in *Harper's Weekly* was by no means alone. Many journalistic observers commented upon the possibilities of the model city, especially the model industrial city. The planned city was an opportunity to incorporate all of the newest thoughts on social control, industrial technology, and urban order. The planners had a chance to conceive of their vision without limitations on space, structures, or topography. "Here in Gary all is different," remarked reformer Graham Romeyn Taylor, "planned at the onset on an enormous scale, it was unnecessary even remotely to consider space limitations." The mapping of the model city, then, became a mapping of modernity. The shape the cities took reflected the ways people understood and chose to deal with the urban conditions of modernity.[2]

Because of these conditions, many journalists and urban theorists paid close attention to the creation and shape of the city. As Taylor wrote in the philanthropic magazine *Survey*, "Gary, by reason of its industrial significance and the marvelous growth of its community life, is a marked place for the student of social, civic, and industrial advance."[3] The new space of Gary allowed observers to read onto the city that which they most desired or most feared. The building of Gary, therefore, was as much an imagined construction as a physical one. Because it was a new space being newly invented and newly created, Gary had no established narratives. Instead, it became essential for observers, planners, and residents to create an order and narrative when they spoke of Gary. Yet in order to do so, people searched for established tropes and narratives to plug the story and city of Gary into. Some spoke of Gary as a triumph of capital, while others saw it as the problems of capital contained. Some borrowed the myths of creation and the awe-inspiring power of science. Still others read the meaning of Gary within the established narratives of social reform and the possibilities of progress. Each of these tropes allowed the observer to imagine Gary in a different way. Yet model spaces on the edges of cities also offered the opportunity to create new narratives and meaning. Building, shaping, and deciphering model industrial spaces became a way for Americans to understand the social realities of industrial society and the possibilities for an industrial future.

By moving their production to the periphery of cities, American industrialists not only attempted to remove themselves and their workers from the influences and problems of the cities and provide more land for expansion and concentration but they also tried to rethink what industrial spaces could be. By creating cities such as Pullman, Illinois, or Gary, Indiana, industrialists sought to prove that capital could be planned and ordered and that new industrial spaces could also be ordered. The model industrial town in particular promised to be a solution not only to the problems of the industrial metropolis but also to the social and cultural problems of modernization. Through a concerted effort, planners could create order and meaning long before the physical spaces existed. This process of imposing order and creating was an imaginary process of comprehension similar in form to mapping. The drawing of a map placed all geography, nature, physical buildings, and people into a two-dimensional plane that could be read, divided, categorized, ordered, and understood. Yet the map was also full of possibilities, and it allowed viewers to read onto the map what they wished the space to be. The story lines attached to the city of Gary gave the same sense of both ordered space and limitless possibility.

This sort of hopeful and ordered mapping had long been a form of applying meaning and possibility onto new spaces. European colonists had drawn both detailed and fanciful maps of the "New World" to capture not only the physical terrain but the dangers and possibilities of the world as well. Throughout the nineteenth century, American mapmakers chose similar ways to view both the American West and the American city. The bird's-eye view of cities gave the viewer a chance to see the scale and power of cities while it also gave a sense of order to city streets—an order that may have been less comprehensible from street level. Maps of western towns stressed the grid pattern of streets (whether those streets existed yet or not), which suggested the possibility if not the inevitability of growth and success. Such images encouraged people to see the city not as it was but as it could be.[4] The process of mapping was especially important for a new space such as Gary. The task for planners became how to transform the lessons they had learned about the social realities of industrialism into physical structures. Construction had the additional role of locking expansive capital into a specific time and space. Thus the planning and mapping is the last time that all possibilities exist. Once the physical structures are built, they immediately begin to age and limit expansion and mobility. At the same time, a dominant narrative becomes locked in the public imagination. Yet within that early moment of Gary's creation, that meaning was not yet determined and all meanings were possible.

"A WONDER TALE": THE SPACE THAT CAPITAL BUILT

Because the U.S. Steel Corporation transformed thousands of acres of mostly uninhabited swamp land and sand dunes into a major center of steel production, the size and scale of the project caught the attention of many. Newspapers declared that the project was the "greatest ever" and that the "plant will be the most complete and best equipped in the world." *Scientific American* declared the site "the largest and most modern steel works in existence." Calling the construction of Gary "a wonder tale," Taylor noted that even "accustomed as Americans of this day are to rapid accomplishment, not one who visits the suddenly created town of Gary ... fails to experience a new thrill of achievement."[5]

The managers of U.S. Steel viewed the construction of the city of Gary not as an act of creation or model utopianism but as part of a larger national plan for expansion and efficiency. Officially the reason for the construction of Gary was to increase the production capacity within the region. While the steel mills on the south side of Chicago produced a great amount of steel, the mills were too confined, the land too expensive, and the regulations too strict to expand production by adding on to these mills. The city of Gary was for the company not a new creation but an extension of the preexisting steel production in the Chicago region. In official terms, the problems of south Chicago and the possibilities of northern Indiana were land and transportation, not class conflict, ethnic community, or urban immorality. It was deemed strictly a financial decision based on efficiency. At the same time, U.S. Steel used the construction of Gary to reimagine the scope of steel production and transportation. In envisioning his new steel mills, Elbert Gary and other officials of U.S. Steel did create a new map. But rather than focus upon the structures and spaces of the city of Gary, U.S. Steel placed the mills of Gary within the larger national map of the steel industry. The mills of Gary became a massive plant with direct access to the shipping lanes of Lake Michigan. This, U.S. Steel officials pointed out, would link the mills directly to the iron fields of northern Minnesota. The building of the mills along the major trunk lines meant direct access to the markets of Chicago, the West, and the East Coast.

During its construction and in the decades that followed, U.S. Steel created promotional maps that encompassed the entire Midwest with the mills of Gary at its center. To make the role of networks and transportation clear, these maps included broad arrows showing how coal, iron, and steel flowed into and out of the Calumet Region. The official vision of Gary was as part of a national system of integration and centralization. The mills of Gary, which the company focused on more than the city, were very important, but that importance stemmed from their place within the larger industrial network. Officially for U.S. Steel, Gary was both an extension of the Chicago market and a centralization of the national market. The actual structures and spaces of the city were far less relevant.

While this may have been the perception of U.S. Steel officials, Gary's planners dealt with more specific issues about what the mills and city would look like and how the site would function. Journalists and other social critics took a very different perspective as they viewed the new steel town. Onto these new spaces they tried to read narrative meaning and draw a comprehensive map. This mapping would be not of Gary within the national system of industrial production but of the city itself. Thus the stories people told of Gary varied greatly. For some, Gary was the ultimate example of technological advance and the victory of man over nature. It was a story of how science could literally turn swamp and sand into steel.

Others saw Gary as a triumph of strategic location and planning. Every aspect of the plant had been designed to maximize its efficiency. This process earned the steel mill the names of "Economy, Indiana," and the "sum of a thousand short cuts." Still others saw Gary as a model industrial city. Some critics hailed its social possibilities, and others criticized its failures and the missed opportunities for social experiments. Despite this variety of descriptions of the building of Gary, each of these narratives tried to construct myth and assign meaning to the place. Whether the story line was about science, order, or progress, the construction of Gary had clearly caught the public's imagination.[6]

The notion of the model city as a social experiment had existed long before the building of Gary. Often these utopian creations were attempts to escape from modernization and return to an idealized notion of a pre-modern and pastoral existence. However, modernists also embraced the idea of the model city. All of the principles of scientific planning could be applied. Because of the emphasis on science and technology, the modern model city often took an industrial form. Through a creation of a model industrial city, the lurking threat of industry could be removed from the larger city, and because of the intricate planning, the new city could diffuse this threat. Designed as a production center for George Pullman's sleeping car, the city of Pullman was just such an attempt at model industrialism. Pullman tried to alleviate the dangerous conditions and bad influences of modern society, including but not limited to bad water, worker radicalism, and improper entertainments.

Because George Pullman sought to control and reform the lives of his workers through planning and structure, he envisioned his city as a social utopia. Clean water, library books, and green spaces were supposed to eliminate social tensions and class conflicts. The great promise of a social utopia was that none of the modern problems of industrialization would be present in such a planned and utopian environment. Such conflicts, tensions, and upheavals seemed not to be inevitable outcomes of modernization, but stemmed from the improper practices of modern society. What separated Pullman from previous utopian plans was its embrace of large-scale modernization and its faith that the answers to modern problems lay in scientific technology and sanitation. Long an advocate for sanitary and moral reforms in Chicago, Oscar C. DeWolf looked to Pullman as confirmation of his ideals. "The erection of such towns as Pullman . . . has a very valuable and decided sanitary educational influence on the general population," he wrote, and "such towns, by improving the social surroundings of the working classes, tend to diminish the unrest, which is one great factor in capital and labor conflicts." By providing uplift instead of support, Pullman provided a model of social and moral reform. "This field is one which especially deserves the attention of philanthropists," DeWolf continued, "since it increases the power of the person aided to help himself, does not take from him self-respect, and therefore has no paupering tendencies, like the greatest number of other philanthropic schemes."[7]

Although Dr. DeWolf believed that the utopian schemes of Pullman maintained workers' self-respect, the foundation of Pullman's social utopia was paternalistic control. Workers not only had to embrace the middle-class standards of moral uplift, leisure, and entertainment; they also had to accept the company's ownership and control of everything. At the same time, while the social planning and reliance on moral uplift assumed that social unrest could be planned away, the economics of capital and labor relations remained an important part of social relations in the city. These paternalistic controls, a series of wage cuts, and the continued high rents in company houses led to a major strike in 1894. For a city that assumed that labor unrest could not occur within its planned environment, the strike shook the foundations of the experiment. The strikers in Pullman were soon joined by the American Railway Union, led by Eugene Debs, which refused to carry Pullman cars. By claiming that the strike was preventing the delivery of the mail, President Grover Cleveland secured a court order to end the conflict. He also sent in federal troops to uphold this order. The result was violence in Pullman between strikers and soldiers that resulted in twelve deaths.[8]

In the aftermath of the Pullman strike, it became clear to all that Pullman's paternalism and his attempt at social utopia had failed. Among those hardest hit by Pullman's failure were the social reformers and urban planners who had placed so much hope in the idea of the social utopia.

After the strike, Jane Addams, founder of Hull House in Chicago, wrote of Pullman:

> The sense of duty held by the president of the Pullman company doubtless represents the ideal in the minds of the best of the present employers as to their obligations toward their employees, but he projected this ideal more magnificently than the others. He alone gave his men a model town, such perfect surroundings. The magnitude of his indulgence and failure corresponded and we are forced to challenge the ideal itself: the same ideal which, more or less clearly defined, is floating in the minds of all philanthropic employers.

For Addams, Pullman represented a modern King Lear. Just as Lear tried to give all to his daughters yet was ultimately rejected, so did Pullman try to indulge his workers without fully understanding what they desired. In *Survey*, Graham Taylor also lamented the end of the Pullman experiment:

> For those who early hailed the town as providing that alchemy by which the labor problem was to be transmuted into Utopian paternalism, the mention of the name [Pullman] brings memories ... [of a] dream which vanished.... For "practical" men it signifies the futility of social betterment schemes and marks the battleground where law and order triumphed over anarchy.... But for the host of warm-hearted, sane believers in the better day that is coming, it stands for a great human tragedy.[9]

The failure of Pullman made many question the viability of the model town and the possibility of social utopianism. The discourse surrounding Gary, coming only fifteen years after the end of Pullman, developed out of these uncertainties. Many of the same assumptions in Pullman were also applied to Gary, yet the meaning of Gary was slightly different. While Pullman aimed to be a social utopia, U.S. Steel conceived of Gary as only a center of production guided by geography, not philanthropy, thus reflecting many shifts in the contemporary understanding of modernity and the urban experience.

Pullman represented an attempt at social utopia because it sought to better its residents and eliminate industrial strife and conflict. Through betterment, the working class of Pullman would cease to be the dangerous element that they were in Chicago. In addition, the scientific planning of production and the general cleanliness of the city would make the structures of industry less imposing upon the urban landscape, with no smokestacks vomiting smoke and disease in Pullman. Indeed, the factories that produced the Pullman sleeping cars were only part of the master plan for the city. To accomplish social betterment, the factories would have to work in conjunction with libraries, schools, shared housing, and other elements of worker life. In essence, the city of Pullman sought to solve the problems and anxieties of modernization. The creators of Gary made no such attempt in their construction. They assumed that the problems of industrialization and urbanization were inherent within modernization. The cause of anxiety within the modern city was not the presence of industry and the working class. It was the uncontrolled interaction between, and the lack of definition of, urban spaces. Thus the creators of Gary sought to clearly define, confine, and restrain the spaces of their city. The mapping of space became an important aspect of Gary because the seemingly unlimited space available made the process of delineation and separation possible. This mapping of Gary sought to separate space and to ensure that the production of steel could continue uninterrupted. The planners of Gary assumed the presence of potentially chaotic elements and that urban upheaval and violence were inevitable.

Chief among these spatial dividers was the Grand Calumet River. Up until 1906, the river was a meandering creek that often flooded large areas of the region. However, at the onset of construction, engineers of U.S. Steel moved the river a quarter of a mile south and confined it to a concrete channel. Ostensibly this was to give the mill room to grow and develop its own rail lines, but the river also served as a barrier between the mill and the town. The moat effect was not lost on observers. Commenting on the newly relocated river, the lake, and the boat channel created for loading and unloading, Henry Fuller of *Harper's Weekly* commented:

> The mills will thus be surrounded on three sides by water. This strategic position indicates a premonition of trouble. The Gary steel mills will be an open shop, and the swarming hordes of Huns and Polacks will think twice—or at least try twice—before crossing the medieval moat to gain the industrial stronghold beyond.

Fuller was not the only one to comment on the fortresslike shape the mills had taken. After echoing Fuller's comments on the construction of the moat, Graham Taylor adds:

with the lake front so extensively controlled by the company, strikebreakers and suppliers by the boat load from the numerous ports on the Great Lakes could be brought directly to the plants without risk. It is pointed out that under such conditions, a repetition of the Homestead strike would be impossible, and that possibly no great industrial plant or series of plants occupies a position so impregnable to mob attack and so calculated to withstand a prolonged industrial siege.

Planners designed Gary not to prevent but to survive the very kind of violence that had ended the experiment in Pullman.[10]

Many contemporaries picked up on the shift in utopian discourse in Gary. Some critics suggested that U.S. Steel was interested in, as *Survey* phrased it, "avoiding the mistakes of Pullman." At the same time the planning of the mills in Gary also looked toward the strike and violence of Homestead in 1892. It was there that Andrew Carnegie and Henry Clay Frick turned the steel mill into a fortified stronghold. So too were the mills at Gary designed to hold off any attempted siege or seizure by strikers. Yet the problem for Frick and Carnegie at Homestead came when the Pinkerton agents they hired arrived by barge in the town where they were met by angry and armed strikers. The battle for Homestead took place not at the walls of the mill but at the riverfront. Gary would not have the same problem. Not only did the river create a protective moat, but the lakefront would ensure that the Gary mills would not be cut off. Thus the construction and planning of Gary represented the culmination and lessons of several different utopian failures. It promised to avoid the naïve assumptions of Pullman, the strategic disadvantages of Homestead, and the lack of control of unplanned industrial areas. "Fresh in the minds of us all," concluded Buffington in *Harper's Weekly*, "is the failure of the Pullman company to maintain its authority over the village affairs." Fuller also suggested that "the new enterprise will avoid the excess of paternalism which put something of a blight on Pullman, and the hit-or-miss planlessness which has filled South Chicago with discord and cross purposes."[11]

"A VIRGIN SITE TO BUILD UPON": THE TABULA RASA OF INDUSTRY

U.S. Steel insisted that, because of its connections via the Great Lakes to the Mesabi iron range of northern Minnesota and its rail connections to major steel markets in the East, Gary was chosen as a site for the mill solely for economic reasons. "The officials of the steel company say frankly," reported *Survey*, "that the building of the town was incidental, that their main concern was to construct a steel plant." Newspaper reports echoed similar justifications. "The selection of Gary as the site of the colossal plant to be constructed," voiced the *Indianapolis News*, "is because of its general understanding that the industry can be assembled there as cheaply as at any place in the United States."[12] U.S. Steel executive Horace S. Norton denied that Gary was a model city. "Gary is really a part of the Chicago development and represents the expansion of Chicago south and east in accordance with the dictates of economic necessity and advantage. . . . It is difficult to tell where Chicago ends and Gary begins." Despite the reluctance to engage in utopian imagery, U.S. Steel did construct an imagined landscape of Gary. It was a form of myth making that centered upon the triumphs of science and the act of creation.

Because of the company's reluctance to proclaim Gary a social experiment, much of the discourse surrounding the construction centered on the economics of location and the technological triumph of the mill. Chief among these observers was *Scientific American,* which marveled at the scale of the mill taking shape on the lakeshore: "With such a virgin site to build upon, the designers of the plant were able to work with a free hand; and the component parts of this, the greatest steel plant in existence, were therefore laid out with a strict regard to the economic handling of the enormous masses of raw material and finished product." Throughout the article, the size, scale, and efficiency of the mill astonished *Scientific American*. It walked the reader through every function of the plant, citing numerous statistics regarding the amount of steel the mill was producing. Not surprisingly, given the nature of the magazine, *Scientific American* viewed the construction in Gary as a great scientific and technological achievement. Its only mention of the city was along the same lines as its description of the mill. "The town has been laid out on the most approved modern lines," it boasted, and "everything is being done to render this city comparable with the best model industrial cities of the country."[13]

The *System,* a business magazine, was equally impressed with the size and efficiency of the new mill.

> Because of its magnitude—the world challenging job of creating a new city, a deep-sea harbor, industry's biggest steel mill—Gary has held the attention of four continents since 1906; interest redoubled with the "blowing in" of its first furnace a few days ago. Size, however, is its smallest quality. To the business man its imperative claims are its efficiency, economy, speed. It is the shrine of the short-cut a composite of the best in power, in production, in saving. It is a hundred-million-dollar lesson in the science of making and selling—a demonstration in steel and concrete of the parts foresight, strategy and exact knowledge should play in every business.

Like *Scientific American,* the *System* gives only a few lines of recognition to the city of Gary. For *System,* the mill was the most important aspect of the story because it represented the finest in scientific progress and technological advancement. The Gary mill was the best of modernity written on a giant scale.[14]

Although *Scientific American* and *System* said little about the city, others voiced similar amazement and used much of the same language in their description of the new town. Commenting upon the creation of the city, John Mumford declared Gary a "land of opportunity" and the "city that rose from a sandy waste." He expressed amazement that "three years ago the wild duck used to flock in the lazy reaches of backwater all about the sluggish bends" where now the city of Gary stood. Juxtaposing before-and-after photos, the article shows "how Gary looked two years ago . . . [and] what has been accomplished during eighteen months." The *Survey* concluded that "Gary is probably the single greatest calculated achievement of America's master industry." Embracing the notion of strategic planning, the *Independent* proclaimed that "Gary is an economic condition"; in fact, it represented the "most interesting economic development of all time." "Surely in Gary we see the so-called trust at its best," it concluded. "The old order of things is passing away. Man, the conqueror, and man, the liberator, takes on new dignity and glory as man, the creator."[15]

"ALL IN THE BEST AND MOST ENLIGHTENED WAY": CITY AS SOCIAL LABORATORY

For many urban theorists and social reformers, the building of the city represented both the promise of limitless possibilities and the lost opportunity to engage rather than confine urban problems. The notion of beginning a city anew attracted a great deal of attention. "In Gary, the town," commented Graham Taylor in the *Survey*, "there was absolutely unhampered opportunity to arrange the streets, provide the fundamental necessities of community life, determine the character of its houses, and predestine the lines of growth, all in the best and most enlightened way."

"Each dwelling has been provided with a small garden," noted the *Chicago Tribune*. "It is clean and has adequate space for the family which it is designed to accommodate." Buffington, writing in *Harper's Weekly*, stated that "Gary is nothing more than the product of effort along practical lines to secure right living conditions around a steel-manufacturing plant." Even a skeptical Fuller concluded that, although Gary was built to order by U.S. Steel for the production of steel, "the general scheme for the new city seems almost philanthropic."

Despite this celebration of the possibilities of urban planning, however, the shape of Gary disappointed many others. "While it may fall short in its community features," lamented Taylor, "there are those who see in it an extraordinary degree of industrial strategy." Among the complaints Taylor leveled at the planners of Gary were the use of a rectangular street pattern instead of a more modern design utilizing diagonal streets, the monopoly by the corporation of the lakeshore thus preventing the development of Chicago style parks, and the boom of saloons within the city. In essence Taylor wanted to apply the newest notions of urban planning popularized by Haussmann and proposed for Chicago by Daniel Burnham. Yet Taylor was most concerned about health, the deterioration of sanitation, and the quality of low-income housing. "The failure of the company to work out the housing needs of its low-paid immigrant labor," he concluded, "was emphasized by its apparent indifference as to where the 'hunkies' found a new abode." Fuller saw the development of low-income areas as a threat to the very idea of the planned community. "Once across the 'Wabash Tracks,'" he declared, "one's sense of the self-assertiveness of private initiative is even augmented. It hangs like a heavy fringe upon the fabric of the original ideal; and the monumental character of the Great Enterprise, as first conceived, vanishes. . . . Once across those tracks, we leave the region of prohibition and propriety behind and enter the free-and-easy realm of the red light." Perhaps Buffington best understood the industrial utopian nature of Gary and the role U.S. Steel sought to play in social questions. "The material welfare of Gary is an accomplished fact," he wrote. "Its social welfare is held within the desires and aspirations of its future citizens." U.S. Steel, it seemed, was not responsible for the development, success, or future of the city of Gary.[16]

If Graham Taylor led the voices of disappointment for the missed opportunities for social and progressive planning, he also tried to place the growth of Gary into the larger context of urban and industrial development. While many of his articles focused on U.S. Steel's failure to take full advantage of Gary's new construction, he also penned a series of articles that examined the phenomenon of industrial peripheries. Serialized first in *Survey* and then collected as a book, Taylor's articles examined the development of what he called "satellite cities." These places were industrial centers that grew upon the periphery of larger urban centers and retained economic and cultural connections to the larger city. Taylor included in this list not only Gary but also cities such as East St. Louis, Illinois, and Norwood, Ohio.[17] While these cities shared the criteria that Taylor used to call them satellite cities, none were planned company towns in the same way that Gary was. Taylor's satellite city declaration, then, placed the creation and development of Gary within a very different category. Far from the acts of creation, the triumph of science, or the possibilities of social planning, the satellite city analysis suggested that Gary's development was part of a larger process of urban and industrial growth. Gone were the personal and corporate intentions, the decisions and oversights, and the narratives that attached symbolic importance to the science and scale. Gary had become a product of urban expansion that, while worth comment and analysis, was not unique but part of a group of similar cities.

CONCLUSION: "SUBURB OF CHICAGO THOUGH IT IS"

By the end of the nineteenth century, cities wishing to call themselves modern looked to Paris as a model. For Chicago, this meant that its periphery was to play an important role. A key part of Baron Georges Haussmann's plans for Paris was the development of the city's outskirts. In addition to the widening of city streets, which also made them harder to barricade, and the introduction of sweeping boulevards with the visual quality and the impressive scale of the capital of an imperial power, Haussmann also moved out of the city all the dangerous elements that could not be controlled. Chicago's peripheral development occurred along different lines, however. Gary was not a dumping ground for all that could not be planned; it was part of a new concept that valued the periphery greatly as an indispensable part of proper city functioning. In modern industrialized urbanism, the periphery was not peripheral at all but central. Gary was no longer just the industrial periphery of a new model Chicago. It was a model industrial city in its own right. It was this possibility that led Henry Fuller to anoint the city an "industrial utopia."

Yet such utopian dreams were short-lived in Gary. Not only had Lewis Mumford declared the possibility of utopia dead in 1922, but utopian language had stopped being applied to Gary. Observers remarked upon Gary's rapid growth and its integration into global steel markets and Chicago's urban world. It was a magic city because of U.S. Steel's role in building it. If the first years of Gary's existence represented an opportunity to debate the meaning of the new city, by 1920 the narrative of industrial relocation had become the most dominant of mythologies. In a section of a guide book to Chicago entitled "The extraordinary making of Gary," Robert Shackleton made this industrial origin clear. "The making of the city of Gary was a huge and remarkable achievement," he wrote, due almost entirely to the leadership of Elbert Gary, "one of America's greatest financiers, who for years displayed his grasp of enormous financial problems as the directing spirit of the billion dollar steel corporation, the greatest single business organization in the world."[18]

As for the city, it was both an extension of Chicago and a tabula rasa for industrial order. "Gary stands where most people, except Chicagoans themselves, think that Chicago stands," he explains, "at the southern end of Lake Michigan." This location was carefully chosen by the corporation "in order to gain real geographical advantages, with its really central situation, its harbor possibilities, its possibilities of railway connections, the ease with which raw material could be gathered and with which manufactured products could be shipped." "Gary is so completely down at the foot—or head—of the lake—Lake Michigan stands on its head, that it is actually over the line in Indiana, suburb of Chicago as it is. It is only twenty-six miles from the heart of the great city" and fully integrated into the world of Chicago. But there is more to Gary beyond its location. It is planned and orderly and a triumph of industrial relocation. And here, much like *Scientific American*'s description of the mill, Shackleton slips into the passive voice to explain its presence. "Enormous steel mills went up as if by magic, and workmen were sent by the thousands. Their families, too, were sent, for homes went up as the mills went up and from the first there was comfort in family living. . . . The city started, unhampered by the mistakes of past generations."[19]

For his part, Eugene Buffington was convinced that Gary was its own industrial center and that the future of American industry and thus the future of modern society had to be sorted out in just such industrial cities. The best way, perhaps the only way, to sort out these difficult issues and alleviate the dangerous tensions of modernization was by designing and constructing better model industrial cities. Far from a tabula rasa unhampered by the efforts of previous generations, Gary, Buffington argued, was the latest in a fine tradition of model cities such as Pullman, Illinois, and Vandergrift, Pennsylvania. Many other observers and social reformers saw the same thing in Gary. They all hoped that its structures, its planning, and its order could solve the basic problems of modern industrial society. But important differences existed between these various attempts at model urbanism. Pullman was an effort to force uplift and eliminate industrial strife through paternalistic control and sanitary conditions. Rather than eliminate industrial strife, Gary sought to control and contain it.

When George McMutry planned his industrial city of Vandergrift, Pennsylvania, he largely eliminated the paternalistic control of Pullman and encouraged individual home ownership (except for the lowest of wage workers, who were forced to live elsewhere). The thinking was to discourage industrial strife by encouraging company loyalty and carefully selecting proper employees. This effort proved useful during the 1901 strike against the newly created U.S. Steel. Vandergrift did, however, keep Pullman's obsession with sanitation and nature. Indeed McMutry hired Frederick Law Olmsted to design the parks and curvilinear streets of his city.[20] The planners of Gary made no such efforts to ensure the sanitation or natural conditions of the city. By claiming all of the lakefront property of the city, the mills virtually ensured the lack of nature in the city. Ostensibly the planners of Gary embraced the Vandergrift model of individual homes rather than the Pullman or Lowell model of rented housing. Yet U.S. Steel made little to no effort to either control or encourage home construction. Instead, the steel company went out of its way to insist that Gary was a venture of strategic location and industrial growth, not an experiment in model industrialism. Despite the dreams and desires that others applied to Gary, for U.S. Steel the hope for order in Gary was purely structural, not utopian.

Observers came to Gary and read onto the new space different ideas about what industrial order, or perhaps industrial utopia, might look like. Gary mattered, within the American imagination, because of what it might represent. It became what observers wished it to be.

PART TWO

A City Built on Sand

I went to Gary prepossessed against it. I was familiar with duke-owned towns of England, as they were before the World War, where titled men actually owned factories and stores and homes and controlled every means of labor and life, and I remembered the sad hopelessness of aspect of the workingmen, and I feared to find something of the same unhappiness and dolor in the atmosphere of this corporation-owned city of Gary. But I found only a breezy manliness, an atmosphere of satisfaction, of positive happiness; and instead of the black and dismal streets that I had known in Sheffield, the most important of the cities that were owned by so-called nobility, I found, in Gary, clean and wide and open streets, with prosperous-looking business buildings and alert and happy people.

ROBERT SHACKLETON, *THE BOOK OF CHICAGO,* 1920

THREE

"The Youngest City in the World"

THE EARLY YEARS OF AN INDUSTRIAL FRONTIER

There could be little doubt that the election of 1912 was going to be about the issue of reform. Each of the four candidates offered a reform agenda, yet each candidate differed on what he saw as the major problem that needed reform. With their shared yet complicated visions of Square Deal government and trust management, William Howard Taft and Theodore Roosevelt battled over the progressive wing of the Republican Party and the schism that was the "Bull Moose" Progressive Party. Eugene Debs had tied into the more radical socialist visions of America's problems and possibilities. Democrat Woodrow Wilson, then, had to choose a different path. On the advice of Louis Brandeis, Wilson made the problem of trusts paramount to his campaign and their elimination vital to the success of "real" Americans. Unlike the Republicans, "the Democratic platform is the only platform," Wilson claimed, "which says that private monopoly is indefensible and intolerable." To make his point more real, Wilson then juxtaposed two different Americas. "I know in Indiana, for example, town after town was pointed out to me that still has the American characteristic," he told audiences, "in which there are factories upon factories, owned by men who live in the place—independent enterprises still unabsorbed by the great economic combinations which have become so threateningly inhuman in our economic organization—and it seems to me that these are outposts and symbols of the older and freer America." Then Wilson told of his journeys further north to a place within Indiana but not quite Indianan, within the United States but not quite American. "And after I had traveled through that series of towns and met the sturdy people that live in them, I entered in the city of Gary, which is a little ways outside of Chicago, and realized that I had come from the older America into the newer America. But this was a town owned and built by a single monopolistic corporation. And I wondered which kind of America the people of America, if they could see this picture as I saw it, would choose?"[1] For Wilson, Gary existed because it was "a town patronized by some great combination of capitalists who pick it out as a suitable place to plant their industry and draw you into their employment." This made the city the epitome of the industrial threats to the very principles of American life. It was the center of monopoly, it was emasculating, and it was dangerous.

Between 1906 and 1912, the descriptions of Gary tended to fall into a couple of categories. The technological might of U.S. Steel and the application of modern scientific principles marked Gary as the new center of modern industry. The limitless possibilities of social planning and spatial separation meant, for some, that Gary might represent a new age of social relations and industrial utopianism. Such stories gave positive meaning to the newly created city. Yet Wilson's vision of Gary was as a place, and a nation, gone horribly wrong. If the process of construction in Gary meant the mapping of established narratives onto the new spaces of the city, it is clear that, by 1912, a number of different, and indeed at times contradictory, visions had emerged. While this process of applying meaning for the structures of Gary was critical in the establishment of the map of the city, it created a map that did not have a permanent and cross-cultural legend. Both the imagined and physical maps of Gary could be read in a number of ways. Even after the opening of the mills in 1909, the meaning and symbolism of the city remained open to interpretation. When people chose to reinterpret the symbolic grids and spatial meanings of Gary, they tended to use very different narratives than those used to define its creation. The existence of Gary prompted narratives that tended to either see Gary and Chicago as the potential for a modern future or the remnants of a wild past. At the same time worker narratives of the city focused less on the physical structures of the mill and the city and more on the new potential for work and community. Without a hegemonic legend, the mapping of Gary remained an interpretative and highly contradictory process. This debate, however, was framed by a progressive reformist agenda, and major themes did emerge. Was Gary an example of industrial progress or monopolistic power? Was it a quintessentially American space or an un-American place? Was it redeemable, reformable, or salvageable? Each participant would have his own interpretation of these questions.

Despite the rhetoric of industrial utopianism that surrounded the creation of Gary and Wilson's political critique of the city, the mythology that most people used to describe the early years of Gary tended to focus on the image of Gary as a frontier. In 1893 Frederick Jackson Turner declared that not only had the American frontier closed but with it ended the first epoch of American history. The process of acquiring, conquering, and taming the frontier, Jackson said to the American Historical Association at the Chicago World's Fair, had defined the American experience. However, by the frontier, Jackson meant the closing of the "West," itself both a physical and imagined space full of mythology and competing narratives. With the "closing" of the West also came, many assumed, the end of both the individual opportunities and the romantic wildness of the frontier. Thus American society began to look for new frontiers and new opportunities, especially abroad in the Philippines and Cuba. Such places offered the same romance, masculinity, savagery, and triumph that the West had provided.[2]

Yet Gary promised much of the same in the first two decades of the twentieth century because it was new and largely unsettled. Young single men streamed in for the economic and entertainment possibilities. Its streets were active, violent, and even bloody. The "Patch," the working-class district south of the Wabash Railroad tracks, was marked by over 200 saloons with names such as the "First and Last Chance," "Jack Johnson's Gambling Joint," and the "Bucket of Blood." This frontier mythology with its focus on youth, opportunity, and violence offered, as Richard Slotkin has argued, a chance for regeneration and renewal. Far from the rest of modernizing America, Gary seemed lawless, violent, exciting, chaotic, and romantic, all within the shadow of the most modern steel-producing center in the world. But above all the frontier image of Gary was profoundly male.[3]

Gary was also a factory town with the identifying markers of poverty, immigrants, substandard housing, and pollution. Because U.S. Steel paid little to no attention to city development below the railroad tracks, the Patch developed poor, overcrowded housing. A government study stated that two-thirds of children of foreign-born workers had no milk, fruit, or eggs in their daily diet. Half had no vegetables, and one-third had no meat.[4] The images out of Gary, then, were convoluted. It was one part frontier town of masculine violence and opportunity and one part factory town of starving children and immigrant families. It held the excitement of a frontier cattle town and the potential for social upheaval that existed in industrial districts.

"MODERN INDUSTRIAL COMMUNITIES": THE POTENTIAL FOR REFORM IN GARY

In his study of the mythology of the frontier, Slotkin suggests that there were, by the early twentieth century, two competing but not necessarily mutually exclusive ideologies of the frontier: the progressive and populist mythologies. A "progressive" image of the frontier saw the 1890s as a crisis in American development. The challenge of this new industrial frontier was to continue the slow transformation that proponents saw as the key to American historical development. Through the implementation of technology and the use of power by a trained managerial class, the rough edges and excesses of this new wilderness could be tamed. Instead of radical labor leaders and monomaniacal industrialists, order and civilization could be established by cooler heads and trained professionals. It was a mythology of conquering, taming, and modernizing wild spaces.

Such a vision of professionalism and modernization certainly played a major role in the image of Gary. During the construction, urban planners and social utopianists certainly saw in Gary a possibility to try out new forms of social planning and social control. Yet even after 1909, when many came to see Gary as a wild frontier, some progressives still saw the possibility of taming both the wildness of Gary and the excesses of industrial culture through centralization of power and scientific planning. Thus while earlier progressives tried to impose order in the creation of Gary, this new generation saw Gary as wild, untamed, and disordered—a place in need of reforming.

Chief among these reformers was William A. Wirt. A student of Thomas Dewey and an advocate of universal public education, Wirt was intrigued by the opportunity to build a new school system in Gary from scratch. The way to Americanize immigrants, educate working-class children, and restore order to city streets was, for Wirt, through his new platoon system of comprehensive education. In July 1907, Wirt became the superintendent of Gary schools and began to institute his work-study-play concepts. He sought to combine the principles of industrial work education with intellectual subjects. The schools in Gary became a social laboratory for the intellectual and social uplift of working-class children. In his study of the rise and fall of the Gary Plan of education, Ronald D. Cohen argues that Wirt's idea for progressive education is notable for its progressive ideologies and because it represents the first attempt at mass education created for complex multiracial and multiethnic urban communities. Wirt and other high-profile members of the school board were closely tied to the business community of Gary, thus one of the functions of the schools was to educate students in the culture of corporate capitalism. The system did divide students into winners and losers based largely on race, ethnicity, and class. Yet Wirt did not exercise total control, and people took the school system of Gary seriously because it offered the image, if not the reality, of an open and equitable society. At the same time, the schools in Gary tried to educate children but also offered other services including babysitting, adult education, and social welfare. While the Gary Plan was essentially an exercise in instilling corporate capitalism, the schools' central place within the community also made them a battleground of resistance.[5]

Discussion of the Gary Plan tended to confirm reformist visions for Gary's present and its future. Much like the discussions of the city's founding, these descriptions stressed the planning, vision, and modern efficiency of the plan. Stressing the science and efficiency of the system, many publications lauded the scientific expertise of Wirt. One editorial referred to Wirt as an "Educational Engineer [and] Constructive Genius of the Gary System." The Gary Plan, much like the city of Gary itself, became a vision of tomorrow. John Dewey even entitled his book on educational reform, which details the experiment in Gary, *Schools of To-Morrow*.[6] In answering the question of "how should young men train for the future" in a feature entitled *Business To-Morrow,* Elbert Gary pointed to the modern qualities of the school system. "Mr. Wirt's work is the first successful attempt to bring the teaching in public schools into any real adjustment with the conditions of life in modern industrial communities.[7] Such were the model possibilities for a modern industrial educational system that many argued the Gary Plan should be copied in other cities.

In addition to scientific reformers who adored its modernism, religious advocates were also enamored of the system because it set aside time for religious education.[8] New York did adopt a similar system, to the delight of many and the concern of some. Advocates argued that the Gary Plan was more efficient, cost less, and provided better education, while some critics pointed out that the Gary Plan could not possibly be replicated because "conditions in Gary are so different from those in most cities. No old buildings or special school traditions existed to hamper the success of the plan."[9]

Therein lay the debate not only about Gary schools or reform in Gary but about the city of Gary itself. For some, Gary was an urban laboratory, born out of industrial expansion and corporate capitalism. All was modern and new, and thus new models of social reform, urban education, religious integration, and Americanization could be tried, refined, perfected, and eventually exported to other industrial cities. The success of the Gary Plan had the possibility to trump even the grand narrative of U.S. Steel's remarkable act of creation. "The 'steel city' of Gary, Indiana—built to order on barren sand-dunes near Chicago by the United States Steel Company for its colossal modern industrial plant," offered *Current Opinion*, "stands a chance of becoming even more famous for its Engineer of Education, William A. Wirt." So too did the *Survey* suggest that "it is the story of the vocational training system at Gary which bids fair to give that town a greater claim on public recognition than the steel mills or the drama of its growth."[10] For others such as Wilson or the critics of New York's adoption of the Gary Plan, Gary was not a microcosm of American industrialism but an aberration. Too new, too modern, too foreign, or too controlled by industrial interests, Gary, in this view, was not a model for exportation but a site desperately in need of transformation. In her comparative study of settlement homes in Indianapolis and Gary, Ruth Crocker shows how progressive reformers often functioned as missionaries who sought to impose their vision of Americanism on immigrant populations. Far from seeing Gary as a new modern site, settlement workers tried to "restore" a sense of domesticity and home life that stressed not cultural pluralism, women's independence, or racial equality but discipline and modernization. The irony was that settlement workers, the earliest of whom (Kate and Jane Williams) arrived in Gary in February 1909, the same year that the mills began to function, sought to restore order and modernize the population in a space that was entirely new.[11] For progressives, Gary combined the mythologies of the rugged frontier that needed to be conquered and modernized and the ethnic industrial city that needed to be controlled and Americanized.

"A WIDE OPEN TOWN": THE POTENTIAL FOR EXCITEMENT AND WEALTH IN GARY

If some observers saw in Gary a frontier in need of civilization and reform, others saw very different possibilities. The other frontier mythology that Slotkin describes was also readily present in the early years of Gary. The "populist" ideology of the frontier, Slotkin argues, came not from technological modernization but rather out of the individualist strain of Jeffersonian and Jacksonian political traditions. Instead of advocating the centralization of power and the rise of a managerial class, the populist vision regarded equal opportunity and decentralized power as the chief markers of the frontier. Instead of chaos that had to be tamed, the frontier represented opportunity that could be grasped. While the progressive ideology focused on Gary's industrial and ethnic realities, the more populist strain concentrated on Gary's almost western possibilities. "I hadn't read much but what I read I remembered. One thing that stuck in my memory was the advice of Horace Greeley: 'Go West, young man,'" recalled Harry Hall, "Gary wasn't very far west but it was new. Besides there was no other place for me to go." Many others saw in Gary the economic opportunities of western mining and cattle towns. "When I got off the train and looked about one minute, I said to myself, this is my town," remembered Albert Lee Anchors. "What I could see looked like a brand new gold mining camp. Everybody busy, everybody hurrying. Graders, carpenters, mill construction workers. I knew how to handle myself in a mining camp and knew what to do here." Within the populist narrative, Gary was a site of economic and social possibility.[12]

The tensions between these two visions played themselves out most clearly in the politics of early Gary. Despite founding the city and giving it his name, Elbert Gary spent very little time there and had little influence over its development. The voice of U.S. Steel in Gary was divided between Horace S. Norton, the head of the Gary Land Company (a U.S.

Steel subsidiary charged with building the city of Gary), and William Palmer Gleason, the superintendent of the Gary Works. The Gary Land Company concentrated most of its energy in developing the First Subdivision. This section of city closest to the mills had graded and paved streets, concrete sidewalks, and rich topsoil that the company brought in so that trees and grass might grow. This section quickly became not only the home of U.S. Steel foremen and executives but also the center of political power in Gary. Yet the booming portion of Gary was below the Wabash tracks in the Patch where neither Gleason nor Norton held much political power. Instead, political power in the Patch belonged to Thomas E. Knotts.[13]

A veteran of the western frontier, Knotts spent much of the 1880s teaching Sioux Indians in Wyoming and the Dakotas. He settled in Hammond, Ind., where he served as both a policeman and an editor of a Populist-leaning newspaper. In an early display of political leanings, he was jailed in 1894 for urging workers to defy court injunctions during the Pullman strike. He would later name one of his children after Eugene V. Debs. After his older brother, Armanis, helped persuade U.S. Steel to build its new plant on the Indiana site, Knotts himself relocated to Gary and, in 1906, became the postmaster. On July 28 he was elected onto the first town board. Soon questions over the success of Gary Land company sales and the profiteering of the Knotts brothers chilled the relationship between Knotts and Norton. This animosity developed into a feud when Knotts gave the city's trolley franchise to the Gary Interurban Company. Not only did the contract not go to the Gary and Hammond Traction Company (a U.S. Steel subsidiary) but Gary Interurban planned to build its trolley north and south along Broadway instead of east and west along 5th Avenue. This meant instead of the town growing on company-owned land on 5th Avenue, it would grow along Broadway, much of which was owned by the Knotts family.[14] What began as a personal battle over land and real estate profits quickly became a struggle over control over the city. While Norton represented the company interests and the First Division, Knotts became the champion of the Patch.

In the city's first mayoral election in 1909, Norton and the company threw their support behind John A. Brennan. Fearing that he was being criticized by the editorials in the city's only newspaper, the *Daily Tribune*, Knotts created the *Evening Post* to trumpet his virtues. In fine frontier fashion, the Republican sheriff of Lake County arrested Knotts and the entire Gary police force on the eve of the election for defamation of character. Yet, because of overwhelming support from the Patch, Knotts won by 71 votes out of 3,500 cast. The victory of town forces against the company would be short-lived, however. In 1913, the company threw its support behind Roswell O. Johnson, who was running on the ostensibly nonpartisan Citizens' Party ticket. Knotts, who had been arrested 24 times yet never convicted, was voted out of office.[15]

What the careers and successes of Armanis and Thomas Knotts demonstrate is the narrative of individual success and opportunity that permeated early Gary. It was, according to mythology, a western frontier town in the east. Knotts's image was not tarnished by his less than legal activities; indeed, his status was enhanced by these acts. If there were things that tied Knotts, Hall, and Anchors together, it was their understanding of Gary's landscape and their success in exploiting it. This is what distinguished them from William Wirt or Horace Norton, who sought to tame Gary's landscape and transform its citizens.

The popular frontier narrative suggested that Gary was a space where the common rules of etiquette and civility no longer applied. It was violent, it was hyper-masculine, it was bawdy in its entertainments, and above all it was exciting. Gary resident Harry King evoked such a space when he remembered Gary as a "wide open town." Likewise, Gary's first police chief described the Patch as "hell on wheels." And indeed this description of Gary did focus on the Patch, for it was there that the entertainments and excitements of a wild lawless town would be enjoyed. "In the early days of Gary," recalled Charles MacKay, "it was not so law-abiding. By reason of its rapid growth and industrial development, men of all types including those criminally inclined, drifted into our city from far and near. Nothing much was safe that was portable. Our rails through the city were about all we could be sure of finding in the morning when we came around."[16]

Gun battles such as the "Turk riot" on January 15, 1908, between Serbian immigrants and police took on less of the narrative of industrial class violence than the gunplay of the Wild West. "In the early days of Gary it was easy to see men with revolvers," remembered Paul Dremeley. "Sometimes they wore them in the wide belt that held up there [sic] pants on Sunday like a decoration.... One night we were playing by the bakery in back of Sarkotich's saloon on 22nd and Jefferson and it was summer (about 1916) when we heard an argument at one of the card tables. Then one guy pulled his gun and shot Steve and Johnny Janda's father and he fell dead. We ran like hell. There was shooting like this in the saloons many times. After dark you could usually hear shots from somewhere almost every night.... A .22 revolver cost about $5. Mr. Yambrosich on 22nd and Adams had a .44. He said it had killed Indians out west." Dremeley also recalled the active social life of the Patch including the various saloons and boarding houses, the demonstration of dancing bears, and the introduction of nickelodeon theaters and various shows. For Dremeley, Gary was a "shootin' tootin' twon [sic] in the early days."[17]

Such connections to the narratives of the West would certainly have been persuasive for generations of young men who had grown up with dime novel heroes such as Deadwood Dick and the mythological if not historical Jesse James. If dime novels were, as Michael Denning suggests, both a site of contestation and a compromise between "popular" tastes and profits, then the city of Gary for some represented a chance to play out these same fantasies and popular tastes.[18] Tying the lifestyle of Gary to the West made the city more exciting and less controllable. If the progressive mythology of the frontier focused on national narratives of progress and civilization, the populist frontier represented the possibilities of the American character. Far from Frederick Jackson Turner's dire warnings, the populist frontier for many was not closed but remained open in Gary. While the residents of Gary may not have experienced the excitements and adventure of the West, at least they could experience Gary. If Mr. Yambrosich himself had not killed Indians, then at least the revolver had. Much of this local vision of the city ignored the industrial origins of the city or the presence of the massive steel mills. The frontier narratives of the city were visions not of the rigid science of the mills or the planned structure of the First Subdivision but rather the fluid social possibilities and unwritten narratives of the Patch.

"DON'T GO THERE, IT'S A BAD PLACE": STEEL WORK AND ETHNIC COMMUNITY IN GARY

For their part many of the workers who moved to Gary brought with them still another vision of an industrial city. Contrary to the reformer conceptualization of a model society and the industrialist vision of an ordered place of production, worker conceptions of industrial society focused on the possibilities for work and community. David Montgomery argues that one of the guiding factors in working-class actions and organizations in the late nineteenth century was a demand for control over the workplace. In response to the centralization of production, the mechanization of labor, and the industrialists' obsession with efficiency, workers strove to exercise some control over their lives by controlling labor on the shop floor. Roy Rosenzweig shows how workers' culture and leisure emerged as a site of contestation between middle-class reformer ideals and the working-class community.[19]

In his study of Chicago's meatpacking district, James Barrett argues that working-class life in the last decades of the nineteenth century was driven by four connected and often overlapping concerns. The first was the experience of mass production work. Just as mechanization seemed rational through the eyes of managers and Taylorists, it brought more chaos and uncertainty to workers in the plants. Second, the standard of living within working-class districts was tied to industrial work but was also shaped by the family economy. Labor struggles, then, were part of an effort to exercise control over communities and homes as much as workplaces. These efforts at control led to working-class unity as well as fragmentation. The changing shape of fragmentation, which is echoed in Richard Oestreicher's study of Detroit, formed the third key issue. Finally, working-class action and concerns served as a counter to corporate liberalism and company paternalism. While working-class visions were efforts at control and stability, the method of contestation was often class conflict. On Chicago's south side, Barrett concludes, workplace and community flowed into each other and the concerns of one became the conflicts of the other.[20]

If the key to working-class solidarity and action on Chicago's south side was the easy flow between work and community, then U.S. Steel's greatest accomplishment in the construction of Gary may well have been the separation of these two. The steel corporation went to great lengths to ensure that firm boundaries between work and home were built into the city. Thus there were two Garys: Gary Works and Gary the city. The historiography of labor, immigration, and migration all demonstrate the importance of community to working-class visions and expectations.

People came to Gary not to reject industrial work and industrial society but to embrace it. Yet they wished to do so on their own terms. These ideals were not the order and production of industrialists nor the model of reform and stability of middle-class idealists. Working-class visions of Gary concentrated on the possibilities of work and the continuation of familial connections. For immigrants arriving in industrial cities, many of these concerns over community were similar. Yet as John Bodnar has argued, immigrants at the turn of the century were driven not by grand ideologies of class or ethnicity but by focused notions of family. The expectations of work, community, progress, and control were shaped by images of family networks and close-knit ethnic communities governed largely by traditional ethnic institutions. Far from the image of the unskilled and pre-industrial peasant, most immigrants were already part of the modern industrial system and, by choosing to migrate into industrial cities, had come to embrace both the realities and potentials of the industrial economy.

Helen Baxter Hansen, for instance, remembered that her father had been a locomotive engineer in Scotland before the family immigrated to the United States and made their way to Gary to find work.

> So he came over. And there were a lot of Scotch people that came over at that time. They all worked in the Gary Steel Mill. The city of Gary is a, was a funny town. In the east side, where we lived, was a whole bunch of Scotch people and then, like on the south side there was a lot of Slavic and, you know, Polish and what else was there? Just, you know, the Slavic people in another end of town, and they were all kind of clannish, you know. But they got along, but they were kind of clannish.... You kept to your own.[21]

William Solyom remembered that before his family's arrival in Gary, others tried to warn them of the dangerous industrial conditions. "After we left Chicago, of course, they tried to tell us you know that there's a lot of Hungarians in Gary, you know, they were telling us in Hungarian. And ah, but he said, 'Don't go there,' he said, 'It's a bad place. You'll get consumption right away, you know, from the sand, you know.'" However, Solyom's take on Gary was far more pragmatic about the conditions. "It wasn't so bad at all," he said, "Because you know, they treated the sand with oil, you know, so that it can't get dusty."[22]

In his study of Irish immigrants in Montana, David Emmons argues that immigrants were driven more by a working-class pragmatism than by an idealized radicalism. One of the ways immigrants adjusted to an industrial economy, then, was to narrowly focus their expectations and accept and embrace their surroundings. What workers and immigrants expected in Gary was steel work. Other expectations for familial life and communal identity would come from other places.[23]

These concerns are echoed in the historiography of black migration. Much like the peasant images of European immigrants, there was often the assumption that rural southern blacks were unprepared for industrial life and urban conditions. However, Peter Gottlieb argues that many of the workers and families moving north in the Great Migration were not rural blacks but urbanites from southern cities. The industrial north was the final step in a long process of acculturation to industrial urban realities. In his study of black migration to Milwaukee, Joe Trotter stresses that the emergence of black communities demonstrated the proletarianization of African Americans. Like the immigrants described by Bodnar, Trotter's migrants created communities, organizations, and worldviews that embraced more than rejected industrial society. Like other migrants, African Americans came to Gary looking for work and wages, not order, stability, or model utopianism. These communities were as marked by internal division, especially in terms of class, as racial unity. James Grossman demonstrates how definitions of community shifted among African Americans. While internally divided, there was often a unified rejection of outside organizations such as white unions.[24]

There was a significant difference between the scales of mapping in Gary. For U.S. Steel executives, Gary sat at the center of a national map of exchange and markets. Reformer visions concentrated on the scope of urban structures such as mills, rivers, streets, and other institutions. Still others saw Gary as a necessary outgrowth of Chicago; one that freed up the metropolis to reach its greater destiny. Working-class mapping of Gary was still more focused. It concerned itself less with the scale and integrated methods of the mill complex than the realities of the shop floor. It focused less on the city as a whole than the familial home and the surrounding community. The working-class vision of Gary also narrowly defined the meaning of community. These were fragmented communities separated by race and ethnicity. It was not a broad and inclusive democratic community that emerged in Gary but rather a segmented series of communities that contrasted themselves against others.

CONCLUSION: "MEN OF THE GARY MILLS"

For the first decade of its existence, the image of Gary was contained within a couple of contradictory story lines. For U.S. Steel it was a triumph of industrial consolidation, planning, and modernity. Advocates for the steel corporation tried to distance the city from its rougher frontier image. Calling Gary the "youngest city in the world," *Domestic Engineering* declared that "the pioneers of Gary aren't 'forty-niners,' nor are they ex-hunters or trappers." But rather "they are active, up-and-doing business men, still in the prime of life." This sort of order was made possible by the city's creation. "Gary is unique. That is to say, it is not a town that 'just happened,' as most of our American cities are," the magazine concluded. "Gary was built upon a site chosen, and from plans completed by the United States Steel Corporation."[25] For other urban planners and reformers, the city was a model city of order and efficiency, a grand experiment in social reform and industrial education, a lost opportunity to implement new planning strategies, or an outdated paradigm to be replaced by newer garden cities. While U.S. Steel had "taken a leading part" in providing industrial housing in Gary, Ralph Warner wrote, "Unfortunately . . . none of the desirable features which modern city planning recognizes were incorporated in this plan, and no breadth of vision was shown with respect to the future needs of the community. The result has been that the city has grown without any direction to meet the urgent needs for expansion."[26] Newer industrial suburbs with proper planning of housing would avoid such disorder and land speculation.

For Woodrow Wilson and others like him, Gary was an aberration. Unlike the nostalgia-laced "real" America of small industries and highly regarded artisans, Gary was a different pattern of monopolistic power, foreign populations, and danger. For the workers of Gary, their city was less a grand metaphor for the future of industrial modernity than a series of smaller communities defined by ethnicity, family, and steel work. What would ultimately challenge these notions of segmented communities and fragmented identities were new definitions of working-class unionism and wartime citizenship. The nationalism of the war would also complicate Wilson's vision of two Americas, and the destruction and chaos of the war would undermine U.S. Steel's vision of massive and benevolent technology. American involvement in the Great War, the booming steel industry during the war, and the push for "100 percent Americanism" helped to create new national narratives, of which Gary was an important element. By 1919, Americans were creating a new understanding of who they were and how they fit into a modern and mechanized society. Far from being on the periphery of these narratives, Gary stood well within, and helped to shape, these national trends, events, and tropes.

Chief among these were two different but interrelated movements. The first was an effort to redefine Americanism and citizenship. A debate emerged between those who tried to impose a strict Americanism down on recent immigrants and ethnics to replace ethnic identity and a subaltern interpretation that incorporated ethnic traditions and working-class realities into a new vision of American citizenship. Closely related was the renewed effort to unionize the plants of U.S. Steel by the Amalgamated Association of Iron and Steel Workers of North America. Both of these would not only challenge the relationship between the corporation and the residents of its town but also reshape the communal identities of and social relations between the residents of Gary.

From its very creation in 1901, U.S. Steel faced the issue of in-plant unionization. The 1901 strike by the Amalgamated Association had both tested and confirmed the corporation's power to deny union efforts. The strike had left a strengthened corporation, a weakened union, and a deep distrust between the two. Over the next eight years the company came to believe that union organization interfered with two of the basic principles of the new men of finance who were running U.S. Steel. First the Amalgamated increased labor costs and stifled the kind of large-scale improvements and developments that had created places such as Gary Works. Second, unionism interfered with company paternalism. Unionism challenged the way the company ran their business and the larger notion of industrial social control.

Given these conclusions, U.S. Steel decided that keeping unions out of its plants was a worthy and vital cause. On June 1, 1909, U.S. Steel announced that "all of its plants after June 20, 1909, will be operated as 'open plants.'" This battle with the union, however, was to be delayed and altered by the coming of the First World War. Steel was in high demand throughout the war, and the steel plants around the nation increased production as much as possible. With increased production and consumption came increased profits. Yet with these profits came new labor conflicts and waves of strikes. In December 1915, a strike in Youngstown, Ohio, ended in rioting. In May 1916, Pittsburgh also experienced strike-related violence. By voluntarily increasing pay, steel companies tried to avoid strikes while maintaining the ideologies of the open shop and company paternalism. Such pay increases pushed the common labor rate from 20 cents an hour to 42 cents. Thus the war became very good to both steel managers and steel workers.[27]

While voluntary pay increases may have held off labor conflicts and unionization, steel companies could not maintain their complete domination and independence during the war. In order to ensure constant and uninterrupted production of goods, the administration of Woodrow Wilson created the War Labor Policies Board. The state became directly involved in establishing work hours, conditions, pay, and production speeds. Even more tantalizing for union organizers, the board seemed to support the right of workers to organize. Steel owners, however, saw government intervention and pay increases quite differently. The board was an unwelcome intrusion into the relationship between capital and labor. However, the profits from wartime production were a welcome benefit. Many steel companies tried to wait out the course of the war and the existence of the board. Elbert Gary concluded that the question of the open shop should "be postponed until after the war and until the difficulties surrounding the war have passed away."[28]

However, the war itself brought important changes in the relationship between capitalist and worker—or, more precisely, the rhetoric of war created important changes. The Americanization efforts of the war tried to convince immigrant laborers that they not only could and should be American but that, in many cases, they already were. Propaganda told workers that their work was essential to the war effort and that they were taking part in a large national and international struggle. The steel industry also created patriotic campaigns to promote increased productivity. "Men of the Gary Mills," the company-run *Gary Works Circle* proclaimed in February 1918, "you are building the wall of steel that holds back the mailed fist of our enemies. You have broken many production records, there are many more to be broken. Make the sky your limit, the forced peace of the entire world your goal." The city created youth brigades to encourage patriotic participation. As Edward Newell, a member of the organization, recalled, "This I feel was a privilege which at the age of thirteen gave me a sense of social responsibility as our various duties made me feel we were in our small way actually participating in the war effort to the best of our ability."[29]

At the same time, workers themselves were challenging the very definitions of Americanization and citizenship. Alongside top-down efforts at cultural assimilation existed a working-class Americanism or what James Barrett has called "Americanization from the bottom up." Class politics by the turn of the century necessitated interethnic organizations and cooperation. By helping to create a new notion of "common grievances," unionization served as both a form of socialization for new immigrant groups and a path to interethnic cooperation. The language of democracy and patriotism utilized during the First World War helped to transform this new interethnic class identity into a working-class Americanism.[30] Thus the rhetoric of the war changed the very definitions of citizenship and contribution. While Americanization efforts and war hysteria were pushing German ethnicity outside of Americanism, it gave steel workers a claim to full citizenship and patriotism. This was especially important in Gary, a city where, in 1910, 70.9 percent of the population was either foreign-born or had foreign-born parents. In 1920, that percentage was still 60.5 percent. In addition, steel work itself became a patriotic endeavor. An industrial war in the machine age meant that workers creating the machines were also part of the war effort. And Gary was very much part of the larger nation.[31]

FOUR

"The Gibraltar of the Steel Corporation"

NARRATIVE AND MEANING IN A STEEL STRIKE

By September 1919, the lines had been drawn in the struggle over union recognition in the steel industry. As a large-scale strike loomed a couple of days away, the *Chicago Tribune* began preparing its readers for the climatic conflict. "Commanders of both sides in the steel controversy tonight are drawing their lines of battle—for the strike Monday morning of all workers in the steel and iron trades is to be a fight to a finish," it reported on September 20. A key part of this battle was to be the new industrial center of Gary, Indiana, and the battle plans there took on especially important roles. "The policy of the Gary city administration with regard to the coming strike," the *Tribune* continued, "was answered yesterday by Mayor William F. Hodges, who declared in a proclamation that 'order will be maintained. . . . The laws of our city, the state of Indiana, and our nation shall be respected and order shall be maintained.'" Despite these assurances, the *Tribune* still warned of the impending crisis in the Steel City:

> Regarded by organized labor as the Gibraltar of the Steel corporation, Gary has been singled out as the most important objective of the steel workers' union. . . . "As Gary goes, so goes the strike," said E. A. Lux, organizer for the Amalgamated Association of Iron, Steel, and Tin Workers. "This is the stronghold of the trust. It built the town and runs it. E. H. Gary gave the city his name, its $500,000 Y.M.C.A., and its library. If we win in Gary the trust is licked."

As the steel crisis loomed, the attention of the nation, it seemed, had refocused on Gary, Indiana.

For the first decade of the city's existence, the meaning of Gary was still open to interpretation. For some, Gary remained the model city of industrial planning and social control. For others, the steel district had become sort of a new frontier. Some saw possibility, some saw lawlessness. For some, it was chaos or teetering on chaos. Others read a romantic and exciting quality into a place that was born out of American industrial modernization yet seemed somehow foreign and exotic. There was no single narrative of the city. Gary was a site where multiple, and at times contradictory, political and cultural ideologies could exist at the same time. The 1919 steel strike would change all of that.

As the labor crisis unfolded, Gary stood at the very center of events. By 1918, the American Federation of Labor (AFL) felt that the time was right for an organized campaign targeting steel. Following the breaking of the Homestead strike in 1892, steel unions had suffered a string of failures including the 1901 and 1909 strikes against U.S. Steel. But new campaigns had proven successful in the meatpacking industry, which was under the same sort of wartime production pressure. In April 1918, John Fitzpatrick of the Chicago Federation of Labor and William Z. Foster of the AFL proposed a unified and organized drive in steel. In August, the AFL created the National Committee for Organizing Iron and Steel Workers and focused their initial campaign to the steel mills of the Chicago region. They found a responsive audience, and throughout the Chicago region, membership swelled quickly.[1]

The steel industry responded by pursuing both company unions and retaliation in the form of discharges, blacklists, and espionage. Yet as David Brody points out, "The steelmakers could not counteract the union tide. Neither benevolence nor repression dissuaded workers from joining unions." Brody concludes that rank-and-file militancy pressured the organizers into a difficult position. The end of the war and the dissolution of the War Labor Board eliminated the union's best advantage right when it needed it most. While most leaders wanted to wait for an organization strong enough to take on the industry, new members demanded recognition from the company and action from the union. Because of this militancy, the committee felt forced to take a strike vote (one which they counted as slowly as possible). On August 20, 1919, the committee tabulated that 98 percent of members favored a work stoppage. Thus began the "steel crisis."[2]

As the union demanded recognition (and tried to stall its own members), the steel industry, under the leadership of Elbert Gary, repeated its stance on the open shop. Newspapers began to fret over the potential chaos and upheaval of a steel war. Periodicals such as the *Chicago Daily News* began to publish maps of the "sections in Chicago and adjacent territory where strike is expected to tie up plants." The *Daily News* also published an updated list of plants that would be affected and the number of employees in each mill. On September 10, the committee set a strike date of September 22. Immediately the White House, in its limited role as mediator, asked for a three-week postponement. Afraid to delay the rank and file any longer, the committee declined the offer. On September 22, 1919, the long-awaited showdown began.[3]

If the steel strike was a national event for Gary, it was also a profoundly local event. Gary was still a very young city; the mills had only been running for ten years. As a social and economic experiment, the model city had yet to be tested with industrial strife. While planning the construction of the mill and city, U.S. Steel had not envisioned preventing conflict (like Pullman had attempted) but rather withstanding it. In 1919, it was still unclear whether such a plan could work. Gary had reached roughly the age Pullman had when the strike of 1894 upended its utopian visions. Could the Steel City function? Would it continue to function? The feat of planning and constructing both a "model" city and a concentrated superstructure of a mill had been proven to be possible, but would it prove to have been foolish?

Meanwhile, deep questions remained about the city itself. It was still growing quickly and haphazardly, spreading out along the twin lines of Fifth Avenue and Broadway. Beyond the steel complex dominating the lakefront, no real city center or public commons had been established. Very few residents had lived in Gary for long, and few had much, if anything, in common with their neighbors and coworkers. This meant that not only were all residents new to the city, but the city also had no long-standing traditions of neighborhood, community, separation, or segregation. Gary was equally a blank slate for all these social categories. For some residents of Gary, the steel strike became an opportunity to impose their own vision of order and segregation on the city by defining the city in terms of masculinity, working-class ethnicity, and racial segregation.

Residents and nonresidents of Gary read and understood the process and meaning of the strike very differently. For outside observers, it was a chance to judge the success of Gary the experiment as well as an opportunity to disparage Gary the industrial center. It was a testing ground for a potentially new kind of industrial war in new cities with new tactics involving new immigrants. For critics and observers of Gary, the steel strike was a chance to create and impose a final and lasting meaning and legacy onto the city. And for some city residents, it was a chance to redraw the racial lines of the city and impose their own version of order. Surrounding the social and political events of the strike was a discussion of who controlled the city and who should have the power to define its image, its purpose, and the meaning of its events. This chapter is a study of the language of the steel strike. It examines the different ways the story of the strike was told and the forms, words, impressions, and implications that came to symbolize it. The language, symbolism, and narrative form of the strike became the processes by which Gary became its own city. How people understood and participated in that process shaped both Gary's urban image and the relationships of power within the city.

"THIS INDUSTRIAL WAR": THE *CHICAGO TRIBUNE* MAKES SENSE OF GARY

As the steel strike loomed, newspapers such as the *Chicago Tribune* tried to make narrative sense of the crisis. On September 18, it published Judge Gary's letter to the presidents of U.S. Steel's subsidiaries on the company's open shop policies. "We do not negotiate with labor unions," he declared, "because it would indicate the closing of our shops against nonunion labor." Based upon Gary's letter, the *Tribune* concluded that the steel strike was near if not inevitable. The next day it published the twelve demands of the union and detailed the lack of movement in negotiations. In the same issue it included a cartoon showing a worker lighting a box of matches labeled "strikes" in a room of dynamite, TNT, and powder; a room labeled "industrial crisis." On September 20, the paper began commenting on the preparations in Gary for protecting the plant and drawing maps of the strike's national scope. The following day the headline read, "Big Steel Strike Starts; Thousands of Guards at Plants Being Armed." The newspaper also said that Gary was not only the origin of the strike but would be at the center of the conflict. Despite the tension and the published threats of workers that there would be either "organized labor or organized riot," on the 22nd the paper reported that the "Steel Strike Starts Quietly." The paper also confirmed that strikers in Gary, despite the city's "babel of

tongues," saw themselves as the "heart of the steel fight." The *Tribune* culminated its buildup of the crisis with a front-page cartoon on September
23 of Uncle Sam watching the steel industry in flames with shipping, oil,
telephone and telegraph, meat packing, railroads, and mines at his back
wondering if "we can localize this industrial war."

If the first stage of the *Tribune's* narrative was about the looming crisis, the key players, and the role of Gary and the Chicago region, then the
second stage was about the slow turning of the tide. The paper reported
both sides claiming gains, the rise of mobs and clashes with guards, and
the specter of damage in the Gary mills. On September 24, it offered
photos of the empty mill in Gary as the "inside facts on steel strike," and
reported that the Gary plant was a "stricken giant" with "mill after mill
silent as a graveyard, others with only half a dozen men struggling to oper-
ate a portion. . . . All but four of the twelve blast furnaces were blanked."
But on September 25 the strike turned. "Defy Strike; Open Mill," declared
the headline as the *Tribune* reported on the "first organized attempt . . . to
resume partial operation of its Gary mills in spite of the strike." Included
in this issue was an aerial photo of the sprawling Gary Works with a description by a *Tribune* pilot who flew over the plant and saw "real soft coal
smoke coming out of Gary stacks."

With the momentum of the strike shifting, the *Tribune* began to focus
on the defensive positions of the Gary steel mills. A day after its aerial
photo, the paper ran a large drawing of the Gary mills that described in
detail all of the defensive precautions taken to protect the plant. Much
like the social commentators from a decade earlier, the paper saw the
Grand Calumet River as a protective moat and declared the mills "pro-
tected as within a fort." Because it had been "built with the strategic eye of
a war lord," the works were "almost impregnable." Included now, however,
were new modern updates of the original plan:

> A man with a machine gun could man the entire south side. There are several
> yards of railroad tracks which must be crossed before the wall is reached. All
> along the wall and deployed at short intervals along the lake front are guards
> who know how to handle a rifle.

Because "desperate citizens met a desperate situation with desperate
measures," the paper reported that Gary's citizens, or at least those the
Tribune considered citizens, had formed themselves into a military police

organization and vowed to keep the mill open. Rifles were brought into the plant and the "battle for Gary was joined."[4]

Thus the paper's narrative of the strike entered its final stage. As "citizens" armed themselves and fortified their position, workers began coming back to work and steel production began to slowly increase. On October 1, the *Tribune* headlines read, "Mills of Gary near Basis of Fifty Per Cent" and "Evidence of Breaking Big Strike." On October 2, the paper again ran a large photo of the Gary works, except this time its smoke stacks were pumping out smoke. "The Steel Giants have lighted their pipes again," the paper said. The *Tribune*'s story seemed complete: the strike began, the crisis loomed, the conflict turned, and the plants reopened.[5]

Then on October 4, violence erupted. The following day the *Chicago Tribune* described the scene:

> The riot in Gary started shortly after 5 o'clock when the crowds of strikers leaving the mass meeting came upon the street car filled with strike breakers, which had been halted at Tenth street by a passing Michigan and Central train. The crowd surged about and began jeering.
>
> The motorman got the car started, but the throng surged in front of it and all around it, impeding progress. By the time Fourteenth street was reached the crowd had swelled to 5,000. Some one jerked the trolley from the wire and twenty-five strikers climbed into the car to single out the strikebreakers.
>
> "Yank them off," shouted a striker from the crowd that was gathering around the car. One of the Negroes is said to have drawn a knife. Another urged him to use it, according to the pickets. The trolley pole of the car was jerked off and the Negroes thrown off the car. The motorman and conductor fled, one Negro was beaten into insensibility. The rest tried to escape. Each became the center of a hooting mob.
>
> A Negro deputy worked his way into the jam and rescued the Negro, who had defended himself with the knife. Dragging him to safety, he took his knife from him and sent him home. This enraged the crowd and an attack was made on the deputy, while others chased the Negro.
>
> In five minutes the mob numbered from 5,000 to 6,000. The police, headed by Capt. James McCartney, arrived on the double quick, followed by armed business men in automobiles. A large force of deputy sheriffs arrived at the same time. They organized with the police and charged the mob, which stood its ground. The police formed a wedge and bored in, swinging clubs and blackjacks. Gradually the mob was forced backward to Fifteenth Street.
>
> Some construction is going on at this corner and piles of brick stood in a vacant lot. These were hurled into the lines of advancing police, several of whom were injured. Ordering his men not to fire, Capt. McCartney fought

his way into the lot. Patrol wagons and automobiles were backed into the curb and scores of rioters were overpowered and thrown into the machines. They fought bitterly, several of them reaching out of the patrol wagons to hit whoever stood near.

For nearly two hours, the fighting mass surged up and down Broadway, Gary's main street, between Tenth and Eighteenth streets. The sound of falling bricks and broken glass were interrupted by the clanging bells of ambulances and patrol wagons.

By the end of the day, hundreds had been arrested. Order, it seemed, had finally returned to Gary.

In the way that the *Chicago Tribune* chose to report the urban violence, the paper imposed order on an inherently disordered event. The chronological framework that the paper placed upon the riot gave it a logical beginning and end. Causes and effects seem to follow from the paper's narrative. In addition, it included common tropes to make the riot relevant and understandable. The paper chose to concentrate on the language of race, the imagery of warfare, and the specter of radicalism. By phrasing its discussion in these well-known tropes, the *Tribune* made the violence in Gary resonate with its readership. By assigning a narrative structure to the violence, the *Chicago Tribune* and other newspapers gave meaning and order to Gary while providing the interpretative room for continued disorder.[6]

The construction of a narrative helped to provide order to the riot and a discursive structure to the city. As Arlette Farge and Jacques Revel demonstrate in their study of street violence and riots in France, it is these narratives which give a voice and presence to a city. This urban presence stems from the way that order and narrative are placed upon and help shape the urban landscape. Fritzsche argues that written forms, especially the modern popular newspaper, create a "word city" that imposes order and meaning upon the physical city. The city as place and the city as text exist as separate yet inherently connected entities. The textual city gives a narrative form and cohesiveness to the physical city. This serves to create a single understandable definition of what the city is and what its landscape means. However, Fritzsche points out that between the text and its readership, room exists for interpretative play. "Texts in the city were at once orderly and disruptive," he argues, "they reframed and juxtaposed and reiterated and left unsaid, they led as well as misled, and worked for and against concretions of power. Because it wished to be all things to all people, the word city remained an unstable, pliable form, which allowed readers to make sense of the changing inventory of the city." Through a similar construction of both order and disorder, the *Chicago Tribune* created a word city of Gary.[7]

One way the *Tribune* gave order to the city and provided interpretative room for disorder to its readers was through the layout of its paper. Articles on other strikes both in the United States and abroad often ran next to discussions of the violence in Gary. On October 5, the first day of reporting on the riots, the *Tribune* dedicated its main heading and most of a full page to the incident. However, next to the pictures of violent strikers, the paper ran a story on congressional investigations into the nationwide steel strike. The story's headline declared that a "Sovietized Mill Aim of Strikers." A vast conspiracy, it went on to say, existed which threatened not only American workers and employers but also the American government. Other stories on Gary were juxtaposed against violence in other American cities, the threat of communist conspiracies, and the "Great British Rail Strike." These stories had little to do with one another, yet the way the paper combined and contrasted these stories gave readers a chance to create their own sense of collective order or chaos. The *Tribune* stressed the eventual triumph of order. In its headlines, the paper announced the success of the police or military before it discussed the breakdown of order that had caused the crisis. While the headlines emphasized the maintenance of order, the common themes revealed the possibility for disorder and chaos. By its placement of seemingly unconnected stories, the *Tribune* could manipulate their impact.

In its coverage the *Tribune* relied on three story lines that would have been readily comprehensible to its readership. On the first day of coverage, it had already cloaked the violence in the language of the race riot. By suggesting that the violence was an outgrowth of racial hatred, the paper assigned order and causality but also gave the riots an intense meaning for its readers. Earlier that summer, racial violence and rioting had rocked the city of Chicago. Although the violence in Gary was confined to a small section of town and was rooted in an industrial labor struggle, the two riots were linked by the application of the title of "race riot." For the readership of the *Tribune,* the notion of a race riot was immediately recognizable and conjured up memories of Chicago's past.[8]

Like the language of the race riot, the paper also utilized the imagery and discourse of war to assign order and meaning to the violence. By October 6, the *Tribune* had already labeled the violence in Gary, Indiana Harbor, and South Chicago as the "Steel War." With this label came several maps with numbers and arrows pointing to the places of conflict and the movement of police and troops. In the days surrounding the publication of the Steel War map, the paper printed other maps in an identical format that detailed the military conflict in Russia. These maps closely resembled the battle maps that readers had grown accustomed to deciphering over the past five years. The *Tribune* also alluded to a military conflict with references to battle-hardened soldiers "sent to the front" to take on the unruly strikers. Photos portrayed the troops as ready with full armaments of rifles, grenades, and machine guns. The *Tribune* not only cloaked the violence and the reestablishment of order in military language but also suggested that Gary was the center of actual military conflict.

The *Tribune* also placed the violence within the context of communist infiltration and agitation. As early as October 5, the paper talked of "radical elements" that had instigated the violence. As the threat of further riots was subdued by military occupation, the paper and, in fact, the military leaders themselves increasingly turned their attention to "red" agitators. Such a discussion helped to explain the causes of the riot and give further legitimacy to the military occupation of the city. The *Tribune* continued to report on vast communist conspiracies uncovered within Gary that threatened both the city's and the country's industrial order. Given the postwar crackdown on vocal radicals such as Emma Goldman, the infiltration and breakup of organizations such as the Industrial Workers of the World, the veracity of the criminal raids led by Attorney General A. Mitchell Palmer, and the overall atmosphere of the 1919 red scare, the presence of radicals in Gary was an accusation that readers could quickly and easily understand and that carried immediate ramifications.

Like any good narrative, the *Tribune*'s coverage of the Gary riots provided both a beginning and an ending. The paper's story concluded on October 7 with Indiana governor James P. Goodrich's declaration of martial law, which the paper printed in full. Shortly after this declaration, Major General Leonard Wood arrived in Gary, along with over 1,000 members of the Fourth Infantry Division of the U.S. Army "armed with field pieces, trench mortars, hand grenades, machine guns, and rifles." Early the next morning members of the Sixth Infantry Division from Omaha, Nebraska, also entered the city, leading the *Tribune* to boast that "by 10 o'clock this morning there will be 4,000 federal shock troops in the steel city—all veterans of the war." In addition, the paper published several pictures of the soldiers and their machine guns. It even declared that the "AEF [American Expeditionary Force] veterans" had been "sent to the 'front' in steel strike." The "U.S. Regulars," the paper boasted, "rule Gary."

The declaration of martial law and the arrival of federal troops served to conclude two of the paper's main themes in its coverage of the riots. With martial law, the violence of the race rioters would no longer be possible. The soldiers had reestablished order in the city. At the same time, the presence of the heavily armed and highly experienced troops created an image of a military victory in the paper's "steel war." So total was the triumph that the paper boasted on October 7 that "the army of the Yanks that swoops down upon Gary, the city of steel, to quell all uprisings against law and order, found no trouble with the strikers yesterday and turned itself upon the radicals." With the cessation of violence and disorder, the paper turned exclusively to the exposure of the "radical conspiracy" that had created the upheaval in the first place. In the following editions, the *Tribune* reported that the army had found tons of "red propaganda," detained radicals and members of the "red element," and uncovered a vast "bolshevist movement." The paper quoted Wood in stating that "most of the trouble had come from red agitators whose only desire seemed to be to foment riots." The causes of the violence, it seemed, had shifted from racial hatred to manipulation by radicals. Finally on October 9, the U.S. Army placed a censorship ban on the media's coverage concerning the military's pursuit of communist agitators. This act brought the *Tribune's* final story line and its narrative coverage of the Gary riots to an end. In its closing thoughts, the paper suggested that "the radical element [had been] rubbed off the slate and order once more assured."

"GARY THE MODEL CITY AS UNDER MILITARY CONTROL": OTHER VERSIONS OF THE STRIKE

The journalistic constructions that the *Tribune* used to create the textual landscape of Gary differed considerably from the narratives of other prominent newspapers. While the *Chicago Tribune* called the "race question" a factor in its earliest reporting and by the second day labeled the violence "race rioting," the coverage in the *New York Times* presented the events in very different language. The only time that the *Times* mentioned race was in passing: "The trouble started," it reported on October 5, "when several thousand strikers, leaving a mass meeting, came upon a street car bearing about forty strikebreakers—many of them Negroes—to work in the United States Steel Corporation mills." In the coverage of the same day, the *Tribune* included a similar sentence. "Bitterness over the race question also developed and the strikers leaving the meeting made for a streetcar bearing strike breakers—most of them Negroes—to the mills of the United States Steel corporation." The difference between the two, then, is the "race question" that the *Tribune* included not only in the story but also as a subject headline.

For the *New York Times*, the violence in Gary was of no great importance. Its coverage focused on the low-key nature of the violence and the quick restoration of order. It pointed with admiration to the fact that during the altercation, "both sides avoided the use of firearms," utilizing their fists and brickbats instead. Likewise, the riot police were commended because, despite their possession of riot guns, they "did not fire a shot." In a similar fashion the London *Times* reported on what it called "Steel Strike Riots." Instead of race, it chose to stress the veteran status of many of the participants in the "street disturbances." The London *Times* also combined the story of Gary's martial law and the opening of the National Industrial Conference. Thus, for English readers, the situation in Gary was defined in terms of industrial classes and conflicts.[9]

Racial violence and race rioting were not a part of the coverage offered by the *Indiana Daily Times*. Not once in its coverage of the events in Gary did this Indianapolis-based paper mention race or suggest that the violence stemmed from racial hatred or the race of the potential strikebreakers. The paper focused on the restoration of order and the breaking of the strike. Its first headline on the riots declared, "Troops Put Down Gary Riots" with the subheading "Mobs Quickly Disperse When Guard Arrives." After the arrival of troops into Gary, the paper stated, "Hundreds of steel workers returned to their places, indicating that the men are ready to work if given protection." For the *Daily Times*, the strike and the picket riots were essentially of no consequence. It was not necessary for the paper to find causes and meaning in the riots through the use of race.

For the *Chicago Tribune,* however, race played an important role from the very beginning. The race question and the "race hatred [that was] breaking out against Negro strike breakers" provided the clearest sense of order to the riot for the *Tribune* and its readership.[10]

Distance from the events can explain some of the difference in the language of the papers. Chicago had a very different relationship to Gary and to the steel strike than did Indianapolis, New York, or London, and thus it understood the events in different terms. Yet other Chicago papers, as well as newspapers from around the Calumet Region, also varied in how they reported the strike. Much of this can be explained by political preferences. By the turn of the century, the *Tribune* had already established itself as a bulwark of conservative causes and Republican policies. However, when Robert McCormick took control of the paper in 1910, the politics of the paper would become even more pronounced. The grandson of the paper's founder, Joseph Medill, and the great-nephew of Chicago industrialist Cyrus McCormick, Robert McCormick helped to establish his paper as one of the most consistently conservative voices in the twentieth century. Other Chicago newspapers, such as the *Daily News,* sought their audiences and political loyalties elsewhere. All of this determined what story lines, connections, and assumptions the newspapers read into Gary's story.

The *Daily News* began publishing maps and charts on which plants and cities would be affected in the Chicago region. On September 22, the headline blared that the "Steel Industry Is Virtually Paralyzed in Chicago District." As it reported on the smokestacks that "no longer belched smoke pall," it also suggested that the strikers seemed quite content and confident. "They are of the smooth faced, Anglo-Saxon type," it described, "the long-mustachioed, matty haired, sloe eyed Balkan, Slavic type: the quick Latin: the more sluggish Teuton type. . . . Everybody is smiling. It is the first day of a great strike that the men believe will win for them recognition of their union and more pay."

Although the crowds were in a "gala mood," they did gather to "jeer carloads of men believed [to be] imported to work in steel plants." While there was a "carnival" atmosphere, there was also a "threat of drama and perhaps melodrama." By September 22, the *Chicago Daily News* had drawn a picture of working-class communities, "smokeless chimneys and striking men." On the 23rd, the paper ran a story on three generations of strikers in Gary. When James Robinson II walked out, so too did his father, despite not being a union member and thus risking his retirement. James III also claimed to be on strike, despite being only a toddler. Thus "family love and loyalty" ranked higher than pensions and security. "Among the dramatic incidents born of the steel strike," the paper concluded, "is a serious comedy entitled 'You strike, I strike.'"

The *Daily News* narrative of the strike balanced impending violence with a slowly collapsing strike. On October 2, the paper reported that "1,500 Gary Strikers Return to Work," yet there was a need to "Add 300 Extra Police." As the strike collapsed, the narrative went, frustrations grew and other options disappeared. "U.S. Troops Armed with Cannon Stop Disorders in Gary," the headlines yelled on October 7. The strike turned with the arrival of federal troops, many of them "veterans of the world war." While strikers may have been brave enough to face the state militia, they were unwilling to face regular troops.

> "They jeered at the state troops," said Col. Mapes, "they held their parades, flaunted their red banners, held open air meetings in defiance of orders. The regulars took command to-day, and you should see those mobs melt before the tin hats. An iron helmet means a regular. . . . Those tin hats were manufactured here, probably some of the men in the crowd helped stamp them. They know what a tin hat is."

Thus the *Daily News* chose different narratives to describe the strike and riot. It was a world of ethnic communities waging a failing strike that was broken by the show of force from the U.S. Army. Such themes were echoed in the coverage provided by the *South Bend News-Times*. It also concluded on October 5 that, upon the order of martial law, "riotous elements loose [*sic*] desire to fight when 4,000 regular troops appear." But the *News-Times* also chose to comment upon the failing utopian ideal of Gary's founding. As the "silk hat of officialdom was supplanted by the tin helmet of Mars . . . Gary, the 'model city,' was under military control."

For the *Daily Calumet*, however, the strike in Gary, the ensuing violence, and the occupation had always been about radicals. In its coverage of the riots and several editorials, the paper blamed radical Bolsheviks and the IWW for the troubles. "The anarchist cares no more for the labor union than he does for the employer. He wants disorder because he can only carry out his designs amid disorder," one editorial on "Gary, Indiana, and Her 'Reds'" concluded. "There is something on which every decent man, woman, and child in our country is unanimous, and that is the vigorous opposition to the injection of the IWW into the controversy," concluded another. The real threat for the *Daily Calumet* was in the radical politics beneath the disorder.[11]

Yet for a paper such as the *Chicago American*, there was no real threat in Gary, either from radicalism or from violence. In an editorial designed to provide "comfort for those that bolshevism frightens," the *American* concluded: "In the mixed populations of great American cities, you will find that different kinds of human beings hate each other, through religious or racial antipathies, more than they hate 'capitalism' or 'the kept press.' Race and religious hatred are older, more bitter than modern, Socialistic or Bolshevist hatreds."[12]

In terms of the strike, the paper also downplayed the potential for violence. On September 23, it reported that "strikers maintain order in Great Chicago Steel Strike." Unlike the *Daily News's* potential mobs, the *American* showed "crowds of striking steel workers cheering but otherwise quiet." The *American* also published an article about a striker's wife who complained of long hours that took her husband's leisure time away from her and her children. Because the strike offered little potential violence, when the disturbances in Gary came, the paper suggested that they were of little importance. Instead of tin hats facing down crowds, the *American* called the troops in Gary "keepers of the peace." While the troops were there to track down the "lawless" and chase out radicals, their chief duty was to maintain the peace in an already peaceful place. "Arrival of the federal troops in Gary," the paper suggested, "was heralded as a victory for the strikers by John H. De Young, secretary of the Chicago committee. . . . 'The feeling among the strikers in Gary today is one of great relief,' he said." As the roundup of a few lawless reds continued, the soldiers, according to the *American*, enjoyed their stay in the Steel City. Across a picture of a soldier in full uniform holding children in his lap, the paper asked, "So this is riot duty! Regulars play with Gary children." "This doughboy doesn't mind a little thing like a steel strike," the paper concluded on October 9. "'Duck soup!' says he."

If the narrative form of the *Chicago Daily News* was imposed order, the *Daily Calumet's* was radicalism, and the *Chicago American's* was uninterrupted peace, then the *Chicago Herald-Examiner* offered yet another twist. The paper, which called itself "the Soldier's paper—the Sailor's paper," wove an exciting tale of daring and danger into the strike and disturbances. On October 5, the paper stated that "a riot in which almost 5,000 men were pitted against the whole police and fire department of Gary broke out." Although the paper does mention the origins of the violence as racial conflict between white strikers and black workers, the main story was the battle that quickly ensued between the large and unruly crowds and the police.

> Captain James McCartney arrested a man who had taken part in the fighting and the crowd tried to rescue him. The captain swung his club left and right with all his might, several of his men gathered about him and after smashing a dozen of heads they got the prisoner into the police patrol wagon. Then the crowd stoned the patrol as long as it was in reach.

As the violence continued, so too did the paper's exciting narrative. On October 7, it declared that Chicago had sent "1,000 troops and machine guns" to Gary. Beside a portrait of Major General Leonard Wood, the paper wove a story in which "regulars dash through the city in autos . . . [while] mobs led by former soldiers threaten jail delivery."

> One thousand troops . . . were rushed into Gary last night in answer to appeals to the War Department. . . . The Fort Sheridan soldiers carried with them into Gary equipment of sufficient force to awe any mob into quiet. Three three-inch filed pieces, with special auto truck mounts were in the van of the procession. These weapons fire pound-and-a-half shells at the rate of ten a minute. Automobiles laden with machine guns also were rushed into the line. In order to carry the extra machine guns and equipment private automobiles were commandeered.

For the *Herald Examiner,* the conflict in Gary was a full-scale battle with all the proper levels of chaos, bravery, and scientific use of machines and technology.

The choices a paper made to describe the strike and street violence could have taken any number of variations. For some it was an exciting battle, for others an anticlimactic peacekeeping assignment. For some it was the proof of an underlying dangerous radicalism, for others a few lawless malcontents comprised the radical element. It could be about class conflict, or racial divides, or nationality, or masculinity. But each narrative explanation was carefully constructed to appeal to readers and

allow them to draw conclusions about the violence and the political, social, and cultural implications of that violence. Often the coverage itself
contained elements for both narrative order and interpretational disorder. Although the articles on the riots stressed the eventual acquisition
or maintenance of law and order, they also contained the possibilities
for massive disorder and chaos. Thus the way a paper chose to construct
its pages and the potential chaos that was often left unspoken within its
stories created a textual city of Gary. From this journalistic construction of the urban landscape, readers could apply meaning to the physical
landscape of Gary.

When the *Tribune* raised the specter of race rioting, it was clearly
tying into an established story line that readers would readily recognize. The summer of 1919 saw a number of major and bloody race riots
(including Chicago). Stories of Bolshevik radicalism would have had
an immediate resonance as well. Papers such as the *Tribune* were con-
stantly mentioning radicalism and the threat of revolution, whether it
was an alarmist piece on radical agitators or a cartoon depicting a mob
converging on a man in the street who is shouting, "Hurrah fer th' Reds,"
only to learn the man was following the World Series between the Cincinnati Reds and the Chicago White Sox ("A Radical Ballsheviki," the
paper called him). Still even this cartoon was placed next to an article
describing the strike in Gary. The implications were clear: Chicago and
the United States were not safe places in 1919. In his study of the red scare
and the red summer, William Tuttle argues that this combination of
race rioting and radicals was no coincidence. Following the chaos of the
world war, Americans were angry and frustrated, uncertain about jobs
and the economy, and looking desperately for a common enemy. Race
and radicalism dovetailed together in this postwar summer. As far as the
Tribune was concerned, the disturbances in Gary were a continuation of
both narratives.[13]

CONCLUSION: "SMOKELESS CHIMNEYS AND STRIKING MEN"

Bigger Thomas understood how the racial politics of Chicago worked.
Whether it had been his intention to kill or not, the main character in
Richard Wright's novel *Native Son* was going to be held accountable for

the death of the white woman Mary. As more people began to suspect his role in the disappearance, Thomas fled into the Black Belt of South Chicago. Yet, although the racial lines in Chicago in the early twentieth century were starkly drawn, they were also easily crossed. As violence of the 1919 race riot in Chicago crossed in and out of the Black Belt and its surrounding neighborhoods, the angry crowds began to circle the south side in search of Thomas. "He could not leave Chicago; all roads were blocked, and all trains, buses and autos were being stopped and searched," writes Wright. "It would have been much better if he had tried to leave town at once. He should have gone to some other place, perhaps Gary, Indiana, or Evanston."[14] While Thomas's destinations are largely based on the single criterion of not being Chicago, it is both apropos and ironic that he would dream of escaping into Gary. For just as the racial politics of 1919 transformed Chicago, so too had the steel strike changed the city of Gary.

While Gary as an economic experiment in strategic location and fortresslike construction may have been proven successful by the 1919 strike, Gary as a social experiment (or at least what some had hoped was a social experiment) of control and order had failed in the wake of the riots, occupation, and red hunts. The racial images and discourses that emerged out of the steel strike effectively marked the end of the reformist hopes for order. For many social reformers, Gary, like so many other attempts at institutional order, held such great potential. After 1919, within Gary, as well as the larger American culture, very few cared to create social and moral reforms. Instead, people saw a city divided by a color line, which, as W.E.B. Du Bois predicted, would become the key political issue of the twentieth century. After 1919, new ideologies, new divisions, and new issues consumed the nation. With the Great Migration of southern African Americans into northern industrial cities, racial divisions and racialized language would replace many of the older categories of class, cleanliness, and civilization. The chaos of the Great War blunted much of the enthusiasm for technological answers and progressive reform. And the pandemic of influenza along with the Russian Revolution had dampened the faith in modern society's ability to quarantine crisis and danger. If the problems at the turn of the century were symbolized by the industrial districts in Upton Sinclair's *Jungle,* then modern society after 1919 resembled more closely Bigger Thomas's Chicago, where neither separation nor comprehension of the other is entirely possible. While some papers saw in the steel strike a community of "smokeless chimneys and striking men," after October the story line became mostly about racial divisions and radicalism.

Yet, for many in Gary, the strike and riot meant something more complicated. The *Chicago Tribune* was clearly ready to label the violence in Gary a race riot, but this did not have the same form or outcome as the 1919 riots in places such as Omaha, Tulsa, or Chicago. The riots in Gary took place in one central location and did not involve the lynchings, roving gangs, or street deaths that had become the ritual of the race riot. The location of the riot was highly symbolic. Stemming from its founding, Gary was a physically divided city. After 1909, three distinct areas emerged: the mills of the Gary Works, which were separated from the city by the Grand Calumet River; the First Subdivision, which was a housing district reserved for foremen, clerks, and skilled laborers; and the poorer district known as the "Patch," an area that U.S. Steel spent no time or effort in planning. The first day of the riots took place on Broadway. This street and the streetcar that ran along it tied together the three districts. Thus the riots may have served as a way for workers to claim the city, the street, and the streetcar as their own. In addition, the paths to the plants themselves were closed off. In some ways, attacking the streetcar was the only available form of resistance against not only strikebreakers but the steel corporation as well. Strikers could deny their own labor, the labor of others, and the means of transportation for workers to get to the defended industrial fortress. At the same time, workers claimed a public role by practicing political action in the streets.

The strike and riots became, in some ways, the "making" of the Gary working class. Yet Gary residents did not have the kind of deep traditions or the rituals of work and play that would have created a working class in the way that E. P. Thompson describes for workers in Britain. They were new residents to a new city. In their study of racial and ethnic patterns in Gary, Raymond Mohl and Neil Betten conclude that the steel strike was not a radical event precisely because of the sojourner status of the immigrant population. But immigrant populations have proven themselves capable of radicalism, and migrant workers have shown themselves capable of class identity. So we should not dismiss the collective identities of Gary's residents. The methods, images, and rituals of protest during the strike suggest the origins of a complicated worker identity in Gary that included and incorporated ideas of ethnicity and race.[15]

Yet there were clearly racial implications in the October violence. One of the categories strikers and sympathizers used to help create a sense of commonality was race. In this way the workers of Gary follow the rhetoric of class-consciousness and "whiteness" detailed by David Roediger. Certainly behind many of the crowd's actions was a sense of racial entitlement and group consciousness created out of attacks upon a racial other. While racial language allowed for the formation of class-consciousness, it did not create bonds between "white" workers and "white" steel owners; rather, it combined and conflated the categories of white and black, striker and strikebreaker, and resident and outsider. The strike was a chance for workers in Gary to claim the city as their own, but who got to claim the city was limited.[16]

FIVE

"You're a Damned Liar—It's Utopia"

IMAGINING INDUSTRIALISM BETWEEN THE WARS

The chaos and uncertainty of the Great War, the Russian Revolution, and the Red Scare had not been kind to people's faith in modernity and industrialism. American critics began not only to question the results of industrialism but to view industrialism itself as a grave danger. In a 1922 collection of essays edited by Harold Stearns, thirty authors explored different aspects of American culture, analyzed its shortcomings, and predicted its fate. In his preface, Stearns was broad about what anxieties and concerns triggered this volume, but reviewers of the collection were less uncertain. Lauding the authors who held "an old fashioned definition [of civilization] which stresses the traditional graces of the mind, and which recognizes our main problem in the spread of industrialism over every phase of American life," one reviewer concluded that "this Inquiry into American Civilization is essentially a study of the peril of industrialism." However, this left the reviewer with a deep concern. "Industrialism is the mode of the modern world, as feudalism was once the mode of Europe," he worries, "and if the shadow is heavy upon our country, it is darkening also elsewhere, even in France and the South Seas; and what other paradise has the young American heard of?" Some of the essays, especially Lewis Mumford's piece on the American city, eased his concern. "Fortunately there are pages in this book which tell us the way to face industrialism," he concludes. "It cannot be removed or avoided, but it can be controlled and transformed. Civilization must take charge of it, not run away from it."[1]

Mumford made the same juxtaposition of "civilization" and "industrialism" in his essay. He traces the de-evolution of the American city from the provincial city of New England where a "genuine community" existed through the rise of western commercial centers such as Pittsburgh and Cincinnati where, instead of commons and churches, commercial hotels and railroad stations dominated the landscape and any "cultural institutions" and intellectual life were lacking. Mumford is even less pleased by the next development. Industrial cities such as Chicago "did not represent the creative values in civilization: it stood for a new form of barbarism." Here was "an environment much more harsh, antagonistic, and brutal than anything the pioneers had encountered." Given the "alternative of humanizing the industrial city or de-humanizing the population," most urban reformers as well as industrialists, he argues, have chosen the latter. Surely such a critic of industrial cities, factories, modern architecture, and scientific efficiency would despise the city of Gary, Indiana, in much the same way that he disliked Pittsburgh or Chicago. Yet the steel city held great promise for Mumford. This promise, however, was the exact opposite of earlier assumptions about Gary. Instead of the ordered efficiency of the mills juxtaposed against the disorder of the city, Mumford saw possibility in reform: "With the beginning of the second decade of this century there is some evidence of an attempt to make a genuine culture out of industrialism—instead of attempting to escape from industrialism into a culture which, though doubtless genuine enough, has the misfortune to be dead," he declared. "The schoolhouses of Gary, Indiana, have some of the better qualities of a Gary steel plant. That symptom is all to the good. It points perhaps to a time when the Gary steel plant may have some of the educational virtues of a Gary school."[2]

When Mumford saw hope for order in Gary, he looked not to the planned mills but to the innovative educational system. By 1919, the city was viewed by many as a failed experiment. It was a strange city filled with foreign workers doing dangerous work in a dangerous place. Yet it seemed remarkably functional for a failure. While the city may not have solved the crises of industrial modernity, it did produce steel. Gary's image as a rough, masculine city gave it an aura that attracted attention. Carl Sandburg comments on this in his collection of poems dedicated to smoke and steel.

> And I said good-by to the Mayor of Gary and I went out from the city hall and turned the corner into Broadway. And I saw workmen wearing leather shoes scruffed with fire and cinders, and pitted with little holes from running molten steel, And some had bunches of specialized muscles around their

shoulder blades hard as pig iron, muscles of their forearms were sheet steel and they looked to me like men who had been somewhere.[3]

Here was not a dystopian city of failed expectations but a city of men, where rough work and rough play complemented each other.

After 1919, the meanings attached to Gary changed dramatically. While founded as an industrial center that, through scientific planning and strict separation, would impose order on industrial production, Gary had emerged as a city of competing, often contradictory, and mostly disconnected visions. Gary could serve as both an industrial dystopia and a fiat city of U.S. Steel. It could be both dangerous and alluring. Others saw an urban laboratory for social experiments. By 1919, however, it had become clear that the industrial reformist visions that drove the creation had effectively been dashed. No longer was Gary a model of industrial planning; it became a flawed industrial space in need of reforming. While an official narrative of technological advancement and massive scale still existed, it applied largely to the mills of the Gary Works and not to the city. The visions of Gary began to shift between a national narrative that depicted the city as a dangerous dystopia with a functioning steel plant and alternative visions that combined definitions of work, race, masculinity, and violence to both praise and problematize life in Gary. All of these competing and coexisting narratives portrayed opportunities, possibilities, successes, and failures, but they did so in very different ways.

"A DREAM OF INDUSTRIAL UTOPIA": AFTERMATH OF THE STEEL STRIKE

It was the strike, riot, and occupation of 1919 which had ended many of the reformist visions of Gary. Where the city had once been a unique place of social experiment, after 1919 it had become, for many reformers, a failed attempt at social control and industrial order. "Gary, Magic Dream City, Now Weird Nightmare," reported Felix Bruner in the *Indianapolis Daily Tribune*. The city, he continues, had begun with such promise:

> Built almost in a day, it was a dream realized. The lords of steel spoke and as if one of the magi of ancient Persia had waved a magic wand there appeared a wondrous city—a city without the gleaming minarets of those fabled cities—but with grim black smokestacks belching forth dark clouds from the roaring interiors of mills.... From these mills come great

skyscrapers, bridges spanning wide rivers, cannon bringing destruction to thousands and everything which can be made from that most useful of all materials—steel.

It was a city that was supposed to be different.

> A dream of industrial Utopia had become temporarily a nightmare. Gary was to have been a city where workers were to be happy. It is a city of model cottages and wide shady streets. These cottages and streets are marred by the great network of railroads and the frowning background of the bills, but the city is not the usual factory city of squalor and poverty. It is far above the usual factory city and it was meant to be above it. Then came the great industrial conflict.

Just like it had in other model cities such as Pullman, industrial conflict had undermined the hopes of utopianists such as Bruner. While "soldiers and their guns will keep order," nothing would return the possibilities of Gary. For social and moral reformers, Gary after the strike came to represent the lost hope in peaceful order and social planning. Gary, it seems, had an inherent flaw. "Gary is American in architecture," concluded Bruner, "the streets are streets of America, certainly the mills are American—but the population is the population of Europe, of that part of Europe that is in constant turmoil." How could an American utopia exist in a city where "eighty per cent of the people were not born in America."[4]

For U.S. Steel, however, the city worked exactly as it should. The company never claimed that it was attempting to create any kind of social experiment. Quite the contrary, the company went to great lengths to say that the city and mill were about economic location only. The planning that U.S. Steel put into Gary focused on large-scale efficient production and the ability to withstand industrial strife. No strikers or protesters came near the heavily guarded plant, and production slowly resumed. By 1924, the company was planning to expand the Gary Works.[5] Yet the steel strike exposed the shifting understanding of industrial expansion. While it was the size of U.S. Steel, its reserves of expansion capital and its integrated system of production and distribution that made the creation of Gary possible were the very same economic forces that made model cities obsolete. While the company could physically protect the mill from attacking strikers, it could not protect the city from such national issues as labor, patriotism, masculinity, and race. The very nature of U.S. Steel's integrated system incorporated Gary into the larger national system. U.S. Steel did not need to shelter the city from these larger national issues as long as the mills produced steel. It did not need to create a workers' utopia. Thus the notion that the mills of Gary were an industrial and technological accomplishment survived the strike unscathed.

Mother Jones remembered the outcomes and meaning of the steel strike quite differently than did U.S. Steel. For Jones, the breaking of the strike in Indiana was not only an example of the corporation's power over its fiefdom but also a deep betrayal of the wartime ideals of citizenship. "I saw the parade in Gary. Parades were forbidden in the Steel King's own town," she wrote in 1925.

> Some two hundred soldiers who had come back from Europe where they had fought to make America safe from tyrants, marched. They were steel workers. They had on their faded uniforms and the steel hats which protected them from German bombs. In the line of march I saw young fellows with arms gone, with crutches, with deep scars across the face—heroes they were! Workers in the cheap cotton clothes of the working class fell in behind them. Silently the thousands walked through the streets and alleys of Gary. Saying no word. With no martial music such as sent the boys into the fight with the Kaiser across the water. Marching in silence. Disbanding in silence.

The steel strike in Gary, however, was broken not only through the resistance and heartlessness of the corporation but also through the cooperation of newspapers and the government. "The next day the newspapers carried across the country a story of "mob violence" in Gary," Jones states.

> Then I saw another parade. Into Gary marched United States soldiers under General Wood. They brought their bayonets, their long range guns, trucks with mounted machine guns, field artillery. Then came violence. The soldiers broke up the picket line. Worse than that, they broke the ideal in the hearts of thousands of foreigners, their ideal of America. Into the blast furnace along with steel went their dream that America was a government for the people—the poor, the oppressed.[6]

If one of the guiding questions of Gary, Indiana, dating back to Wilson's juxtaposition of different Americas, was just how American was the city, Jones made it clear in her depiction of the strikers that she considered them fully American and fully patriotic. Alas, for Jones, it was the steel corporation that undermined this "dream of America."

Once the strike was broken, she lamented, "[Judge] Gary and his gang celebrated the victory with banquets and rejoicing. Three hundred thousand workers, living below the living wage, ate the bread of bitterness." And herein lay the important lessons of the strike for Jones: not only were the industrialists of U.S. Steel ultimately to blame, but the outcome of the strike meant the inevitability of larger and angrier conflicts. "I say, as I said in the town of Gary, it is the damn gang of robbers and their band of political thieves who will start the next American Revolution; just as it was they who started this strike," she concluded. "Fifty thousand American lads died on the battle fields of Europe that the world might be more democratic. Their buddies came home and fought the American workingman when he protested an autocracy beyond the dream of the Kaiser." While some hope remained for Jones, "had these same soldiers helped the steel workers, we could have given Gary, Morgan, and his gang a free pass to hell," she lamented. Still, the outcome of the steel strike was a bad omen. "All the world's history has produced no more brutal and savage times than these, and this nation will perish if we do not change these conditions."[7]

If there were anyone who came out of the steel strike in Gary with a better reputation, it was General Leonard Wood. "He showed us the stuff he was made of in his handling of the steel strike at Gary, Indiana," wrote one supporter to the *Independent*. "He did not force the issue between labor and capital, but met the situation like a diplomat and submitted it to arbitration."[8] In its survey of the political preferences of its readership, the *Independent* found that while most liked Herbert Hoover as their top Republican candidate in 1920, General Wood ranked very closely behind. Wood's presence in Gary and his actions to put down the strike and chase out the radicals were major parts of his appeal as a national candidate for the presidency. "On my way to Chicago I had passed through Gary, Indiana, where the troops were patrolling the streets during the steel strike, and I had heard so much about revolution and Reds that an uneasy excitement seemed to be in the air," wrote Evan David for *Outlook*. Yet, "when I was ushered into the presence of Leonard Wood, I was tremendously impressed by the feeling of serenity and steadfastness which the man personified." David describes a "powerfully built man, with deep chest, broad shoulders, [and a] large massive face and head," whose presence allayed the reporter's fears of traveling into the unsettling city of Gary.[9] David then interviewed Wood about his views on labor problems and the danger of immigrant radicalism. Much of Wood's national profile was built upon his actions in Gary. "Probably every man in public life would be willing to stand for the statement, 'I believe in law and order.' Most men have stood for it. But this simple phrase would mean one thing if put forward by Leonard Wood," stated the same magazine three months later. "From Leonard Wood this statement is to be understood against the background of his constructive achievements in establishing law in Cuba, in establishing order in the Philippines, and maintaining law and order in Gary, Indiana."[10] All three places, it was assumed, were very foreign, very radical, very dangerous, and had been brought under control by General Wood.

"MASTER WORKSHOPS OF AMERICA": BUSINESS LEADERS TALK OF GARY

While social reformers had abandoned the experiment of utopian Gary, the raw power and industrial might that industrialists had created remained an important part of how people spoke of Gary. "The world's largest business concern is the United States Steel Corporation," wrote Edward Purinton in 1920. "That makes it the world's largest school of industry, efficiency, economy, safety, concentration, coöperation, ideation, will and character. If you want to know the rules and rewards of life—learn them from the leaders of an industry like this." And what better place to learn these lessons than its model city:

> We regard the conception, creation and operation of the model city of Gary, Indiana, as the most original and important educational service rendered the nation by U.S. Steel. . . . Fifteen years ago, the site of Gary was a desolate sand dune, where wild fowl resorted, and nothing grew but sage brush and scrub oak. Now the world's largest steel mills operate here. . . . Almost everyone here works, and thinks at the same time, and does both for a common purpose in a common cause.

So impressed by Gary and U.S. Steel was Purinton that he called the city one of the "master workshops of America." At the end of the issue, the *Independent* issued a series of reading comprehension questions about

Purinton's article and thus about its view of Gary. "Why did the United States Steel Corporation build a new city 'from the ground up' at Gary, Indiana?" it asked. "Study a map, paying particular attention to the location of iron and coal mining regions, rail and water routes, and the neighborhood of great commercial centers. In view of these conditions do you think Gary was a good location for a steel manufacturing center?" It also asked its readers to compare their city with the well-run factory town of Gary. "What triumphs of municipal government has Gary, Indiana, achieved? What features of Gary's civic life does your town lack?"[11]

Charles Flint praised U.S. Steel for its strategic planning and ruthless efficiency. "A Trades Union is a combination of labor. A University is a combination of intelligence. A Bank is a combination of capital. An Industrial Consolidation is a combination of labor, intelligence, and capital. The mere combination of these factors, however, is not enough—it must function through the most complete coöperation of work, brains, and money for the highest efficiency . . . but the Steel Company went still further and made a great reduction in unnecessary transportation by plant relocation." All of which culminated in the building of a "new city, scientifically located—Gary, Indiana. Here, at a point precisely engineered between cheap, water-transported ore and fuel, and the centre of distribution of the finished products, great modern mills, homes, churches, schools, etc. were erected upon what had been desert sand dunes." Flint concludes, "Such a plan for efficiency could not have been carried out on such a scale except by a gigantic industrial consolidation."[12]

When she was looking to be awed by American industrial might on her visit in 1926, Queen Marie of Rumania visited the mills of Gary to see the "thrilling cascades of moulten metal" where "amid the glare of the furnaces her regal and commanding presence was revealed at last in an approximately iridescent milieu."[13]

The narrative of the Gary Works remained a symbol of industrial triumph and strategic planning. Plans for industrializing the port of San Francisco, for example, used the steel city as a model. "The heavy industries, because of the superior facilities of this well developed industrial port will be able to offer lower prices on half products and thereby make it a decided advantage for the light industries to locate in the same district," wrote Virginia Lee. "This is the economic foundation for the rapid growth of Gary, Indiana, far beyond the direct requirements of the United States Steel plant."[14] Gone was the rhetoric that infused these industrial spaces with hopes for social order and peaceful class relations. Discussions of Gary largely centered on the mills, their industrial output, and the foresight and technological expertise of their builders. When the city of Gary and U.S. Steel celebrated the twenty-fifth anniversary of construction, reports read like U.S. Steel mythology.

> One day late in 1905 Elbert Henry Gary, board chairman of U. S. Steel Corp., set a well-manicured finger firmly down on a map of northern Indiana. Said he to his directors: "This will be our metropolis. We'll build near the railroad junction of Chicago where acres of land can be had for almost the asking, midway between the ore regions of the North and the coal lands of the South and East." The Steel directors nodded consent. Purchased were 8,000 acres of barren sand dunes. On March 12, 1906, surveyors drove their first stakes among the tumbleweeds for U.S. Steel's fiat city. Streets were laid out, houses built, water and gas mains sunk. Top soil was brought in to spread over the sand, to grow trees and grass in. Great scoopers chewed a mile-long harbor back from Lake Michigan. Railroad connections were made. Against the sky began to rise the jagged outlines of steel mills, foundries, tin-plate plants.

"Within a year," *Time* magazine concluded in a story on what it called a "fiat city" of U.S. Steel, "$100,000,000 was dumped into this desolate Indiana waste and out of it by industrial magic rose Gary, greatest single steel city in the U.S."[15]

In his article where he calls Gary "Steel's Greatest Achievement," Charles Longnecker traces much of the creation mythology of the "magical" origins of the mills. "Until industry waved its magic wand over the land upon which the vast steel mills of Gary now stand," he begins, "the place was none other than a bleak, sandy waste." However, "industry with its wand, as potent as Aladdin's lamp, had transformed this section of sand driven desert into one of the most active and progressive manufacturing centers." For Longnecker, this transformation was not about triumphs of industrial planning and modern science. The mills of Gary were a triumph of personal leadership, vision, and "sane and wise counsel, together with his unusual ability" from Judge Gary. Longnecker imagines the vast passage of time over the Calumet Region sand dunes. "Our mythical observer would . . . have seen the missionaries," such as Pere Marquette,

Louis Joliet, and Sieur de La Salle, pass over the territory. He would have watched the Pottawatomie come and go and have seen the land change hands several times. Yet the important moment was the passing of a settler through the Calumet on his way to Warrenville, Illinois, west of Chicago in 1831. "It was he—Erastus Gary—whose surname would, through his son, be given to the world's largest steel works, and to one of the world's largest industrial cities." Other founders, such as general superintendent William Gleason, land lawyer A. F. Knotts, and current U.S. Steel president B. F. Fairless, also receive praise in Longnecker's reassessment of Gary's origins and meaning.[16] Such foresight and strategic planning, it seemed, had created an ordered if not utopian industrial center. Even as the industrial conflicts of the Great Depression loomed, *Time* noted that Gary remained U.S. Steel's "private stronghold in the Midwest," as the company prepared its defensive positions for "what looked like a major industrial war."[17]

The success of this industrial vision of Gary is perhaps best shown by the fact that U.S. Steel continued to replicate this form of industrial expansion. Almost on the completion of Gary, U.S. Steel launched a new company town in Fairfield, Alabama. Although executives had been adamant in denying social planning and paternalistic control for Gary, the new streets, homes, and organization of Fairfield were intricately planned and ordered. Yet Fairfield was a much smaller community and followed the industrial model of the southern company mill town rather than the urban industrial center. In 1951, however, the company announced its plan to open its new and massive Fairless Works outside of Trenton, New Jersey. Named after company chairman Benjamin Franklin Fairless, the new works were a mile outside of Trenton on the Delaware River with access to the markets of Trenton and Philadelphia as well as the "ore ships that will come from Venezuela." Just as it had forty-five years earlier, U.S. Steel's construction captured the imagination because of its scale. Calling the site "the largest steelworks ever built at one time," *Time* was awed by the "giant earthmovers . . . clawing across 3,800 acres of bean fields and tomato patches." "When the whole complex is completed," the magazine concluded, "the Fairless Works will boost Big Steel's 34-million-ton yearly capacity by a whopping 1,800,000 tons, enough to make 90,000 autos—or 45,000 more tanks—a year."[18]

Like Gary, the Fairless Works demanded new housing for the steel workers. For this site, however, the answer lay in sprawling postwar housing. Across the river, in Pennsylvania's rural Bucks County, a 16,000-home Levittown promised to house the majority of workers next to a smaller, and more expensive, neighborhood called Fairless Hills. Yet while the language of technological awe and audacious scale as well as the basic structure of worker housing physically separated from the mill site remained the same from Gary to Fairless, few saw in the Fairless Works a possibility to solve industrial conflict. *Time* warned that "amid the cheerful clatter and roar of expansion" the dangers of a strike still loomed for the company.[19] The strike of 1919 and its aftermath had proven to many that the Gary model could withstand, if not prevent, industrial conflict, just as the officials of U.S. Steel had planned and hoped it would. Unlike Pullman two decades earlier, the onset of industrial violence only helped to confirm this notion of Gary.

However, as U.S. Steel's official narrative about Gary, which stressed the wisdom of the founders, the audacity of the project, and the culmination of strategic industrial planning, became slowly hegemonic, a basic paradox emerged. These tales about Gary focused on the mills and their capacity for steel production, not the urban conditions of the city. For reformers and others, the creation of the city of Gary held great potential for order and progress. After the First World War, however, the easy connections between industrial planning, audacious scale, and social betterment were gone. Responding to an earlier article and defending the culture of New England, a letter sent to the *Independent* in 1925 made this evaluation of industrial spaces clear. "For, after all, the shoe factories and the cotton mills, the bank clearings, population increase, and unfilled orders for pig iron are not the only indices either of the vitality of a community or of the depth and fineness of its civilization," stated the author. "If they were, Gary, Indiana, would be a nobler human habitation than Athens ever was."[20]

No other observer recognized both the importance of image to Gary and the basic contradiction of its narratives better than Arthur Shumway. Writing in *American Parade* in 1929, Shumway, a former reporter for the *Gary Post-Tribune*, declares that because Gary existed as a "Shrine of the Steel God" of U.S. Steel, the boosters of the city were unreasonable about their conceptions of the city. The vision they presented, Shumway states, was clearly in stark opposition to the way others saw the city.

> Mention the magic name, Gary, anywhere but in that boisterous young city, and immediately your hearers shudder and draw drab mental pictures of desolate sand flats, smoke-belching steel mills, sweaty "Hunkies," squalid shacks, sun-cracked streets, unbelievable heaps of dirty golden dollars and one great, awesomely intricate School, the whole alternately sweltering and freezing under a pall of black smoke. Your hearers would be right, and they would be wrong. Gary, whatever else, is a paradox. It is busy; it is dull. It is modern; it is backward. It is clean; it is filthy. It is rich; it is poor. It has beautiful homes; it has sordid hovels. It is a typical overgrown American mill-town; it is a unique new city of the old world. It has a past, but it has no traditions. It has a feeble glow of culture, yet the darkness of prehistoric ignorance. In a word, it has everything, and at the same time has nothing.[21]

But, Shumway continues, the officials of U.S. Steel and the boosters of the city see none of these problems. They see only profit and possibility. Mention of Gary in these circles, jokes Shumway, requires "awesome reverence, with a bow of the head, and if you are inclined to be rheumatic, with at least a mental genuflection."

For himself, Shumway saw Gary as "at its worst . . . interesting," largely because of the variety of social conditions within the city.

> Its smelliest corners are interesting as the slums of a metropolis are interesting to the lily-fingered philanthropist, as the sty is interesting to the visitor from the city, as the cancer to the medico. And it is high time intelligent Americans knew why and how this 22-year-old upstart, this divinely conceived incubator child of the United States Steel Corporation, . . . is interesting to one who has had to scratch its sooty sand for sustenance.

This article is not a call for reform, especially not reform from "lily-fingered philanthropists." For Shumway, what made Gary interesting was the abnormality of the place and the surface optimism that contradicted the seemingly obvious realities of the city.

It was the boosters of the city and the executives of U.S. Steel who created, in Shumway's estimation, this separation of reality and image. He juxtaposes the creation mythology of U.S. Steel, which by 1929 had become the official narrative, with the gritty reality of the city's streets. "The golden power and prosperity of the omnipotent United States Steel Corporation," he jokes, "has gone to the heads of the devotees of the

Great God Steel. . . . Ask one the name of the greatest city in America and listen to him roar: "Gary!" Tell him it's a half-raw, dirty sort of a hole and listen to him hiss: "You're a damned liar—it's Utopia!" Yet Shumway concludes that the optimism of the residents is equally out of step with the actuality of the city. The immigrant laborers of the city, he argues, are "your ingredients for modern, blatant, noisy, self-centered, untutored, yet boundlessly ambitious and hopeful Gary." But this optimism seemed misplaced.

> Carl Sandburg, puissant poet of sweat and steel in a verse about Gary, said of these men on Broadway: 'They looked to me like they had been somewhere." Mr. Sandburg was wise. He said that they had *been,* not that they were going. It is hard to believe many of them are going anywhere. It is equally hard to believe that they have *been.*

Shumway sees neither working-class opportunity nor community. He does not believe the narrative that Gary is a crucible of assimilation and Americanization. "A melting pot, this Gary?" he concludes. "In 50 years, perhaps." He views only dystopian spaces of industrial pollution and dangerous immigrant workers, whom he categorizes as "devoid of the foolish appearance of optimism: Their big backs droop; their feet drag; their eyes look dull. . . . It is conceivable also that many of these, while not the majority, perhaps want to flee from the blazing furnaces, from lonely sand-drifts, from grimy hovels." Among these discontented workers, only one group stands out to Shumway. In an echo of the racialized division and racial stereotypes that would increasingly define Gary throughout the twentieth century, Shumway argues that among all the workers in the dirty and desperate city, only "the sauntering Negro . . . seems to get any real life out of the grimy existence. His laugh is loud, merry, human, and comforting amid the polyglot babble."

Yet the stories remain about Gary, and this is what Shumway is struggling to understand. Despite what he sees as the clear dystopia of the industrial city, legends and images of opportunities and wealth continue to exist, unconnected to the economic and social realities of Gary.

> There has grown out of this amazing upstart city a legend that it is a City of Gold. When young backwoods boys in the wilderness vastness of the Fundamentalist Mississippi, Georgia, and Alabama interior put on shoes and socks and head north, those who select Gary as their promised land

think of it as a wild, wicked and bustling den of the devil, where, despite "furriners" and filth, money can be made in a minute. They vision great heaps of golden cinders pouring like manna on the city. To them every grain of Gary sand is a potential nugget.

In comparing the stories people told about Gary and the realities as he saw them, Shumway recognizes the importance of narrative and imagery to Gary's meaning, but he also demonstrates how far the reformist vision of Gary had fallen. Shumway is deeply cynical and judgmental about the city. It is not only a dystopian wasteland of pollution and poverty; it is also populated by unassimilated immigrants and ignorant migrants wearing shoes for the first time.

This is a far cry from the reformist language of the late nineteenth century, which envisioned model industrial cities as a place of uplift, education, and Americanization. Some tried to counter the imagery of Gary that Shumway presented. The *Gary Post-Tribune* defended itself and its city with a series of essays and rebuttals. In one of these articles, community leader Garry Joel August tried to rebut Shumway's critiques as well as Woodrow Wilson's from 1912. "Gary is America," he concluded. "Every American city is Gary writ large or small."[22] Yet outside commentators and observers saw something else. August, the *Post-Tribune,* and the boosters of Gary may well have tried to defend themselves in their local paper. But in national publications, by 1929 the bloom had fallen off of the model city rose.

"IT'S A LOT LIKE WORKING IN HELL": WORKERS TALK OF GARY

Despite the national narratives and visions of Gary as an industrial site defined by pollution, vice, and strangeness, the working-class residents of Gary retained a sense of pride in themselves and their city. This was a major source of tension for Gary in the middle of the twentieth century: outside critiques belittled the city and declared it a wasteland while local residents clamored to defend the city and redeem its reputation. Such a defense necessitated some kind of local unity, yet from its very founding, Gary was a divided city. U.S. Steel in its planning ensured separation of physical spaces, especially spaces of work and home. Immigrants to the steel city grouped themselves into ethnic enclaves. Steel work did offer some possibilities for commonality and community. The strike of 1919 helped to create a culture of labor, as steelworkers and families claimed the streets as their own, even as they did so utilizing racialized categories and imagery. The success of the Congress of Industrial Organizations in unionizing U.S. Steel in 1937 and the emergence of Gary as a union town reconfirmed the sense that Gary was a good place for working families. Organized labor served as a counternarrative to the racial divisions and separations of Gary's working class. In his oral histories of workers in the Calumet Region, Staughton Lynd identified a tradition of radical labor organizing that just as often defied the CIO as U.S. Steel. Calling this tradition "guerilla history," Lynd argues that, especially in Gary, radicalism was a very real tradition, and a more radical union was a real possibility in the 1930s. While not quite the radicalism that Lynd documents, the Federal Writers' Project of the Works Progress Administration classified Gary, in 1939, as a mill town because so much of its urban culture revolved around the production of steel. Many residents took great pride in their capacity for work and steel production. In this way, the residents of Gary took the official narrative of U.S. Steel and made it their own. It was, in this vision, a site of large-scale steel production, vast mills, ethnic communities, and hard work.[23]

One version of workers' Gary centered largely around the idea that Gary was a good place to be from because of strong ethnic communities and the creation of a proud work ethic. "Gary was a company town, one hour's drive along Lake Michigan," writes actor Karl Malden. "My father moved us there when I was five years old. He was following the money, so he left behind a job shellacking doors and window frames in a lumber yard to work in the higher paying Gary steel mills." Because immigrants and migrants from all over were moving to Gary, Malden points out that the Gary of his youth "was a checkerboard of nationalities. . . . Where you lived meant who you were. Irish, Scottish, Polish, Hungarian, Bulgarian, Greek, Serb. That was us. The Serbs. Living at 457 Connecticut Street in Gary, Indiana, U.S.A. But it may as well have been Yugoslavia."[24]

While the notion of ethnic diversity and old world customs had long been part of the dystopian critique of Gary, for Malden (or, as he was born, Mladen George Sekulovich), this helped create a sense of belonging and community within the ethnic enclave. So too was Malden moved by the Americanization efforts during the Great War. "It was a time when contributing to your country, even with a small ball of tin foil, could make a small child feel very worthwhile," writes Malden. "I think that silly ball of foil meant something particularly special to me; it meant I really was an American after all."[25]

If Malden's memories of growing up in Gary turn the dystopian images of foreignness, ethnicity, and Americanization on their heads, then so too do his descriptions of Gary's social conditions and air qualities. "As much as Gary was still undeveloped at that time, the mills had already become the heart of the city. At night, the flames from the blast furnace lit up the sky for blocks," remembers Malden. "The mills rained a fine, gray dust over the city. But no one cared. The dust meant work."[26] This connection between economy and ecology was echoed often in the local narratives of Gary. An early cartoon in the *Gary Works Circle*, the official plant publication, made this link directly. Entitled "The eyes of the world are on Gary," the cartoon shows a globe looking into the smoky distance and pondering "Where is all that smoke coming from?" only to be answered by the Gary worker, "Oh, that's the Big Smoke from the Billet Mill."[27] For Gary, belching smokestacks meant wealth, work, and stability.

For Gary residents such as Malden, however, the relationship with industrial pollution was far from simple. While smoke and soot did promise work, most still recognized that it was a compromise they had made. For Malden, the omnipresence of the mills and the layers of soot could be as much about oppression as opportunity. While the dust may have meant work, he continues, "the dust coated everything and, in a way, smothered the dreams of most everyone who lived under it, who breathed it in, like a coat of grimy reality." While his father did find work in Gary:

> It was a dangerous job that my dad detested, though he spent twelve long years working with the heavy equipment, often in the mouth of the furnace where the heat would be so intense you could hardly catch your breath. There was little relief. No salt pills, no water coolers, only big buckets of water. They had to sprinkle oatmeal on top to absorb the flu dust so that the men would have to scrape the scum away in order to dip down for a drink.[28]

Eventually, "like every good Gary son," Malden himself found work in the steel mills. "Sparks fly like fireworks and the molten ore flows like lava. In reality, it is a terrifying, dangerous place to be. It's a lot like working in hell." This kind of rough and dangerous work had long been central to

Gary's self-image of a steel town. For Malden, the work in the mills was anything but fulfilling.

> I worked in the mills for a total of three years. All the while the same thought plagued me until the sound of it reverberating in my head became almost unbearable. "This is where my life is going to end up." I tried to remind myself that I was lucky to have a job. It was still the Depression after all. . . . It was hard to feel lucky laboring at backbreaking work that I loathed. I felt trapped.[29]

The worker's vision of Gary had its limits. Throughout his autobiography, Malden often cites his origins as motivation for work effort and success, yet the rest of the story that Malden tells is how he got away from Gary. For residents such as Malden, Gary was often a better place to be from than to live in.

A closely related version sees the city of Gary as not just a laboratory for learning hard knocks and work ethic but also a close-knit, if somewhat narrowly defined, community that offered unconditional support and loyalty. Unlike the Malden story line, which ultimately explained what one learned in Gary and then how one escaped, this vision of community suggested a much closer and mutually beneficial relationship between the youth and his surrounding environment. This vision often focused on athletic achievement, so the tale was almost always reserved for young men. While these stories are repeated often, involving different people including boxer Tony Zale and football players George Taliaferro and Tom Harmon, they tend to contain the same narrative arc. A young man, a son of a steelworker, learns the value of hard work, perseverance, and sacrifice. After a brief stint in the steel mills, which shapes him in profound ways, the man moves on to great success and proves the value of Gary's working-class masculinity. After such success, he returns home to be the favorite son of Gary.[30]

Born in 1913 on the south side of Gary, Anthony Florian Zaleski came of age in a city that still, as James Lane has pointed out, "had a male dominated, frontier quality." Tony Zale grew up in the Polish Community of the south side that centered on Saint Hedwig Church at the corner of Seventeenth and Connecticut. Zale's father, Josef, worked as a fitter for the American Bridge Company, a subsidiary of U.S. Steel, until his untimely death. From the school at Saint Hedwig, Zale moved to Froebel

High School, the recognized immigrant school of Gary and one of the experimental sites of William Wirt. Zale and his brothers began to box as amateurs in the Silver Bells Club, an extension of the Polish National Alliance. When Gary began to hold Golden Gloves competitions in 1930, Zale entered and won the first of three city titles. By 1934, the weight of the Great Depression combined with the absence of his father drove Zale to turn professional to provide for his mother, Katherine. Untrained and poorly used by his manager, Zale spent the next year splitting bouts and taking beatings. In 1935, he quit boxing and began to work in the steel mills. He returned to the ring in 1937, better trained and better managed. In January 1940, Zale received his first big bout, a nontitle fight with National Boxing Association middleweight Al Hostak. What was supposed to be an exhibition victory for Hostak quickly became a battle, as Zale "beat on Hostak's ribs like the madcap vaudeville performer, Professor Lamberti, banging on his xylophone." Zale won the bout by decision. In a July rematch, the referee ended the fight in the thirteenth round, and Zale became the NBA middleweight champion. His status as champion was confirmed with a second round knockout of Hostak in a third fight and a November 1941 decision over George Abrams.[31]

Like so many other careers, Zale's boxing was suspended by American involvement in the Second World War. Zale entered the navy, where he served as a physical instructor and spent four years without boxing. Still his reputation preceded him, as Shirley Povich would report in the *Washington Post*. As he checked in at the Great Lakes Naval Training Station, he stated his name and occupation as "Anthony Zaleski, professional boxer, middleweight." To which the naval clerk responded, "I'd hate to be in your shoes, Zaleski. Tony Zale's due here this week."[32] However, afraid of losing his edge if he pulled punches or hurting his sparing partners if he did not, Zale chose to do no fighting. Yet he still exited the navy as middleweight champion. After six tune-up bouts, all won by knockouts, Zale faced his first real contender, Rocky Graziano. The two met for their first bout on September 27, 1946, in Yankee Stadium. Graziano dominated the champion for the first several rounds, yet Zale absorbed Graziano's best punches, and by the sixth round, having turned the momentum, he had knocked out the challenger. Zale was hailed in his return to Gary as a conquering hero and was presented with the key to the city. In July 1947, Zale and Graziano would meet again in Chicago. This time Graziano

would emerge from the sixth round as middleweight champion. The following summer, Zale would regain his title with a third round knockout
of Graziano. In 1949, after being beaten by Marcel Cerdan, Zale retired
from boxing and returned to Gary.

For many boxing fans and sports writers, the three Zale-Graziano
fights rank highly as some of the best boxing matches of the twentieth
century. But at the time, the coverage and meaning of the fights meant
quite a bit more. Upon his return from New York, just as they had when
Zale returned from his Hostak fights, residents of Gary embraced the
fighter as a favorite son who embodied all of the qualities of their city.
Zale's career was a confirmation of the city's work ethic, ethnic and communal pride, persistence, and strong-willed masculinity. Much of the
coverage of Zale picked up on these same themes. Like Malden, Zale
was the son of a steelworker who had worked in the steel mills himself.
Here he had learned both the harsh realities of life and the work ethic
that would eventually pay off for him. The steel mills shaped (dare one
say "forged") his determination and toughness and literally shaped his
physique and strength. "I knew I'd never be any good as a fighter as long
as my side bothered me," he told the *Saturday Evening Post*. "So I got the
kind of work that would strengthen it." The heavy work of the steel mill,
the lifting of beams, the shoveling of ore, became the path to greater success. This story, along with his origins in Gary, his willingness to fight
through illness and injury, and a tendency to take beatings early in bouts,
led many to label Zale the "Man of Steel."[33]

Although in Gary Zale represented a working identity of work ethic
and determination, this story line often ran counter to what people outside of Gary expected to see from such a boxer. Zale's exploits, for Howard Roberts of the *Saturday Evening Post*, "suggest a barroom brawler,
as rough as ten-cent whisky, with a heavyweight ego in a middleweight
frame," basically what people had long expected from residents of frontier
Gary. Yet Roberts was surprised to find that Zale was "a mild, soft-spo-
ken, and modest man whose life outside the ring is as quiet and amiable
as his fighting style is furious." Here was a fighter "who does not smoke,
drink, or swear, who lectures boys on sportsmanship [and] clean living."
Writing after the first Graziano fight, Roberts lamented the unfortunate
career of Zale. "Fate has rubbed rosin in Zale's eyes for years," he claimed,
because Zale had made so little money and had lost so many years serv-

ing in the navy. Roberts then juxtaposed this "hard-luck champion" with Rocky Graziano, "who looked like the hottest thing in years. The kid from the streets of New York was young, cocky, infinitely dangerous." In so doing, Roberts made Zale into a national personification of the American working man. Adored within the iconography of New Deal liberalism, the honest worker was clearly different from the street punk and juvenile delinquent who contributed little to the common good. At the same time, Zale's victory served as a celebration of the sacrifice of wartime veterans, for Graziano "had been fighting regularly while Zale was sweating out his last months in uniform." "Zale's victory," Roberts stated, "delighted many men who, like him, had spent what might have been their decisive years in service." Graziano's defeat was a well deserved comeuppance that the impending rematch would not change. "Win or lose this one against the bumptious Rocky Graziano," Roberts concluded. "Tony Zale will retain a place in the hearts of boxing fans . . . [that] Graziano can never usurp."

Of course, Roberts's predictions proved quite wrong. Although the Zale-Graziano fights remain well regarded, it is Rocky Graziano who is far better remembered from this golden age of boxing, largely due to the popularity of Graziano's book, *Somebody Up There Likes Me*.[34] The Man of Steel maintained a consistent level of popularity in Gary and Chicago (to the chagrin of residents of the Calumet, who felt that Mayor Daley was claiming Zale as his own). For the next several decades, Zale made public appearances. Yet his legacy as a boxer, which once symbolized the ultimate triumph of the New Deal worker, once again became a symbol of working-class perseverance and struggle. "He was considered impervious to pain," the International Boxing Hall of Fame would note upon inducting him. "He managed to endure endless punishment and time and time again would snatch victory from the jaws of defeat."

While George Taliaferro would not carry the same kind of symbolic imagery as the midcentury boxer, his story was also a tale of hard work, community, and wartime sacrifice. Taliaferro remembered having a very close community of supporters as he rose to gridiron stardom at Gary Roosevelt High School. He had fond memories of the Gary of his youth, which he remembered as fairly socially integrated, friendly, and well kept. He told of playing with children of different races and ethnicities, although Gary Roosevelt was an all-black school that was not allowed by the state to compete against white schools, such as Emerson or Lew Wallace, in contact sports. A nonscheduled game against East Chicago Roosevelt was the one major exception. This game introduced Taliaferro to a wider Calumet audience and reinforced the pride that the black community held for him. Taliaferro felt that the community support of Gary gave him the security and confidence to tackle larger challenges. At one point he toyed with going straight into full-time work in the steel mills. (He had worked weekends as a teenager as a part of wartime peak production.) It was his father who ultimately discouraged him from steel work, telling him that such work was man's work and that "there is no room for two men in this house, and I am the man in this house."[35] However, unlike Malden, whose steel work experience drove him to acting, the possibility of steel work gave Taliaferro a safety net; seemingly, there was always work available in the mills.[36] Leaving Gary after high school, Taliaferro would play football at Indiana University and, after a brief stint in the military, would become the first African American player drafted by an NFL franchise.

In the interwar period, workers' stories of Gary offered stark contrasts to both U.S. Steel's master narrative of efficient industrialism and outsider assumptions about pollution, ethnicity, division, and industrial life. The workers' vision of the city offered different interpretations of Gary's social conditions. Yet a basic problem lay at the center of this kind of resistance. As much as these are responses to outsider critiques of the city, they become outsider narratives as well. Malden and Taliaferro, for instance, recall their childhood in Gary from a position outside of the city. As memory is wont to do, they manufacture a folklore of their city to explain who they became. So too does the meaning of the CIO and labor agitation become shaped by labor activists and labor historians who wish to see in Gary the possibilities for working-class solidarity, social justice, or other ideals. For instance, Alice and Staughton Lynd collected oral histories on labor radicalism in the Calumet Region and Chicago through the Labor History Workshop in Gary in 1971. Many of these appeared in their collection, *Rank and File*. While he was writing about radicalism and "guerilla history" of the working class in Gary during the 1930s, Lynd was actively involved in social movements, including both labor and antiwar movements, that advocated similar tactics and policies. "If we had a better idea how radicals should have acted while unions were being organized," he argues, "we might better understand how they should act today." The Lynds, it seems, came to Gary for many of the same reasons that Graham Taylor and other urban planners did before them. Gary represented what the nation/movement/culture could be or should be. It remained a screen for outsider projection of hopes and fears, even those of the historian.[37]

Many Gary residents would take great pride in their steel work and would brag of never missing a day. The city, its schools, and its mills may have been tough places, but this, within the workers' narrative, created tough people who shared the soot, pollution, and ethnic community. However, the political realities in Gary were based far more on intense divisions, especially racial divisions, than this narrative admits. In the depths of the Great Depression, a column in the *Gary Post-Tribune* dedicated to the "Voice of the People" lashed out at "outsiders, aliens, hillbillies, and women" who were taking away precious jobs. One of the primary targets for this rage was the city's Mexican population. As early as 1924, the city's police began an "anti-vagrancy" campaign that criminalized the presence of Mexican workers, who, being exempted by the stringent immigration laws, were actively recruited by the steel corporation. The anxieties of the Great Depression accentuated these patterns. During the 1930s, roughly 1,500 Mexicans were repatriated by the city, some voluntarily, other forced. But like the rest of Depression-era politics and culture, Gary was part of larger national trends. Nationwide, nearly half a million Mexican workers were sent south.[38] While narratives of industrialism may have shaped the meaning of Gary, the politics and social realities of the city were driven by national politics and racial divisions.

CONCLUSION: "STRETCHES OF INDUSTRIAL WASTELAND"

While the mills of Gary would still appear in national discussions of steel policy and labor relations, and its sanitation efforts and water works continued to interest sanitary engineering publications, discussions of the city often told a very different story.[39] For the most part Gary remained a strange and foreign place of adventure and danger. In some folklore, Gary became the place where Chicago's gangsters would hide from the law and make their hits. In the 1930s, John Dillinger's popular career in and around Lake County, Indiana, only enhanced this lawless and populist image. When Walter Kelly, the boss of the numbers game in Gary known as "De King," was killed in 1939, his funeral became a public event. "There was a $5,000 bronze casket smothered with tea roses," reported the *American Mercury*.

> A former Congressman, Oscar De Priest, led the mourners, and Joe Louis sent a huge wreath. Maurice Cooper, star of the *Swing Mikado,* sang "Goin' Home," and 7,000 Negroes swarmed around the church, crushing each other to glimpse the bier of the man who had, in their minds, walked with the gods and toiled with the devil.

According to the *American Mercury,* Gary was mourning not only the loss of a larger-than-life crime figure but also the "Robin Hood of the Numbers Game." Assuming that Kelly served a benevolent communal role in his activities, the magazine pointed out that "less than a week after his murder, three hundred Negro families in Gary applied for Relief; he had been supporting them."[40]

During the height of Prohibition, blind pigs, gambling joints, and other illegal activities dominated the discussions of Gary. The *Chicago Herald-Examiner,* for instance, ran a story about the massive police sweeps that were "cleaning up Gary stills." Despite the raids that had seized 1,173 stills in the city the previous year, the paper expressed little hope that the Volstead Act could be enforced in Gary.[41] Many of these stories about Gary stressed not only crime but political corruption and the foreignness of the population as well. In a 1923 article, *Outlook* described the conviction of Gary's mayor and fifty-four other city officials as the "Gary Liquor Scandal." In detailing the crimes, the magazine stressed the strange otherness of the city. "It has been said that the American 'melting-pot' had never been even thawed out in Gary: that Gary is Hoosier only as far as geography is concerned. What an example the city officials have set for the overwhelming foreign population, among which sentiment might be expected to be adverse to the enforcement of prohibition! What a lesson in 'Americanism' had been set for them."[42] The *Peoria Transcript* agreed that Gary's population was by nature against prohibition and thus would not care to see enforcement of the law. Such communities, the paper concluded, "will always ignore the Federal laws and make but slight efforts to enforce them." Other papers may have been more positive in their assessment of the value of the raids. The *Pittsburgh Gazette Times,* for instance, concluded that the "Gary case may prove of great value as a warning, and also an illustration of what can be achieved in upholding the law."[43] Yet all assumed that Gary was a lawless and foreign place where crime and corruption were tolerated.

Among the other consistent narratives about Gary was its industrial pollution and decay. Alongside political corruption and "othered" populations (either black or foreign), Gary was often described as a dirty and decaying town. It is an ironic narrative given both the technological and utopianist founding of the city and U.S. Steel's persistent official narrative that stressed the modern science of the steel mills. Gary was still a very young city, but for many it seemed a city that had aged beyond its years. In a 1931 article on bank failures, *Time* magazine set the scene by reminding its readers that "Gary, Ind., is essentially a steel city, its murky horizon is sliced jagged by towering smokestacks. An efficient Chamber of Commerce boasts to visitors that Gary has 515 acres of golf links, parks and playgrounds, a $1,000,000 community Church, a model public school plan. The visitor will listen politely. But he will always remember Gary as a grey city of steel and flame and smoke." The article even prefaced the failure of the bank by pointing out that "its location is in that part of Gary known as 'across the tracks,' the great flat area where thousands of steelworkers dwell."[44]

Often Gary would serve as a comparison for other decayed and polluted places. "The Garden State of New Jersey," announced one *Time* article, "boasts some of the most remarkably unsylvan areas east of the city dump at Gary, Ind."[45] When Paramount needed gritty city streets for its 1951 film *Appointment with Danger*, it found the "littered alleys, poolrooms, shabby hotels, and stretches of industrial wasteland" on location in Gary.[46]

If there is a single lasting image of Gary within American popular culture in the twentieth century, however, it probably comes from Meredith Willson's musical *The Music Man*. The plot revolves around Harold Hill, a traveling salesman/confidence man, who comes to River City, Iowa, pretending to sell residents musical instruments and band uniforms with the promise that he will then lead a city band. As proof of his musical pedigree, Hill claims to have graduated from the Gary Conservatory of Music, class of '05. In order to sell his commitment to the institution and the city, Hill sings fondly of the city of Gary.

Gary, Indiana! What a wonderful name,
Named for Elbert Gary of judiciary fame.
Gary, Indiana, as a Shakespeare would say,
Trips along softly on the tongue this way—
Gary, Indiana, Gary, Indiana, Gary, Indiana, Let me say it once again.
Gary, Indiana, Gary, Indiana, Gary, Indiana, That's the town that "knew
    me when."
If you'd like to have a logical explanation,
How I happened on this elegant syncopation,
There is just one place that can light my face.
Gary, Indiana, Gary Indiana, Not Louisiana, Paris, France, New York, or
    Rome, but—
Gary, Indiana, Gary, Indiana, Gary Indiana, My home sweet home

The mention of the steel city serves as a basic plot point. Hill's lies are exposed when the town's librarian discovers that Gary did not exist until 1906. At the same time, there is an unspoken joke that twentieth-century audiences would clearly be in on. So naïve and unworldly are the rubes of River City that they are willing to buy the notion of Gary, Indiana, as a center of high art and culture and a producer of musical expertise. Clearly the Iowans do not know what the audience knows: Gary's real products were steel, smoke, crime, and vice.

The mention of Gary within *The Music Man* played off of the dominant dystopian visions of Gary in the early twentieth century. There was the official narrative that focused on the Gary Works as a site of steel mills and a place of corporate, scientific, and technological advancement. This vision was an image of machines that produced steel—not social reform, industrial order, or uplift. At the same time, a popular narrative of Gary the city emerged that described the place as an untamed frontier wilderness that could be a dystopian wasteland of pollution and irredeemable otherness, a profoundly masculine space of limitless potential or a clean slate for redemptive social engineering. Other visions focused on Gary as a cauldron from which emerged strong communities and strong workers. Such stories of Gary were a long way from the cultural center of which Harold Hill sang so longingly.

PART THREE

The Very Model of Modern Urban Decay: Decline and Fall

DECLINE AND FALL

For Gary was built on shifty sand: it was built in the sandy dune country. It was set up in a bit of savagery. And even now, in spite of the miles of street pavement and sidewalks, in spite of the thousands of orderly homes and business blocks, the sand is all about and in between and is always vastly threatening. Let a householder but stir with a stick in his back yard, on a windy day, and the treacherous sand begins to move and cloud and whirl. And, close hemming the city, are areas of sand, shifting and blowing and always threatening. And the fancy comes, that if the people were to be taken away for a little while, and the town left to itself, it would be blotted out; one feels that its houses would become hills and knolls of sand, that its streets, now thronged by day and brilliantly lighted by night, would become sand valleys, that scrub-oaks and pines would begin to grow here and that the city of Gary would vanish from sight as magically as it arose, with only a few mill chimneys standing up mysteriously to puzzle wondering travelers, until even those last signs of human life should rust and topple and disappear.

ROBERT SHACKLETON, *THE BOOK OF CHICAGO*, 1920

SIX

"Gary Is a Steel Town, Young, Lusty, Brawling"

DECLENSION NARRATIVES ABOUT GARY

The war effort had been about inclusive democracy, communal sacrifice, and the rejection of racial categories and racialized hatred. Or at least this was the official war narrative created by the Office of War Information (OWI). While much of American culture had focused on proper hatred of the enemy that was, especially for the Pacific theater, often racialized, the OWI centered on the perils of fascism and racial ideologies of German Nazism. It was little wonder then that the postwar attitude suggested a possible paradigm shift in American social relations. The Serviceman's Readjustment Act had promised significant changes in education and housing, regardless of race, and the massive wartime mobilization had undermined many Americans' notions of community, ethnicity, and region. In total, the narratives of the Second World War had created a culture of optimism. It was this postwar optimism that the song "The House I Live In," sung by Frank Sinatra, captured.

> What is America to me?
> A name, a map, or a flag I see?
> A certain word, "democracy"?
> What is America to me?
> The house I live in, a plot of earth, a street,
> The grocer and the butcher or the people that I meet.
> The children in the playground, the faces that I see,
> all races and religions, that's America to me.[1]

It was apropos, then, that Sinatra would become an ambassador of sorts for the new postwar paradigm of race relations. Racial segregation and racial violence had long been a part of American society, especially in northern cities since the Great Migration during the First World War.

They had a long history in Gary, especially in housing and education. Given the idealism of the era, this no longer seemed acceptable. Thus when the white students of Froebel High School walked out of classes to protest the inclusion of black students, Sinatra flew to Gary to offer this new vision of toleration.[2]

Yet this vision of postwar optimism was short-lived. What had been the self-assurance at the end of the war quickly became the paranoia of the cold war. What had been the democratic community and sacrifice of Frank Capra's *It's a Wonderful Life* became the national concern over Alfred Kinsey's discussions of sexuality, the uncontrollable nature of runaway youth, and the deceit and betrayal of film noir. Even the racial promise of the GI Bill faced the reentrenchment of Jim Crow laws throughout the American South. The promise of a new racial paradigm was even shorter-lived in Gary. Despite the high-profile visit of Sinatra, education in the steel city remained segregated, and white students seemed determined to ensure that it stayed that way. Only two years after Sinatra came to town, students from Emerson, another Gary high school, walked out to protest integration. By 1947, even the national press had grown cynical about Gary's chances of changing its social realities. Calling the city a "crucible of steel and humanity," *Time* concluded that there had been no gain in Gary. "Two years ago Crooner Frank Sinatra flew from Hollywood to Gary to try to persuade Froebel High students to end a strike over Negro pupils. The bobby-soxers squealed with delight but didn't take any of his line of reasoning."[3]

Time was not the first national publication to see in Gary a "crucible of humanity." The city of Gary had long been shaped by the visions and images others placed upon it. As the concerns and obsessions shifted throughout the twentieth century, so did the snapshots of Gary that the larger American public saw. As postwar America's fears shifted from political corruption and liquor-law violations to the morality of public sexuality and youth, so too did the descriptions of Gary. In a 1948 piece for the *Saturday Evening Post*, J. D. Ratcliff described in detail the rash of traffic accidents in Gary: "Motor-vehicle injuries and deaths have risen to a point where they represent a major national sickness. Bombarding the public with gruesome statistics won't help. A close-up view of the dead and dying may." While Ratcliff suggests that these dangerous conditions do exist "in one degree or another" in every city, still there is an inherent lawlessness that permeates Gary's urban image. The article begins by recognizing this image. "The chime sounds when an ambulance arrives with an emergency case," writes Ratcliff. "It may be a cutting, a shooting, or the results of a tavern row. Gary is a steel town, young, lusty, and brawling, and such things are common."[4]

The story lines about Gary had several things in common. The first was that, after the Second World War, Gary became somehow representative of the larger American experience, the "crucible of humanity." What happened in Gary mattered because it had larger meaning in terms of race relations, public morality, and industrial might. At the same time, these stories about Gary were tales of decline. Each contained a moment where the city went wrong and the Americanism represented in Gary was a corrupted Americanism. Yet every story had its own turning point. For some it was the moral debauchery of the 1950s; for others it was the rise of black power and politics in the 1960s; for still others it was the white backlash against civil rights. Within the stories people told about Gary, the city seemed to always be in decline (this despite the empirical evidence of growing populations and increased steel production). When outsiders viewed Gary in the postwar period, they could agree that Gary represented something important, and they agreed that something was wrong, but they never agreed upon what that problem was. But two culprits often emerged: vice and race.

"CHALKED UP AS AN INCORRIGIBLE SIN CITY": NARRATIVES OF VICE AND REFORM

The complicated nature of postwar anxiety, however, was that the sensationalist press, within which much of this anxiety was contained, was often as tantalized by the material as it was appalled. In a May 1955 sensationalist exposé of Gary's nightlife entitled "Steel and Sex," *Quick* magazine claimed that the "vice dens are hotter than the blast furnaces." Detailing the number of bars and clubs that "spawn sin, crime, and open immorality," the magazine describes the conditions that created such open immorality.

> Over one hundred thousand brawny steel-workers clean up $17 million
> a month and spend it on sex, gambling and dope right in their own back
> yard! Recent investigations uncovered 64 gambling halls and "joy houses"

> operating full tilt within the city limits of Gary, Indiana! Dressed up in gaudy eye-catching outfits, swarms of gals walk the streets, invade the markets, theaters, stations, and bars in search of their share of that 17 million bucks! Hungry racketeers have moved in to grab their share, and the dope peddlers are firmly entrenched in this wide-open steel town.

Connecting industrial pollution and immorality directly, the magazine states that "for years now the thick, choking black pall of smoke from the steelmills seem to have shrouded Gary with an impenetrable cloak that hides Gary's crime and sin from the outside." The city "has been chalked up as an incorrigible sin city that probably will never change."

In a 1966 exposé, *Time* declared that Lake County in northwest Indiana was "the abandoned county." While efforts at controlling vice in Chicago may have changed the locations of vice, it had not changed its existence.

> The once racy North Side is as dead as Gomorrah. Calumet City, thanks to another crusading police chief, has only darkened flesh parlors to show for its long career as Chicago's sin suburb. Even Al Capone's Cicero has quieted down. No matter. If he insists on drinking life to the lees, the conventioneer can still find paradise now an hour away in Gary or East Chicago, across the state line in Indiana's grimy Lake County.

Classifying the region as a "hard-boiled area of steel mills and oil refineries with an abrasive ethnic mix," the article suggests that Gary has developed "every problem, vice, and crime known to man." However, "the fundamental problem is political," the magazine declares. "The county has been solidly Democratic since 1932, and its politicians have made corruption a way of life." While private reform organizations such as the Northwest Indiana Crime Commission had "sporadically attempted to clean up the county," their efforts had failed, just as it was assumed why earlier reform efforts had failed, because of a "low budget and the obvious indifference of local and state officialdom."[5]

When *Newsweek* focused on industrial pollution and environmental conditions in 1970, it declared that "along the southern shore of Lake Michigan squats what many ecologists regard as the most concentrated pollution factory in the world." The magazine concluded that the "city of Gary, home of U.S. Steel's largest complex, probably capsulates the area's pollution crisis best." *Newsweek* even turned much of Gary's creation mythology on its head. What had been at the turn of the century a story of barren and useless sand dunes turned magically overnight into productive and modern steel mills became something quite different. "Gary was even conceived by an act of despoliation," concludes Harry Waters, who traveled into Gary for the article. "In 1906, the U.S. Steel Co. . . . carved out some 2,500 acres of open-hearth furnaces and slag heaps on what had been the starkly beautiful Lake Michigan sand dunes." Here for Waters was the tradeoff. Gary the mills provided "pay for more than 30,000 Garyites," yet was responsible for "36,000 tons of soot." While some must stay for the money, concluded Waters, there are other reasons that go deeper into what is to him the bizarre culture of the place.

> The Slovaks, Hungarians, Poles, Swedes, Greeks, and Irish who originally settled in the Hammond–East Chicago–Gary steel complex at the beginning of the century took as much pride in their jobs as in their stamina and brawn. They boiled big fish lunches in tin cans over pieces of molten steel, washed it down with coffee made from sludge water, and topped off ten-hour shifts exposed to thousand-degree blasts with a night of wenching in Calumet City. No sissy frissin' thing like pollution was going to bug this breed.[6]

Here again were the older narratives of ethnic pride, masculine virtue, and attractive vice used to explain Gary to an outside audience.

This connection between smoke and work colored Gary's response to the environmental movement of the 1970s, especially the Clean Air Act. "For the first time in a decade, the skies over Gary these days are clean and crisp," reported Seth King in 1971.

> It is now possible to breathe deeply without coughing and see clearly from the lower reaches of Broadway northward to the Indiana Tollway overpass. But the clean air is not a source of much happiness, for it is a result of the fact that since Aug. 1 the four sprawling divisions of the United States Steel Corporation which for years have smothered Gary in a reddish-brown and black blanket, have been operating with only half of their normal work force of 25,000.[7]

The *Fort Lauderdale News and Sun-Sentinel* echoed these sentiments with a headline declaring "Blue Skies over Gary Mean Unemployment Lines."[8] Again in 1975, the economic well-being of Gary seemed at odds with the efforts of the Environmental Protection Agency. "Ever since New Year's

Day, a familiar sight has been missing from Gary, Ind.," reported *Time*. "For the first time in years, there is no miasma of smoke." While the article points out that this is not merely a case of "economics v. ecology" but rather unfulfilled promises from U.S. Steel to control pollution from its smokestacks, it also says that "almost everyone in Gary would like to see them relit as soon as possible."[9]

Gary's relationship to its environment was complicated, however. While smoke often did mean work, and many workers came to the same sort of understanding that Malden did with his environment, industrial pollution did trigger community responses. The residents of Gary were very much involved in some of the environmental reforms of the mid-1970s. Being a massive industrial center, Gary had been subjected to large doses of industrial pollution. Often the poorest sections of Gary had the worst air and water quality. Yet, beginning in 1972 with the Calumet Environmental and Occupational Health Committee, Gary's residents began to fight for better health and environmental standards. In his study of Gary's environmental movements, Andrew Hurley concludes that, far from being an elite movement to protect nature at the cost of jobs, Gary's environmental concerns created a broad-based coalition of several interests. The community's environmental group, the Community Action to Reverse Pollution (CARP), included members from white middle-class suburbs, organized labor, and the black working class. In fact, since poor blacks were the ones faced with the worst pollution, their participation was essential to CARP's success. When it came to environmental standards, Gary's citizens were willing and able to shape their city's image and destiny.[10]

From 1909 on, the citizens of Gary were also actively involved in various urban politics and social movements. James Lane has documented much of this with decades of oral histories.[11] Yet it was fairly rare for outsider critics, who used Gary as a symbol, to recognize or discuss the resistance and agency of Gary's citizens. When these critiques did discuss the residents of the city, it was often to stress their strangeness. From the early narratives of Gary as a new frontier to Carl Sandburg's description of muscular workers to the postwar exposés of prostitution and gambling, all of the urban images of Gary assumed that it was a city of ethnic working-class men. Outside observers offered alternatives to this dominant narrative of Gary mostly when reform efforts came from outside these assumptions. One such case was the postwar effort of the women of Gary to reinvent their city and their place within it. Their vice campaign captured positive national attention, which was rare for the steel city, largely because it tapped into national interest in new definitions of postwar femininity.

The event that triggered this newest effort at reform was the murder of Mary Cheever on Thursday, March 3, 1949. Described by the *Ladies' Home Journal* as a "spinster schoolteacher . . . highly regarded for both her blue eyes and the firmness of her approach to education," Cheever was mugged and shot on her way home from a PTA meeting.[12] By Saturday, indignation and anger had risen over the killing. On March 8, Prosecutor Ben Schwartz announced a new campaign to find Cheever's killer as well as crack down on the city's vice and gambling, pledging in front of the mayor, deputy prosecutors, and city and county judges "all out assistance to Gary's war on vice." Unappeased, Gary's ministers called upon the FBI to investigate the Gary police department. Outraged about the city's record of crime and its leadership's apparent apathy, thousands of women continued to meet and protest. Throughout the following week, women packed both mass meetings as well as city council meetings to demand that something be done to fix the city. By May 1949, the mass meetings had transformed into the organized meetings of the Women's Citizens Committee (WCC).

Originally formed to prod city and state officials into addressing crime, the WCC quickly expanded to tackle the good governance of the city. The WCC soon formed a subsidiary committee called the Crime Commission. Patterning it after a similar commission in Chicago, the WCC appointed 15 women to carefully screen the names of potential members. They chose 100 men, with an eye to representing "every race, creed, and business, and the two major political parties"; 65 agreed to be part of the organization. In addition to the Crime Commission, which emerged out of the initial outrage over Cheever's murder, the WCC also targeted police reform, judicial corruption, and housing with standing committees on traffic, criminal justice, and taxation. It placed its members outside known brothels and gambling joints to write down license plate numbers and publicize which men frequented the businesses. It championed the mayoral campaign of Hylda Burton, one of its own members, who promised to make "Gary famous instead of notorious throughout the country." Pointing out that she was not connected to any political corruption and that her "hands were not tied," Burton challenged voters to "see what a woman can do for Gary!" But perhaps the case that caught the most attention was the WCC and Crime Commission's placement of a microphone in the office of Blaz Lucas, the chief Gary deputy of Lake County prosecuting attorney Ben Schwartz, thus documenting the deep corruption of the office. With such methods, these "modern Carrie Nations," as the *Chicago Herald-American* would call them, began to gain national attention for their vice campaigns.[13]

"The sins of Gary are red as the fiery glare from the open-hearth furnaces which stretch out along its waterfront," *Newsweek* began when it picked up the story. But the bigger problems, according to the magazine, were the rackets that were tightly controlled by corruption within the mayoral administrations. While the rackets may have run the city, that changed with Cheever's death. Although there was little connection with the culture of political corruption, "Miss Cheever's death burst open the floodgates of public indignation and started the greatest uprising in Gary's 43 years of open lawlessness." The magazine, however, was not optimistic about the city's chances at reform. "The racketeers of Gary, Ind., had not given up," it concluded. "Last week they were offering substantial odds that the heat would die down. 'It always has in the past,' said a member of the syndicate. 'Why, we're running a poor man's Monte Carlo.'"[14] If this early coverage of the vice campaign centered around the well-established narrative of the lawless steel town, national coverage soon became fascinated by the emergence of the women's committee and the reversal of Gary's gendered imagery. Declaring that a "petticoat rebellion subdues Gary," the *Cincinnati Enquirer* reported that "the hands that wash the dishes are wiping up crime in Gary." The *Chicago Daily News* stated that "Gary women prod cops to vice war." The *Chicago Sun-Times* entitled the campaign "the housewives' war." *Time* continued the gendered language: "They barred their menfolk from the building, resolved to march on City Hall four blocks away." On the way over, and only after being so publicly harassed, "clots of men humbly joined them."[15]

The tenor of the reporting changed, however, after the initial protest transformed into the organized campaign of the WCC. It also changed as publications aimed at American women picked up the story and reported the efforts of the women of the WCC very differently. In a piece by A. B.

Hendry entitled "The Angry Housewives of Gary," the *Coronet* declared that the women of Gary had "made history with their smashing crusade to rid the city of vice and crime." The June 1951 piece told the same story of the WCC's origins: the death of Mary Cheever, the outrage, and the spontaneous rallies that turned into a protest march into the city council meeting. But it was the women's presence at the meeting that impressed Hendry. "In the line stood mothers, teachers, club members, neighborhood leaders. . . . It was a civic awakening the like of which Gary has never seen before." Equally important to the magazine was the level of decorum that the women exhibited. "But there was no yelling, no disorder," Hendry reported. "When it was their turn to speak they presented a resolution. . . . The men sat silent, while the women went on." It was this political patience and moral suasion that gave the women of Gary their power and influence.

The *Ladies' Home Journal* also raved about "what women did in Gary." It credited the WCC for driving the racketeers out of town and then keeping them out with their constant vigilance. "Their movements were followed at every turn by housewives and schoolteachers one would have thought too timid to meddle in the affairs of a vice syndicate." It traced the origins of the committee and lauded the tactics of its reform efforts. "The vice mills fell apart swiftly, and beneficial effects began to spread through the community." While the WCC campaign may have been a local movement, its influence was widespread. "Gary proved that crime can be uprooted by an aroused citizenry," the *Coronet* concluded. "And if men are not capable of doing the job, then the women must take over—just as Gary's angry housewives did."[16]

By 1953, however, coverage of the WCC campaign and of Gary began to shift its assumptions. The original story line was how Gary's women rose up to tackle their city's problems and to take on the corruption of male politicians and police officers as well as the indifference of the rest of Gary's male population. This soon gave way to a different take on the city that reemphasized the masculine ethos of the steel city. The first of these was a reimaging of the Crime Commission. Since the commission had originally been an offshoot of the WCC, women from the WCC had held a voting majority on the board. Yet when interviewed for a February 1953 article in *Male* magazine, the former chairman of the Crime Commission, Bernard Spong, gave credit solely to the commission for cleaning up Gary, and he attributed much of the success to the toughness of the male reformers: "If you really want to lick dope peddling, prostitution, gambling, and graft, here's the formula a fighting cleric used to lead his home town to a victory over vice." Not surprisingly for a magazine that specialized in hyper masculine stories of police officers, soldiers, and other heroes, the article by Spong read as an adventure tale. "We said: Something's got to give!" Spong declared. "If we've got to get down and fight them on their level, then that's the way it's going to be." Missing from Spong's interview was the documentation of license plates in front of brothels and the picketing by women in front of gambling sites; instead, his tale focused on the placement of the microphone that "blasted Blaz Lucas and Ben Schwartz out of office," a story complete with a hired detective from New York willing to bend the law, secret recordings, an untimely discovery by the target, and threats of retaliation and intimidation. Only through such action, the article concludes, could the masculine honor of Gary be restored. "We haven't made Gary a paradise, and we don't expect to," wrote Spong. "But women are safe on the streets here now, the red-light district is gone, and there is no syndicate gambling. Hoodlums have stopped coming here, because the town isn't 'wide-open' anymore."[17]

In the note introducing the article, the editor makes no mention of the WCC. Credit is given to Spong and the Crime Commission, an organization "which he helped organize and which he led in a successful fight against the crime-politics alliance." In his interview, Spong also downplays the WCC. He focuses on his own experience in such organizations as the Social Protection Committee and the Social Hygiene Council. Despite these organizations' efforts to document the "deplorable conditions" of Gary, "powerful interests did not want publicity given to the situation, so nothing happened." Then the death of Mary Cheever and the rise of the WCC, an organization that Spong mentions in his piece only once, created an atmosphere of outrage and indignation. The key moment in Gary's salvation was when "the women joined the Teachers' Union and our Social Hygiene Committee to set up a citizens' group called the Gary Crime Commission." Thus in Spong's retelling, the relationship between the WCC and the Crime Commission was transformed from a subsidiary to a collaborative effort.

Even for those who did not write the women of Gary out of the story as *Male* attempted to do, very few, by the end of 1953, were still optimistic about the effect of the WCC. Even the *Ladies' Home Journal* declared that the righteous indignation that had driven the original campaigns had largely died out and the rackets and corruption were working their way back into the city. "Time for another murder," stated one disillusioned resident. "It took Mary Cheever's murder to arouse us into cleaning up Gary the first time—and it looks as if we are going to need something as bad or worse before people will face up to the fact that crime is running the city again."[18]

By 1955, the *Chicago Daily News* agreed fully. "Dice, Cards, Girls—Reform Getting Nowhere in Gary," the June 23 headline declared. "Six years ago—in typical suburbanite fashion—the women of Gary rose up to wipe out crime." "What happened to their citizens' crusade? Today Gary, the restless giant of Chicago suburbs, is going like a blow torch. Hot. Handbooks, dice games, black jack, girls, pinball machines—you name it." The conclusion that the paper came to was the same that many came to. "Bookies, Sin Dives Wide Open," it said, "Despite 6-Year Crime War." Although the coverage of the WCC offered a different take on the city, by 1955 the images of Gary as a wide open town of crime, vice, pollution, and violence were firmly entrenched.

"GONNA BE HERE LONG? NOT LIKELY": TRAVEL NARRATIVES

Visitors to Gary who wrote of their experience would echo these assumptions about the city. In his 1980 autobiography about his transfer to Gary as a FBI agent in 1958, G. Gordon Liddy described it as "the great steel city of the infamous Lake County, by reputation a hotbed of vice, corruption, organized crime, racial discord, and a target of Soviet bloc espionage. I could hardly wait to get there." Describing his arrival into the city, Liddy repeated many of the standard narratives of industrial modernity. As he drove through northern Indiana, "the lush, green flatlands seemed to roll on endlessly into a bright blue sky." But then the landscape began to transform. "From that sky came the first hint of change, a dirty smudge on the horizon, which seemed to grow until, at the outskirts of Gary, it dominated the skyline, then developed into a sooty pall that hung over everything."[19]

Variations on this travel narrative almost always marked Gary as a strange industrial space that triggered shock, awe, concern, and often fear. When Harry Waters of *Newsweek* journeyed to the city to write about the Calumet Region's ecology, he began by describing his trip from his known universe of downtown Chicago into the unknown world of Gary.

> You drive only five minutes out of the Loop on the Chicago Skyway before the huge, gray, flame-flecked cloud mushrooms into view to the southeast. Then the sulphuric fumes hit, overriding the stench from the Chicago stockyards, forcing you to hastily wind up the windows. "Welcome to Gary, Ind—City on the Move" proclaims the grimy green sign off Exit 2. Dingy, three-story buildings slide by, each coated with a curious rusty tinge. The Tivoli movie house ("Gary's Only Adult Theater . . . Police on Duty at All Times") gives way to a soot-blotched replica of the Statue of Liberty (an appurtenance of all U.S. Steel towns) and finally to a gate where a burly guard glares suspiciously at the press credentials. The sign says Gary Sheet and Tin Works. The guard says, "Gonna be here long?" Not likely, officer. The only visitors who stay very long in this drab steel city are duty-bound relatives of the inhabitants.

Waters's journey is not complete until he can leave Gary. "Somehow it's a depressing scene and you hasten to your car and drive north," he concludes. "Through the rear window, the sky smolders in an eerie false sunset, as if a nuclear holocaust were subsiding." Looking for a way to explain his experience, Waters turns to mythology. "You recall that the god of steel towns like Gary is Vulcan, who was banished from his seat on Olympus for being the only ugly immortal. He never made it back."[20]

Although his essay focused on the ramifications on unchecked corporate power in a one-industry town, James O'Gara begins his piece on the steel settlement in 1949 with a similar travel narrative: an ugly trip into an ugly place.

> Much of the area immediately south of Chicago looks like a plot by the Christian anti-industrialists to win friends and influence people. Smokestacks, rather than steeples, dominate this land. When industry is going full blast, a haze of smoke and soot usually obscures the sun. The locomotives which pull long trains of tank and freight cars in and out of the district are pygmied beside towering structures of bizarre shapes and sizes,

whose very purpose is obscure to the layman. Normally the casual observer cannot even see the men who serve the giant machines or who labor near the blast furnaces. This lack of anything recognizably human in the scene provides an added air of unreality.

The story then becomes more mystical.

By night, however, much of the drabness of industrialism is concealed, and one travels through a land still mysterious but no longer ugly. For the steel towns on the fringes of Chicago, every night is the Fourth of July. The sky glows red as it reflects the flames of the giant furnaces and the white heat of molten steel. Giant torches blaze high into the night sky, and showers of sparks erupt into the darkness as the hot steel is poured. Silhouetted against this display of industrial fireworks, some of the odd structures which seemed so obscure in purpose by day take on that austere sort of beauty possible only to the starkly functional. The trip which was an act of penance by day can by night be an unforgettable expedition.

"Gary is a steel town," O'Gara concludes, "When you have said that, you have just about covered the ground." But this conclusion comes with dire consequences. "Without steel in general and Big Steel in particular, Gary would be a ghost town. The steel strike did not succeed in making Gary a ghost town. But the strike did show to a frightening degree how real that threat is to Gary and any town like it." As firm as the future of the mill seems, "the house the steel workers live in is built upon shifting sand."[21]

For some, the experience of traveling through the industrial sites of the Calumet Region were represented by visceral smells. Some were moved by the realization that they had moved into some new realm, whether that meant moving from the pastoral country into the city or from the environs of Chicago into someplace else. For others, the region provided awe at the industrial might and scale of the place. The narrator of Philip Roth's *I Married a Communist,* for instance, feels great comfort when passing through the Calumet.

Coming as I did from industrial north Jersey, I confronted a not unfamiliar landscape. . . . In Newark we had the big factories and the tiny job shops, we had the grime, we had the smells, we had the crisscrossing rail lines and the lots of steel drums and the hills of scrap metal and the hideous dump sites. We had the black smoke rising from high stacks, a lot of smoke coming up everywhere, and the chemical reek, and the malt reek and the Secaucus pig-farm reek sweeping over our neighborhood when the wind blew hard. And we had trains like this one that ran up on the embankments through the marshes, through bulrushes and swamp grass and open water. We had the dirt and we had the stink.

Yet here was also something quite different and foreign.

> Concentrated here was the power of the Midwest. What they had here was a steelmaking operation, miles and miles of it stretching along the lake through two states and vaster than any other in the world, coke furnaces and oxygen furnaces transforming iron ore into steel, overhead ladles carrying tons of molten steel, hot metal pouring like lava into molds, and amid all this flash and dust and danger and noise, working in temperatures of a hundred degrees, sucking in vapors that could ruin them, men at labor around the clock, men at work that was never finished. This was an America that I was not a native of and never would be and that I possessed as an American nonetheless. While I stared from the train window—took in what looked to me to be mightily up-to-date, modern, the very emblem of the industrial twentieth century, and yet an immense archeological site—no fact of my life seemed more serious than that.

Roth's narrator also juxtaposed the sight of postwar industrial might as signified by the mills with the costs of such might.

> To my right I saw block after block of soot-covered bungalows, the steel-workers' houses, with gazebos and birdbaths in the backyards, and beyond the houses the streets lined with low, ignominious-looking stores where their families shopped, and so strong was the impact on me of the sight of a steelworker's everyday world, its crudity, its austerity, the obdurate world of people who were always strapped, in debt, paying things off—so inspiring was the thought. For the hardest work the barest minimum, for breaking their backs the humblest rewards.

Here reconfirmed was the difference between the ideas of Gary the mills and Gary the town. While one was an awe-inspiring if somewhat intimidating triumph, the other was a depressing reminder of the ramifications of industrialism.[22]

The Gary described by Liddy was not only a city of crime, corruption, and the omnipresent "odorous pall of the steel mills" but also a city of bizarre otherness. "I glanced up and stared at something that was to me remarkable: an outdoor advertising sign in which the persons shown happily boosting the product were *black*. I had never seen a black depicted in advertising. Clearly, Gary was going to be something new and different." Liddy also confirms the official U.S. Steel narrative of Gary as a powerful steel center built upon technology and awe-inspiring scale. "The main street ended at the gates of U.S. Steel's gigantic Gary Works, its tall stacks disgorging dense smoke from open-hearth furnaces that symbolized the raw economic power of America in the Eisenhower era." But perhaps most importantly Liddy saw Gary as a city of exciting vice, proper corruption, and limitless masculine adventure. Ironically perhaps for an FBI agent assigned to the city, Liddy felt there was little problem with the corruption. "In 1958 Gary resembled Mayor Daley's Chicago; it was a city that 'worked,'" writes Liddy. "Every ethnic group had a piece of the action, public officials made a fortune from graft, and organized crime flourished on prostitution and gambling. The only serious problem was criminal violence." Liddy argues that the corruption of the city and the control of the syndicate often came in handy, since the FBI could count on their cooperation in chasing down the "real" criminals.[23]

Liddy lamented the end of his Gary, a transformation that he largely blames on Attorney General Robert Kennedy. As Congress and the Justice Department cracked down on corruption and organized crime, the city that "worked" was no longer possible. "Robert Kennedy wrote a book including his experience in Gary called the *Enemy Within*," concludes Liddy. "Not long after he finished his work there, the Gary I knew was gone. Half the public officials had been convicted, and the old way of life—in which the victimless crimes of gambling and prostitution were tolerated and controlled and numerous ethnic groups coexisted, each with a slice of the pie—had been destroyed." Liddy adds, "Whether the current state of affairs in Gary is an improvement, I'll leave it to the judgment of those who live there today." For every story about Gary, there is a moment when the city begins to decline. For Liddy's Gary, that moment was when the "right kind" of corruption and vice disappeared from its streets to be replaced by images of uncontrolled violence and racial division.[24]

"TO KEEP GARY FROM DISINTEGRATING ALTOGETHER": NARRATIVES OF RACE

While wartime messages of racial harmony and optimism may have promised major changes, the new postwar paradigm of race relations did not seem to apply to places such as Gary, Indiana. Yet the forces set in motion by demobilization, civil rights, and suburbanization ensured that the existing paradigm of de facto segregation could not last either. Since the middle of the 1930s, industrial Gary had been a strongly Democratic city and a classic example of the industrial working-class wing of the New Deal coalition. Its politics were a combination of New Deal Democrats, labor, and ethnic organizations all tied together by the political machine run by Mayor George Chacharis. Just as the New Deal coalition was redefined by issues of civil rights and race relations nationwide, so too would the politics of Gary become defined by race and backlash. For instance, in 1964 George Wallace, the segregationist governor of Alabama, carried Lake County in the Indiana Democratic primary. Clearly notions of race, segregation, and separations had changed in Gary between 1945 and 1964. So too would notions of race alter the way people thought and talked about the city. If Sinatra's visit had represented the possibility that Gary was a laboratory for postwar optimism, then Wallace's success made Gary into a crucible of racial conflict.

Between 1920 and 1930, roughly 15,000 black migrants from the South arrived. By 1940, another 20,000 had joined them. Like most northern cities, Gary had its difficulties with segregation and racial violence. As early as the 1919 steel strike, race had been a key determinate in Gary's political culture and vernacular imagery. By the 1920s, this concern with separation and segregation was centered largely upon education in Gary's high schools. In 1927, the white students of Emerson High School, angered that two dozen black students had begun attending the school, walked out in protest. "The next day the 'nice' residential part of Gary," reported *Time* magazine, "was littered and scrawled with placards and signs: 'WE WON'T GO BACK UNTIL EMERSON IS WHITE . . . NO NIGGERS FOR EMERSON . . . EMERSON IS A WHITE MAN'S SCHOOL,' etc. etc." By the second day student protesters numbered 1,357. They demanded that the black students be "segregated in the corners of Emerson classrooms and in the school cafeteria" until they could be transferred to a different school. Students also demanded that "no disciplinary reprisals" be made against them and that they would not have to "make up school work missed during the strike." As the school administrators acquiesced to all of the student demands, the question of Emerson moved to the city council. Before a packed gallery, the council decided to allocate $15,000 toward a "temporary" all-black high school. Although black Alderman A. B. Whitlock protested that "this money wouldn't equip a shack, and the site you propose is in a wilderness. There are no streets, no sewers, no facilities there at all," white Alderman Merritt Martindale countered that "the difference is there and it does no good to try to hide it." Reporting the episode, *Time* declared the situation "Jim Crow, Jr."[25]

Emerson would face the same issues during a student protest over integration in 1947, although this time school authorities were convinced that the strike was instigated by parents more than students. The administration suspended all striking students over the age of 16 and cancelled all activities for the year, including football. Yet 1,300 students still stayed out and were joined by 500 parents in a rally in front of the school. This protest came only two years after the visit from Sinatra during the Froebel strike and suggested that very little in terms of racial separation or racial identity had changed in twenty years in Gary. "On a few occasions, reactionary elements have forced liberal sponsors to cancel their plans to present me in a reading of my poems," wrote Langston Hughes. "I recall that in Gary, Indiana, some years ago the colored teachers were threatened with the loss of their jobs if I accepted their invitation to appear at one of the public schools."[26] Even after the 1954 Supreme Court case of *Brown v. Board of Education*, Gary's schools remained segregated by race. In a 1964 lower court decision that the Supreme Court refused to review, Gary was not obliged to desegregate its schools. Calling the phenomenon "de facto segregation," the Gary school board argued that it was not responsible for integrating unintentional segregation caused by racial separation in neighborhoods.[27]

By the mid-1960s, anxieties and aspirations on both sides played out in the political arena. At the same time that George Wallace's presidential primary campaign strained the New Deal coalition, black voters and politicians began to sever traditional ties to white Democratic candidates. These trends combined in the 1967 mayoral campaign. In the traditionally Democratic city of Gary, incumbent A. Martin Katz had received the endorsement of both the Democratic Party and the United Steelworkers—support that normally would have guaranteed him a victory. In 1967, however, the rules of Gary politics changed. Instead of supporting Katz in the primary, many African American voters supported black candidate Richard Gordon Hatcher. The primary campaign between Katz and Hatcher was fierce and highly racialized. After Hatcher's victory, significant numbers of white voters switched parties and supported the Republican candidate in the general election. The Democratic political machine in Gary cut off Hatcher and refused to support his campaign. Democratic Party boss John Krupa explained this abandonment in terms of radical politics, not race. "I'm not against Dick Hatcher because of his color," he told *Time,* "unless it's because he's a Red." The magazine also points out that along with his color, Hatcher frightened the Democratic machine because he refused their demands for patronage and pledged to clean up corruption.[28] In spite of all the official opposition, Hatcher won the election, and he and Cleveland's Carl Stokes became the first black mayors of major American cities.[29]

For the national media, the election of Hatcher and Stokes represented a triumph not only for black voters but also for moderate reform. "Shouting, dancing Negroes weaved wildly through the six downtown blocks of Gary, Ind.," reported *Time.* "It was not a riot but a rip-roaring victory celebration; their chant was not "Black power!" but "We beat the machine!" Lauding the "nonincendiary power of the ballot box," the magazine presented Hatcher as a candidate of moderate reform and integration, although it also pointed out that the white backlash that helped Wallace in his primary campaign probably helped Hatcher as well. "Openly appealing to anti-Negro voters," it reported, "a third candidate, Bernard Konrady, siphoned off more than 13,000 votes that most likely would have gone to Katz." Yet the fact that the magazine did not see Hatcher as a radical advocate of "black power" led it to believe that he might make good on his "plans to wipe out the prostitution and gambling that have made 'Steel City U.S.A.'—as it boosters like to call it—synonymous with vice."[30] For the most part, Hatcher was hailed in the press specifically because he was not a "fanatical leader" of black power but rather an advocate of the more moderate and more integrationist "black pride."[31]

Hatcher's election touched off a dramatic series of events for Gary. Fear of a city run by a black mayor led many white residents to move away. "For Sale" signs popped up as residents feared declining property values. A rash of white flight of both capital and population occurred. "I been here all my life," reported one white resident to *Harper's.*

> I got me a house I paid $35,000 for, but I'm leavin' it. . . . It's not that I hate the colored or anything, but I'm dumpin' it all. Who the hell wants to live this

way, I ask you. Bein' scared somebody'll hit you on the head all the time, you can't go out of the house after dark. You work all your life for something, and then they start movin' in, and suddenly you don't have anything—it's not yours anymore. First person that makes me any kind of half-ass offer on that house now, it's his, and I'm gone. With one exception—I'm not sellin' to no goddam colored. I'd put a torch to it first.

The prospect of sharing a neighborhood, especially for a city built upon an image of strict separation, was seen as undermining the very thing people had worked for in the mills. "Mr. Hatcher, We are a big group of women, who would like to know a few answers," stated one letter to the new mayor:

> We have nothing against the colored people but we would not like to have them live next door to us. Yet it seems that the colored people are always pushing. . . . Please can you explain to us why the black people want to be near us when we don't want them deep from our hearts & never will.

"Jesus, what do they want, I ask you, what do they want?" asked one resident. "We've passed every law under the sun we could think of for them, they've got their welfare, they even got themselves a Mayor now, but they're still raisin' hell." He concluded, "If the coloreds keep on they gonna find themselves on reservations one of these days just like the Indians. I even predict that. It has about come to that."

The notion that the barriers of racial separation had broken down and integration of neighborhoods was unstoppable drove many of Gary's white residents to look for housing in surrounding communities. But even this did not seem safe to some. "What the people out here in Glen Park foresee now is a tendency for Negroes to invade this area in unmanageable numbers," stated Eugene Kirtland, who was leading the effort to sever the district from the city of Gary. "But, of course, everywhere, ever since man has been on this earth, he has instinctively collected himself together with his own kind for protection." Kirtland defended the racial purity of his community by objectifying and othering the black residents of Gary. There could never be, in his mind, any kind of compromise because any integration would undermine the utopian nature of Glen Park. "By nature or whatever—I don't know what it is—but it seems blacks tend not to be inclined to obey the law," he continued, ". . . and there're all the other lusty things that go on under a lusty group of people. Black people are night-people—you ever notice that?" All of which led *Harper's* to worry about the success of black politics. "If the town is an image of the American crisis, it hints at profound alienations that may be withdrawing beyond the reach of even the truest voices. Hatcher's basic struggle right now is to keep Gary from disintegrating altogether."[32]

Interviewed in 1976, Dorothy Gale, a white liberal who had chosen to live in Gary, explained the shocked response she would receive upon disclosing her residence. "I was tired of getting that reception when I said that I was from Gary," she remarked, "because people acted as if you were a leper. I have never heard anything good said about Gary, even on TV." With the election of Hatcher and the ensuing white flight, Gary's image transformed into a black city with the inner city problems of crime, violence, and drugs. "Gary has declined tremendously," observed a white resident of East Chicago. "The crime over there is fantastic. I haven't been to Gary in years. I wouldn't go to Gary if I had an armored guard of marines to guard me over there." In his study of the folklore of the Calumet Region of northwest Indiana, Richard Dorson determined that every city possessed its own image within the minds of others. "Gary is the black city where nobody goes anymore because of crime, particularly drug crime."[33]

CONCLUSION: "BECAUSE HE SO EASILY AND EERILY REPRESENTS US, EVEN MIRRORS US (ALL OF US)"

When *Time* began its article on Gary by stating that "for all the hosannas sung to it in *The Music Man,* Gary, Ind., is not one of those garden spots that perennially win community-service awards," it was following well established story lines about the city. "Indeed," the magazine concluded, "it is in some respects the very model of modern urban decay." Yet by 1972, the discussions of Gary's crime and Gary's national reputation were increasingly defined in terms of race, which often meant that the crime that Gary had long been associated with began to look more sinister and menacing. "The sons and daughters of the Poles and Slovaks, and Croats, who for generations have worked the foundries," the magazine states, "form a decided minority. Most of the blacks, who make up the town's majority, are law abiding citizens, but a few of them have lately terrorized Gary with mob shootouts that rival New York City's Mafia battles in sanguinary savagery."

The danger, according to *Time,* came from the gang members who called themselves "The Family." Identifiable by their "wide-brimmed hats, black leather jackets, high-heeled boots, and bell-bottom pants," these gangs were responsible for not only protection and prostitution but also the trade in heroin. Commenting on an attempted killing, one investigator pined for the days of "organized" and orderly crime and vice. "These guys are hardly professional," he said, evoking Gary's past. "Can you imagine a Syndicate murderer not waiting around to make sure the guy is dead?" Gone was the romanticism of Gary's wildness. In the minds of many, Gary's crimes were defined by youth, inexperience, and race.[34]

For many of the famous residents of Gary, the steel town was a good place to be from, if not a good place to still live. Although Karl Malden was deeply critical of how depressing he found the city and how close the mills came to trapping him, still he had fond memories of his childhood and the ethnic community he grew up within. For Malden, the ethos of Gary stayed with him. It was a hard-working town of tough guys who asked no favors. It instilled within him a work ethic and worldview that served a supporting actor with an unsightly nose very well. But the notion of Gary as a good place to be from was based on an imagery of ethnic division and steel work. As Gary became increasingly defined in terms of race, dangerous visions of Gary's youth came to largely replace Malden's tough steel town.

Ironically perhaps, as this shift in Gary's descriptions from "hardscrabble steel town" to "the very model of urban decay" occurred, Gary produced its biggest local stars in the Jackson Five. In many ways the Jacksons tended to be a newer version of Malden, Taliaferro, and Zale. They represented the same kind of narrative of hard-working life, local pride, and ultimate success. Yet while the stories told about Tony Zale hinted at some great truth about midcentury working-class toughness, the myths surrounding the Jacksons tended to have an aura of fabrication. Such self-aware mythologizing dates to the group's very origins. Despite their popularity in the region and their contract with Gordon Keith's local label, "Steeltown," Motown Records preferred to create its own story line. Thus their early records identified the group as discovered by Diana Ross. Although Joe Jackson's steel work could have fit the standard narrative of children of Gary, promoters and reviewers tended to place the Jacksons into a story line of black ghettoization, hard streets, and escape. Publications such as *Newsweek*, for instance, identified the family as "growing up in the dingy ghetto of Gary, Ind."[35]

Indeed, Michael Jackson's autobiography in 1988 confirmed much of this background. Unlike Malden, who talked at length of his father's steel work, Jackson makes only one mention. "A big part of my earliest memories is my father's job working in the steel mill," he writes. "It was tough, mind-numbing work and he played music for escape." Much of the rest of the section on Gary focuses on the Jackson home, juxtaposing it against the hard streets of his hometown.

> One day, back in Gary, when I was real little, this man knocked on everybody's door early in the morning. He was bleeding so badly you could see where he'd been around the neighborhood. No one would let him in. Finally he got to our door and he started banging and knocking. Mother let him in at once. . . . I can remember waking up and finding blood on our floor.

The home, the family, and the group became a protective barrier against this dangerous world. "Music was a way of keeping our family together in a neighborhood where gangs recruited kids my brothers' ages." At the same time, unlike Malden, Zale, or Taliaferro, Jackson saw little opportunity or stability in his father's work. "Mom was working part-time at Sears, Dad was still working the mill job, and no one was going hungry, but I think looking back, that things must have seemed like one big dead end." There is an apropos ending to this era of the Jackson family tale: on the drive to Detroit to audition for Motown, an audition that would earn them the contract that would allow them to leave Gary, the children listened to the radio and tried to identify the call letters of different stations. Able to identify most, the children were stumped by WCFL. So little did industrialism and working-class organization mean to the Jackson children that their father had to identify the Chicago Federation of Labor for them.[36]

The timing of this transformation should not surprise us. For one, the Jackson family emerged from a Gary where the multiple narratives of working-class perseverance, struggle, and work ethic or even the critiques of vice, corruption, and foreignness had been reduced to a racial narrative of blackness. Gary, in the public's mind, was a black city; this assumption shaped the way people viewed the Jacksons. At the same time, American culture was shifting from an assumption of authenticity within modernism to the façades, interpretations, and adaptations of postmodernism. Tony Zale was supposed to represent a modernist "truth" about mid-century masculinity and Americanism, but the Jacksons were thought to be a manufactured image no more real than the constructed camp of the New York Dolls or the self-aware transformations of David Bowie.[37] As Michael Eric Dyson has argued, Michael Jackson came to personify postmodernist entertainment.

> Jackson strikes a deep, primal chord in the human psyche, fascinating us, perhaps, because he so easily and eerily represents us, even mirrors us (all of us) at the same time. Thus, if he is not a Nietzschean Übermensch, he is a Promethean allperson who traverses traditional boundaries that separate, categorize, and define differences innocent/shrewd, young/old, black/white, male/female, and religious/secular. Perhaps this is why he frightens us.[38]

Dyson argues that Jackson's art represents the postmodernist "theatricalization" of secular spirituality and popular culture blackness. Through the shifting personalities and identities of his "Thriller" video to the cultural obsession over the "de-Africanization of his face and the Europeanization of his image," Jackson plays with, yet is held captive within, the limits of marginality, difference, and otherness. His self-conscious transformations critique popular culture notions of the black male body; yet at the same time how people choose to read the meaning of Jackson's body, music, and meaning are not within his control. Such a postmodernist screen of shifting identities, fears, hopes, marginalization, and importance fits Fredric Jameson's description of the midcentury shift to the "logic of late capitalism," but it also fits the logic, or lack thereof, of Gary's national image. Far from being outside the story lines of the steel city, perhaps Michael Jackson personifies the shifting assumptions of his hometown better than most.

SEVEN

"Epitaph for a Model City"

RACE, DEINDUSTRIALIZATION, AND DYSTOPIA

Lake County was supposed to be a minefield for Democrats in the 1968 presidential primary. This was, after all, a county that Alabama governor George Wallace had carried in the 1964 primary. After what was to many the surprising popularity of Wallace's primary campaign, many journalists and other commentators began to talk about the politics of "white backlash." Indiana governor Matthew Welsh, a stand-in for President Johnson in 1964, had carried the city of Gary but lost the cities of Hammond, Whiting, and Munster and the more rural areas around Gary. Welsh had also failed to carry any white districts in Gary. The breakdown of votes in 1964 seemed like a new racial paradigm.[1]

Given four years of nationwide white flight, urban riots, contentious race relations, the independent campaign of Wallace, and the law and order mantra of Richard Nixon, Democrats faced a difficult trial in the industrial Calumet in 1968. Failure to address these issues, warned Rowland Evans and Robert Novak of the *Washington Post,* might mean that the county and perhaps the whole state might tip Republican in the general election. Joseph Kraft also predicted that Lake County would test Democrats' ability to wed black politics with the politics of white backlash.[2]

Yet Gary had long been practiced at countering the dire predictions outsiders read into its future. Just as workers found ethnic community and labor possibilities in the hard-scrabble steel town, and as the members of the Women's Citizens Committee tried to reform politics and tackle crime, and as the members of CARP seized control of their own environmental standards and well-being, so too did many of the residents of Lake County forge their own notion of racial cooperation and racial politics. Gary was supposed to be in decline. After the 1964 primary and the election in 1967 of Richard Hatcher, this decline was supposed to take the shape of white flight and backlash identity politics. Yet when Robert Kennedy visited the steel city in 1968 and took a tour of its streets, a very different picture emerged. "At the Gary city line, two men climbed into Robert Kennedy's open car, and stood on either side of him, for the wild hour it took to navigate the clogged, happy streets," remembered Jack Newfield. "One was Tony Zale, the former middleweight boxing champion from Gary, who was a saint to the East Europeans who worked in the steel mills. The other was Richard Hatcher, the thirty-four-year-old Negro Mayor of Gary." Symbolizing for Newfield, and perhaps for the city of Gary, "the Kennedy alliance that might have been," this combination of Gary's white ethnic identity and its newfound black power was all the more remarkable given the support Wallace had received in 1964 and the backlash assumed in 1968. Yet here were the three men "standing on the back seat of the convertible, waving to the cheering citizens of the city that so recently seemed at the edge of a race war."[3]

Robert Kennedy, the same man whom G. Gordon Liddy held responsible for ruining the well-run corruption of Gary of the 1950, went on to win Lake County and the Indiana primary. He put together the same sort of interracial coalition to win the California primary before his assassination. However, Kennedy's campaign did not end the political patterns of racial animosity, nor did the shared ride through Gary's streets with Hatcher and Zale stem the tide of white flight and racial conflict within Lake County. In many ways Evans and Novak were right: the 1968 election did shift Indiana's political loyalties for the next forty years. At the same time, the racial politics of the late 1960s dramatically changed the way people viewed the steel city. "The blue and gold signs at the entrances to the city proclaim in bold lettering: 'WELCOME TO GARY, CITY ON THE MOVE. Richard G. Hatcher, Mayor.'" Godfrey Hodgson and George Crile wrote:

> But the slogan has now taken on an ironic significance. For the most noticeable movement, in a city that was touted as an "urban laboratory" for the nation when Mayor Hatcher took office only five years ago, is a sad one: The whites are moving out of town. . . . The exodus of whites is only the symptom of a whole litany of woes that now beset the city of Gary, and with the best will in the world it is not easy to see where deliverance will come from.

The declension narrative had returned to Gary. Hodgson and Crile reviewed the standard culprits in Gary's decline. "There is the problem of crime, and rumors of crime, encouraging the white flight," they write. Drug wars, violent gangs, rooftop snipers, and sirens shook the city, despite the recently introduced curfew—"a desperate measure enacted to cope with crisis conditions." All of this made for a classic example of an urban crisis. "It is all a vicious cycle," they conclude.

> Crime fears chase out whites. Businesses follow them to the suburbs. Confidence and the tax base erode a bit further. More crime is bred. More flee. More tax money goes. And Gary becomes that much more dependent on federal help—at a time when federal aid is about to be brutally cut back.

Yet in addition to these standard markers of an urban crisis, Hodgson and Crile point to the crisis in education and school funding and the rising rate of unemployment. Despite Gary being U.S. Steel's town, the steel giant had recently sliced employment, laying off nearly half of its workforce and driving the unemployment rate in Gary to nearly 40 percent. While many of these steelworkers were back in the mills, the jobs were far from permanent or stable. In order to compete with Japanese imports, U.S. Steel was actively looking for ways to automate more of its steel production, meaning fewer jobs for Gary residents.[4]

The story of Gary had long been one of capital and industry. The city had been born out of the industrial expansion of Chicago and the efforts by industrialists to consolidate capital and control production. Gary was, first and foremost, a site of steel production and steel work. Every perception of the city had to deal with this basic paradigm. Early narratives about Gary focused on the control of capital and industrial forces through the strict planning and order of urban spaces. By midcentury this had shifted to various tales of decline. For some, Gary was an industrial abomination from the moment it was built; others pointed to moments when the experiment went wrong. Still others could point to the triumphant sons of Gary, if not the city itself, as symbols of work, pride, and struggle. By the mid-1960s, however, as the nation grappled with the issues of civil rights, segregation, and racial politics, the language of race came to define most discussions of Gary.[5] Race not only became the metalanguage of Gary but also reduced the possible declensions of Gary into a single story line—the moment Gary became a black city. The story of capitalism in Gary had shifted from one of space to one of race. Gary had moved from a model city of industrialism to a cauldron of racial politics. Yet even these story lines had to acknowledge the presence of industrial work. The automation of the steel mills beginning in the mid-1960s and accelerating through the early 1980s would sever this relationship. While Gary Works remained a place of steel production, it ceased to be the place of steel work. More than any other event, this transformed the city of Gary and how people spoke of the city.

"A MICROCOSM OF ALL AMERICAN CITIES": GARY AS AN URBAN LABORATORY

When he wrote about Gary for the *Washington Post* in 1966, Wolf Von Eckardt followed many of the standard descriptions. "The sun is all but blacked out in Gary, Ind. Greasy, dark smoke, intermingled with poisonous looking orange vapors, belches forth from a forest of chimneys, triumphant markers of a ruthless industrial age that, in the wake of affluence, devastated much of our environment." Here was the common image of Gary as a dark and dangerous industrial environment. "The industrial jungle lightens as you drive on, . . . still further east, beyond the man-made litter, you catch glimpses of wild swamps and the raw beauty of the Indiana dunes . . . where the cacophony of urbanization dissolves into natural calm." In many ways, Von Eckardt's description could have been from the previous century. Echoing the descriptive tales of Theodore Dreiser or Hamlin Garland upon their (or their imagined characters') arrival into Chicago, Von Eckardt too makes a clear distinction between the pastoral peace of the natural world and the chaotic unnaturalness of the city. Yet Von Eckardt's Gary was unlike earlier descriptions. People who noted the opening of the steel mills in 1909 contrasted the modern design and scientific efficiency of an industrial site carved out of barren and useless sand dunes. What makes Von Eckardt's description really remarkable, however, is that he is not just juxtaposing the natural beauty of the dunes with the dark polluted chaos of the steel mills; rather, he is introducing his readers to a newer steel mill built by Bethlehem Steel in neighboring Burns Harbor. This new mill blends with the dunes, maintains the natural beauty of the lakefront, runs quietly with little pollution, and returns water to the lake, the company promises, cleaner than when it was removed.

"You are struck by how clean this new industrial environment is as you come back out. It is almost aseptic. But," he concludes, "the beauty of this vast plant rests precisely in the fact that here man has so decisively and geometrically imposed his order on nature. He has flattened the dunes and constructed neat, matter-of fact workshops." Elbert Gary could not have done better himself.[6]

The other factor that greatly impressed Von Eckardt was the modern technology. "This brand-new Bethlehem Steel mill . . . represents the modern industrial age, the age of computer control and automation where one man in a business suit and with an advanced degree in complex engineering operates the giant machinery that fills a hall the size of several football fields." While *Scientific American* in 1909 might have liked to imagine a process of making steel that did not involve any workers, the Bethlehem plant with its automation allowed Von Eckardt to actually see such a process. Part of what made possible this automated system that used no workers, had no smokestacks, and created no pollution was that Bethlehem Steel was a rolling mill which did not actually make steel. Still, the creation of the Burns Harbor plant represents an important shift in the city of Gary's relationship to its mills. As Thomas Sugrue has demonstrated in his study of postwar Detroit, there are important structural shifts in economics and work that not only predate but in many ways help to create the urban crises of crime, poverty, and civic unrest. For Detroit, this meant the shifting location of automobile production and changing patterns of employment long before the racial crises of the 1960s. For Gary, the automation of steel may have confirmed the shoreline of Lake Michigan as a site of industrial innovation and reinvention, yet for the city of Gary and its steel workers, automation meant the reduction in work and spikes in unemployment.

Writing six years later, Hodgson and Crile note the rise in unemployment and U.S. Steel's pursuit of automation as part of Gary's "litany of woes," yet structural changes in steel employment do not appear in their pattern of urban decay, which starts with crime, which leads to white flight, which eventually leads to more crime. While the United Steel Workers often connected the fate of Gary with the working conditions of the mills, and Mayor Hatcher often complained about U.S. Steel's policies on layoffs and environmental standards, the descriptions about and assumptions underlying the urban crises of Gary almost always came down to race.[7] In response to criticisms about poverty and crime, Mayor Hatcher argued that "they're not just our problems in Gary. They're the country's, because they exist in some degree in every city." In his description of white flight and crime in Gary, Joel Weisman counters that "every major city problem seems more acute in Gary." While there are multiple "historic drawbacks" for the city, including its dependence on U.S. Steel as a one-industry town and its proximity to Chicago, the major problem in Gary was racial animosity. Weisman quotes real estate salesman Daniel Barrick's assessment of the city: "It seems like everybody wants to leave. . . . I feel like an outsider in my own home town. I don't want to live here. I don't like working here. And, most of all, I feel like they don't want me here." By "they," Barrick meant Gary's black population. "I have my office encased with iron bars over the windows, an iron screen on my door, and I wear a .38 on my hip. Now I ask you, what kind of a way is that to sell real estate?" Despite the numbers that showed Gary's crime rate had declined, city councilman John Bowman, who represented the much wealthier and whiter district of Miller, questions the numbers. "People are still scared to come downtown, and no one goes out at night." Plus, "I don't believe all crimes are reported. And there is no way to record the fear element." Echoing the mayor's complaint, George Applegate, the director of the Gary Chamber of Commerce, argues that Gary's problems are "really not that much worse than those in other cities. But we have an added problem: people exaggerate the dangers here."[8]

Throughout the city's first century, two very different story lines about Gary challenged each other. For some, Gary was a space lost to a dangerous otherness (after 1967, this would be racial politics, crime, and white flight). Others saw in Gary a microcosm of all American cities and thus a laboratory of progressive experiments and modern solutions to industrialism and urbanism. Both of these were counterbalanced by a narrative of local pride and autonomy. With the election of Mayor Hatcher, black residents of Gary took great pride in their city as a symbol of self-empowerment and self-governance, even though automation of U.S. Steel was actively undercutting the economic foundation of this political "experiment." At the same time, Hatcher's national prominence as a black political figure drew national attention to the conditions and possibilities of Gary. His oft-repeated claim that Gary represented the same problems that every American city faced made the city a prime target for the urban renewal plans of President Lyndon Johnson's Great Society programs.

In their study of the rise and fall of the Model Cities program in Gary, Hodgson and Crile offer the usual description of the city. "Gary may not be the most alluring city in the United States. Pollution often hangs over the city like a miasma, and political corruption has often been almost as noxious and pervasive. But Gary's future has not always seemed so dark. The early days of the Hatcher administration were a time of vaulting optimism, a strange time when the city's very problems were viewed as assets rather than liabilities." The steel city, with its multiple problems and complicated past, seemed a perfect place to implement Great Society reforms. Thus the city became "a microcosm of all American cities and chosen as *the* urban laboratory." Federal money flowed into the city, often matched by charitable donations from major foundations. James Gibson from the Potomac Institute in Washington came to oversee the experiments and established a direct link between Indiana and the capital. "For a while people were going around saying Gary was lucky to be in such bad shape," state Hodgson and Crile. "It would get so much help that it would be a model of what could be done to regenerate cities. And for a while it looked as if the experiment might just work."

Many problems and fissures soon emerged in Gary's Model Cities program. Some blamed the failures of the program on shifting politics in Washington. "If we had still had a Democratic administration in Washington," concluded program director Bill Staehle, "Gary really would have been the urban laboratory everyone said it was. The sky would have been the limit." Others pointed to the uniqueness of the city. Gary was far too reliant upon U.S. Steel for both jobs and tax revenue to be a model city. According to Mayor Hatcher, two problems doomed the project. The first was the system of independent commissions. Formed to deal with political corruption, these citizen commissions made management of reform initiatives impossible. Second, a rural-dominated state legislature was little help and often a hindrance in Gary's efforts. In addition to these issues, however, the problem with Great Society spending in Gary, as it would be in other parts of the nation, really came down to racial divisions. Concerned that seemingly all of the spending was aimed at Gary's black community (a constituency that kept Mayor Hatcher in power), the white workers of Gary and other Lake County industrial communities began to form their own advocacy groups and reform organizations. These new political movements tapped the growing sense of industrial discontentment, unemployment, and anger (a phenomenon that Hodgson and Crile call "blue-collar blues").

Within the industrial communities of the Calumet Region, Hodgson and Crile point to several places where disaffected white working-class ethnics could turn, including labor unions, the Catholic Church, and a "host of other liberal organizations, all anxious to justify their existence by addressing themselves to the newly perceived problems of the white working class." On December 5, 1970, leaders from these groups met in Hammond, Indiana, to create the Calumet Community Congress. For many of the participants, this was neither an act of racial backlash nor a shift toward conservative politics. Quite the contrary, many saw the congress as a first step toward creating out of the white ethnic working class a radical new political voice. The four men who were most instrumental in creating this vision were Saul Alinsky, the renowned labor organizer from Chicago, Bishop Andrew Grutka, a longtime friend of Alinsky, Staughton Lynd, the historian and political activist, and steelworker Jim Wright. The chairman of the first meeting was George Patterson, who had been a picket-line captain at the infamous Memorial Day massacre in 1937.

The radical spirit of the congress was short-lived, however. When local politicians learned that Lynd, who had taken part in several peace movements, had traveled to Hanoi, county chairman John Krupa (who had been deeply critical of Richard Hatcher's loyalties in 1967) condemned the congress as a "power grab ... motivated by the godless, atheistic forces of Communism." Due to the controversy, several moderate Protestant groups withdrew their support for the organization even after Lynd was removed from the congress. At the same time, the idea behind the congress was that a similar political organization of blacks would rise at the same time so that the two organizations might double their influence. When Jim Wright enrolled at Alinsky's school for community organizing, Obadiah Simms also enrolled. Yet, critics Hodgson and Crile pointed out, the Hatcher administration was unsupportive of a black political organization that the administration did not control. The Federation of Community Organizations, as the black organization was to be called, never got off the ground. After Wright left the Calumet Region in 1971, a power struggle split the congress into two factions, and by the end of the year the congress was dead as a political movement.

Overall, Hodgson and Crile are fairly negative in their assessment of Gary. Without federal assistance, there was little to keep the city afloat, and federal assistance from the Nixon administration did not seem forthcoming. Thus they conclude that their piece is an "epitaph for a model city." When Arthur Shumway offered his deep critiques of the city in 1929, Garry Joel August responded to the criticisms with a defense of the city. So too did James Gibson of the Potomac Institute and Monsignor Geno Baroni, a founding member of the Calumet Community Congress, respond to the epitaph written for Gary by Hodgson and Crile. Gibson and Baroni took basically the same line of reasoning as August. Gary is an American city, and American cities have a history of conflict, immigration, middle-class alienation and flight, and assimilation. "The American city is a hardy organism," they conclude, and Gary is no different. Gary should be thought of in terms of a "regional city" that is formed out of the confluences of "race, regionalism, and shifting industrial production technologies." There is a larger context and perspective to the urban crisis. "The Hodgson-Crile article is based solely on the limited perspective of crisis rhetoric and draws not at all upon the full and pragmatic story of cities themselves." The fact that these two men coauthored a response to Hodgson and Crile is remarkable in itself. Here were the two poles of Great Society politics in Gary: the federal money flowing into the black administration, and the white ethnic political organization meant to counter Mayor Hatcher. Yet their response shows that they were not necessarily in conflict with each other. As Gibson points out, the nature of an urban laboratory is such that efforts will fail and some problems will not be addressed. Pointing to the failures is not a valid condemnation of the process. Likewise, Baroni criticizes the authors for what he feels is an unfair assumption. Just because so many of the political organizations were based on ethnicity does not make them a product of backlash. Ethnic, he points out, does not mean racist. Despite these criticisms, however, Gibson and Baroni agree with Hodgson and Crile that Gary faces some very real challenges and will need help to overcome them—a point that Hodgson and Crile were happy to make in their own rebuttal.[9]

Neither the rise of ethnic power envisioned by Baroni, nor the radical coalitions imagined by Alinsky and Lynd, nor the urban laboratory promised by Gibson emerged in Gary. Rather, the story in Gary, as it was elsewhere in the United States, was one of increasing white flight, racial animosities, industrial automation, and efforts by surrounding communities such as Glen Park to "de-annex" themselves from the city. Even the fascination Gary held to national audiences as either an urban laboratory or an example of implosion began to wane. Between 1967 and 1974 the *Washington Post* had dedicated a fair amount of its space to covering the racial politics, industrial concerns, and ethnic possibilities of the city. After 1974, that attention would move elsewhere.

"WELCOME HOME TO GARY": THE BLACK METROPOLIS

Racial separation and segregation had long been a part of Gary's history. From the street violence of the 1919 steel strike to the school strikes spanning the 1920s through the 1940s, Gary's spatial divisions were often defined by race. As the mills and the union became more integrated, these divisions within the city seemed all the more important. Yet there were always multiple interpretations to the history of race in Gary. While some saw deep division, others, especially African Americans within the city, saw opportunities for both integration and self-defined community.

For their part, African Americans in Gary responded to segregation with both pessimism and optimism. Dr. John Peoples, who had been raised in Mississippi, spent several years teaching at Froebel and remembered how he learned the patterns of northern segregation. "When I went north, you know, I was naïve enough to think that, hey, this is integration," remembered the former president of the University of Southern Mississippi.

> I was surprised to find that you may have what they call de jure, that's legal integration, but there is a de facto—as a matter of fact it is not so. So I was the first. I found that I was the first black teacher assigned to Froebel High School in Gary, Indiana. Yeah, I didn't realize that I was the first black teacher. Well, the principal told me, he said, "Mr. Peoples," he said, "we're in the process of a year-by-year staff integration of the faculty here. And if you do well, we'll hire some more teachers, more black teachers." So I was a guinea pig, so to speak.

Peoples quickly learned how school segregation worked in Gary.

And now the student body was quote-unquote "integrated," so I thought. I
thought that was integrated.... So I went there that Wednesday night and
went into the auditorium, all black kids. I'd been teaching integrated classes.
I didn't know what to say. I didn't say anything. So I found this one kid, and
I said, "What happened to the white kids?" He said, "Oh, this is the beta
group. The whites are the alpha group. They have their parties on Tuesday."

For Peoples, this was an important lesson to learn. "So that was one experience that I got there, finding out that Gary, Indiana, was not integrated the way I thought it was, you see, so I learned about that.... So we
began to learn that when you go up north, you know, that it's not all that
it's cooked up to be at that time, you know, for integration. We thought
that everything was supposed to be just like you read about sometime.
But still that was part of our learning and growing up and so on and
maturing."[10]

A very different take on school segregation and integration was offered by *Ebony* magazine. Lamenting the violence and resistance that African Americans faced in other industrial cities, *Ebony* lauded the Indiana
city. "Noticeably calm in the current storm is steel-muscled Gary, Indiana, the only city in the North where Negroes make up a third of the total
population," it concluded. "A 50-year-old boomtown with many races and
nationalities among its 150,000 citizens, Gary does not 'view with alarm'
its high proportion of Negroes. Instead, it is quietly lowering its once-high
racial bars." While the magazine recognized the deep problems within
the city and its history of school strikes, it claimed that "Gary's Negroes,
most of whom came to the steel mills from the rural shacks in the Deep
South, are finding their own political strength. Their sons and daughters,
better educated and surer of their rights and responsibilities, are riding
to new power and dignity on their votes." Optimistic about the future,
the article concluded that, while much remained to be done in the city,
"said one city official: 'Of course we have a long way to go in Gary, but
look how far we've come.'"[11]

At the same time that African Americans in Gary struggled to deal
with the realities of segregation and integration, they also embraced the
possibilities that a black Gary offered. While white residents of the Calumet Region criticized the city, and outside observers lamented its decline,
the residents of the black metropolis created an entirely different image
of their city. For many, Gary presented not only the opportunity for work

and upward mobility but also an opportunity for them to define themselves and construct their own sense of blackness within their own black city. After detailing the white image of crime-ridden Gary in his study of the folklore of the Calumet Region, Richard Dorson says that "Gary's black residents expressed a wholly different outlook: the sweet taste of success . . . struggles in the white world that, despite heavy odds, ended in proud achievement." Within the black metropolis, the culture of steel labor and racial pride combined to give Gary's residents some control over their own lives and their perceptions of the city. "The only place I know is Gary," stated black steelworker Robert Jackson. "I love Gary; as far as I'm concerned, there's no other place in the world." On Gary's national image, Jackson admitted that "Gary has a bad reputation for vice, corruption, low-living standards." Yet, he explained, "this is all political. The same things happen in Chicago and New York, but because we are a smaller city, people pay more attention to us. We also have a bad reputation because we are 57 percent black and have a black administration." For black workers such as Jackson, Gary offered the opportunity to take part in consumer society and join the middle class.

> People in Gary aren't buying five-thousand-dollar homes; they're buying forty-five- and fifty-thousand-dollar homes. They buy Mark IVs and Cadillacs, and they buy books, and they go on vacations and wear funny fur coats, with a motherfucking rock on their finger. They don't be stealing; they don't be peddling; they don't be pushing—they flat out be getting it.

"As far as Gary is concerned," concluded Jackson, "we live here because we love this place, because we make more money here than a layman can make anywhere else in the world . . . 'cause that U.S. Steel is open. The doors are always open, twenty-four hours a day." Because of the availability for steel employment, Gary represented a promised land to black steel workers such as Wilbert Harlan because "there's more money in the black community . . . than any other city I know of in America." Some residents of Gary were more cautious about the autonomy of the black community. Robert Anderson, for example, worried in his 1976 interview about the stability of steelwork. With steel companies opening new mills in the South, Anderson commented upon Gary's future: "The key here is the steel mill, what controls? Industry . . . they got this BOF [Basic Oxygen Furnace] process can provide more steel with less men."[12]

At the same time the role of black politics, personified by Mayor Hatcher, gave Harlan a sense of pride in his city. Before 1967, according to Harlan, Gary deserved the title of Sin City, but "along came a guy, Richard Gordon Hatcher. He done more for the black people, I think, than any human being ever. . . . I sincerely believe God sent him, for he sure enough deliver the black people." Others, especially more radical black nationalists from outside of Gary, were more critical. "If we examine Cleveland, Ohio, Gary, Indiana, Washington, D.C., and many other areas populated predominately by Blacks," concluded H. Rap Brown,

> we can see a tactic being used that has often been tried in Africa, Vietnam, and other oppressed countries. It is called neo-colonialism. In other words, when white structures and institutions are threatened whites protect their economic and political interests and maintain control by using members of the oppressed people as their spokesmen. They set up puppet governments headed by individuals with white interests in mind.[13]

For its residents, however, the black metropolis was, for the most part, a special place. After conducting his interviews, Dorson concluded that while "the blighted city [was] spoken of with such fear and disgust by dwellers in other parts of the region . . . these black speakers see a shining metropolis in the inner city. . . . This is the heart of Black Gary, which teems with its own life."[14]

This self-pride was perhaps most evident when Gary hosted the 1972 National Black Political Convention. The city greeted the delegates to the convention with banners that read: "Welcome Home to Gary." "What was proposed as the Unity of Gary presumably was the culmination of a year's worth of meetings," wrote Imamu Amiri Baraka in 1972. What had begun as a discussion of "a Black leadership conference" soon became a call for a broader national black political convention. Gary was chosen to host this convention because, according to Baraka, "Gary is expressive of most of the contradictions existing in Black politics and the Black movement because we consciously tried to draw every element to the convention that we could." Reporting for the Black Panthers, Lloyd Barbee stated that

> the quality and quantity of delegates, leaders, and observers in Gary, March 10, 11, and 12, was impressive despite usual convention falderal and confusion. Individualists, collectivists, militants, and moderates all had

their say and way. . . . In summary, Blacks met together, set up a structure to keep together for the benefit of Black political effectiveness. This was an accomplishment worthy of historical note.[15]

When asked in an interview what impressed him about the current politics of black America, David Maphumzana Sibeko, head of the Pan Africanist Congress, responded that he had "seen also the meeting that has taken place in Gary, Indiana, where the African American people worked for an agreement on a single presidential candidate, and to see that the voices of the African American voter were no longer misused by the racist politicians who merely need them to gain office." "This great desire to unite in a common National struggle," he concluded, "is one of the most important developments."[16]

Other participants were slightly less enthusiastic about the outcomes of the convention. Commenting on the "state of black unity in Gary, Indiana," Bobby Seale stated that "although, on an overall basis, the theme of the Convention had stressed the need for unity in the Black community, the racist U.S. government press attempted in every way, through a bombardment of propaganda, to present a picture of dis-unity among Black people."[17] Despite some disappointments, some conflicts, and what Seale and others took to be unfair press coverage, Baraka and others still remained positive about just what the convention in Gary meant. "Gary was successful in a great many ways," Baraka concluded, "The fact that so many Black People did come together, out of so many different bags, and had to seriously consider each other's opinions, is success enough. . . . What was important about Gary, aside from the agenda, was the functioning of Black people together as a *national community*."[18] Looking back, Baraka fondly recalled everyone's participation. "In Gary, Indiana, in 1972, 8,000 Black People came together to roar our solidarity, our willingness to struggle," he wrote. "And though we did suffer from some of the same lack of science and thorough analysis, we did possess the burning spirit without which, armed even with the best of theories, we could not win!"[19]

The national coverage of Gary almost always defined these events differently. Upon his election Hatcher was hailed as a moderate black reformer who offered an alternative to radical black power. Yet by 1969 opinion had changed toward Hatcher. Two years into this term, Hatcher had been beset by problems and, according to many, was beginning to fail. Likewise, national coverage of the 1972 convention stressed how disorganized the delegates were and how frail the connections had been between the various groups and ideologies. Stories about heroin, crime, and gangs painted a picture of a lawless and dangerous city, and these narratives often stressed the racial background of the city. Gary was, in the national eye, a decaying industrial city and a dangerous black city. Calling the choice of Gary as an "odd place for a convention," the *Washington Post* confirmed much of this thinking in its coverage. "Gary, with its belching smoke stacks and oil refineries, its city streets rutted by railroad tracks and flanked by drab buildings, is not a place where people usually come for conventions." Yet it was the Hatcher administration that made the city "particularly symbolic and appropriate to what this convention is all about."[20]

"THE SUM OF A THOUSAND SHORT CUTS": GARY AS A DEINDUSTRIALIZED MILL TOWN

Much of the image of the thriving black metropolis assumed, as Robert Jackson did, "that U.S. Steel is open. The doors are always open, twenty-four hours a day." However, U.S. Steel had a very different understanding of its role in both the mills and the city of Gary. From the beginning, the Gary Works were dedicated to the idea of capital movement, industrial relocation, and economic production. Almost immediately upon its creation in 1901, the newly minted corporation began to look for ways to increase production and make it more efficient. By 1906, this process had culminated in the construction of Gary. The construction of the massive new mill also allowed the planners to break down the steel-making process into its smallest components and make it as efficient as possible through the system of scientific management. Because they had essentially limitless space and capital, USS could take such measures as slowly curving their railroad tracks, which allowed trains to maintain speed and steam. Such initiatives earned the Gary Works the nicknames of "Economy, Indiana" and the "sum of a thousand short cuts." The dual processes of large-scale capital mobility and the desire to squeeze savings and profits out of existing plants had been a long tradition in the Gary Works; indeed, the Gary Works and the city of Gary were born out of these traditions. Yet this impulse did not end with the construction of Gary. Thus when the steel crisis of the 1980s shook the corporation, it dramatically altered its plan for the mills, which in turn radically changed the fate and fortunes of the city. Even during the worst of the crisis, U.S. Steel continued to upgrade the Gary Works, including a $300 million slab caster that opened in 1986, and designated the works as the corporate flagship. At the same time, the company closed most of its older mills and diverted its money into the acquisition of Marathon Oil, a process that many called "industrial triage."[21]

The story of the USS Gary Works does not fully follow the traditional narrative of deindustrialization.[22] By the mid-1990s, it was producing as much steel as it ever had before. However, through mechanization, it did so with a fraction of the jobs that it once had used. In 1985, after the implementation of U.S. Steel's "rationalization" plan, the mill, which once employed over 20,000, had jobs for only 7,500. Thus, while USS Gary Works may not have undergone deindustrialization in terms of production, the city of Gary certainly felt the effects of industrial job loss. The process of deindustrialization in Gary cannot be defined solely in terms of plant closures or capital reinvestment. The city itself suffered many of the effects of industrial job loss.[23] As the recession of 1981 threw most of the world's economies into disarray, many American businesses, including the steel industry, suffered severe losses and looked to reduce their costs through layoffs and plant closings. The fiscal years of 1981 and 1982 were particularly disastrous for American steel companies. During the steel crisis, American mills ran at only 43.8 percent of capacity, and most companies reported record losses. The recession had left a saturated steel market that would require most of the decade to recover. In addition, most of the "Big Eight" American steel companies who negotiated with the United Steel Workers operated mostly with large, old, and inefficient mills. Thus the steel crisis was deepened by competition from low-cost foreign steel and American mini-mills. By the end of 1982, Japanese and American mini-mills accounted for over 25 percent of the U.S. steel market. Much like other American industries, the solution the steel companies came to was a drastic reduction in cost through wage cuts, outsourcing, massive layoffs, and closure of plants. For many mill towns, particularly those stretching from the Monongahela Valley of Pennsylvania to Chicago's south shore, the steel crisis meant massive job loss and the deindustrialization of their community.[24]

In a 1989 article, *U.S. News & World Report* recognized this trend among steel companies. Calling the steel industry's recovery "a hollow comeback," it reported that, in 1982, Inland Steel Industries in neighboring East Chicago, Indiana, had operating losses of $118 million. In response, it had eliminated 10,000 mill jobs and received salary and work rule concessions from the United Steelworkers of America. By 1988, its stock prices had recovered and continued to rise; there was, however, no rise in employment. The comeback of U.S. Steel had similar ramifications for the city of Gary. While the mill continued to produce vast amounts of steel, the economic hardships of job loss remained for the city. "It's a great success story for the company," stated Gary mayor Thomas Barnes, "but it has been a painful experience for us. The fact is, a business that once employed 21,000 people now employs about 7,500, and that number is probably never going to go any higher."[25] For USS, which renamed itself USX Corp. after buying Marathon Oil, the automation of the Gary Works was another form of reindustrialization. Much as they did with their curving tracks eighty years earlier, they cut corners to make the plant more efficient. For the city of Gary, however, the loss of jobs meant a deindustrialization of their workers' vision of the city.[26]

In 1983, Thomas C. Graham took charge of U.S. Steel's chain of mills and plants. A former executive of Jones & Laughlin Steel, Graham was brought in by the USS board to reverse its economic fortunes and trim its production systems. Seemingly no one was safe; Graham reduced production jobs, executive positions, foreman and plant supervisors, and clerical staff. In addition he began outsourcing aspects of steel production to cheaper outside firms, despite the union contract that forbade such actions. In December 1984 came the masterstroke of what came to be known in USS circles as the "Graham Revolution." USS announced the closing of parts or all of twenty-eight plants and mines, thereby eliminating 15,436 jobs. By 1987, Graham could boast that U.S. Steel, with only 18,000 employees, would match the output of 1983 when it employed 48,600. While they turned around the fortunes of the company, such drastic cuts decimated steel centers such as Gary.[27]

One of the plants Graham closed was the USS Tubing Specialties in Gary. Built in 1926, the mill thrived off the booming oil industry, which consumed most of its tubing products. However, after the collapse of both the oil and steel industries, USS began laying off many of the plant's employees. Explained plant manager John Benda, "The future, unfortunately, became so bleak the powers that be decided it was not in the best interest of U.S. Steel to hang on." In December 1985, USS announced the complete closure of the plant, putting 2,200 employees out of work. After losing his millwright's job in 1982, Sherman Hayes Jr. found employment in Kentucky with Mid-America Canning Corp.; however, it soon closed its doors as well. "It used to bother me, but anymore it's a way of life," remarked Hayes to a *Gary Post-Tribune* survey. "If you hire in anywhere, you just can't count on that job being there." Fellow worker Larry Koker expressed similar sentiments: "It's like watching a very bad movie, and you can't turn the movie off. . . . You have no control." Despite the fact that Koker earned half his mill wage working for the Westville Correctional Center, he was determined to stay optimistic. "The dreams are always there," he stated. "You can't give up. If you give up, you end up in the garage with a shotgun in your mouth."

The layoffs at Tubing Specialties affected many other workers in the same way. "Since the layoffs and shut downs, we have lived through hell," said Patricia Jones. "We are still fighting to be independent again." Amos Schultz Jr. recalled, "The day they told me I was laid off, I went home and my wife told me she had good news. She was pregnant; I didn't know whether to laugh or cry." Likewise, Sharon Haymon remembered the day her husband lost his job: "I was five months pregnant. It was a very emotional pregnancy for me and my husband. His job was gone, but the bills kept coming. We lost our house, car, and on Oct. 5, 1982, which is incidentally my husband's birthday, the gas company shut off our gas." Said Rudy Grasha, "It really hurt me for a long time, fifteen years of my life given to industry was now nothing."[28]

Spouses and children also felt the effect of job loss. "At night, I used to always wake up and hear my mama cry," remembered Mary Perry who was 15 when her mother lost her job. "I knew she was upset because she couldn't get us stuff anymore." When the plant closed, Edith Robinson's son Eric suffered as well. "I went through a lot of hardships and pressure," he stated. "I didn't perform well in school because I was afraid that we might lose the house." The pressures of job loss took a toll on Larry Koker's entire family. "The children became anxious and depressed because they couldn't do the things that their friends could do," he lamented. "Their frustration would sometimes lead to tears that further depressed the wife and I." Shortly after he lost his job, Koker and his wife of eighteen years divorced. "I'm confident that if I hadn't been laid off, my ex-wife and I would still be married," he concluded. "I escaped into alcoholism. It made the hurt go away for a little while. But there's no escape for the children."[29]

In addition to the intense personal tragedies, the loss of steel jobs also had a cumulative effect on the city. Economic downturns and massive layoffs were not new to the city. During a 1972 layoff, unemployment spiked as high as 40 percent. Yet the steel crisis of the 1980s brought permanent unemployment on a scale to which Gary was not accustomed. Beginning in 1982, Gary's unemployment rate topped 20 percent for four straight years. Its downtown became largely a deserted and desolate strip of abandoned shops. By 1985, the city found itself in a financial crisis. A conflict with USS over property taxes (the mill often supplied 40 percent of the city's tax base) had left the city nearly broke. Unable to fund its social programs, the city scaled back its system of welfare. Rising crime had earned for the city the title of murder capital of 1984.

According to a U.S. Census Bureau study, in 1985 one-fifth of Gary's 49,500 households lived below the poverty line. The combination of job loss, crime, and reduction of social aid led one resident to lament, "We've already been designated the murder capital and now we are headed on the road toward becoming the hunger capital." Few saw any way to reverse the fortunes of the city. Lynn Feekin, the director of the Calumet Project for Industrial Jobs, stated frankly, "I haven't seen the new industry that's going to provide the stable manufacturing job base, that's going to replace the enormous job loss the region has suffered." Upon announcing that the Gary Works was to become the flagship of U.S. Steel, company spokesman Thomas R. Ferrall added, "I wouldn't want to suggest any hope for increased employment at this point."[30]

The economic conditions of Gary had grown so bad that any new jobs were a cause for celebration. Such was the case on April 16, 1985, when the mayor, city officials, and many others gathered to celebrate the opening of a Wendy's fast-food restaurant. "Larger cities, like Chicago, would look down their noses at a fast-food franchise," said Mayor Hatcher to commemorate the occasion, "but Wendy's represents 80 jobs." City boosters pointed to the franchise opening as a sign of economic recovery. "I absolutely believe that Gary has reached bottom and is on the way back up," expressed one. Hatcher agreed, suggesting that "there really is a light at the end of the tunnel." The press covering the event, however, was less optimistic. The *Chicago Tribune* stated that the city of Gary was "grasping at rays of hope where it can" and that the opening was a major civic event because "this hardscrabble steel town of 147,532 welcomes any new businesses." Adding an ironic twist to the celebration was the fact that several of the new employees of the restaurant were former steelworkers who had traded their mill wages for $3.35 an hour. "Sure we would rather have the $15- to $20-an-hour jobs that the steel mills used to provide, but that is not reality," explained Hatcher. "From our point of view, we have to get jobs first, then, later on, we can be selective."[31]

Despite his best efforts, however, the mayor could not put a positive spin on his city. His successor in 1987, Thomas Barnes, did no better. In 1988, the city published a promotional pamphlet entitled *Gary!* and sent it to thousands of companies around the world, boasting, "We're a city with a future, make no mistake." The pamphlet even tried to entice prospective companies with its only photograph: a picture of downtown positioned to include the city's only national chains, a Walgreens and its brand-new Wendy's. However, the *Chicago Tribune* observed, "The reality of downtown Gary fits uneasily with these claims." Even the environmental accountability that Gary's residents had sought seemed to fade away. On April 14, 1987, a leak of over 27,000 gallons of hydrochloric acid at a Gary factory created a massive toxic fume cloud and necessitated a mass evacuation of thousands, further tarnishing Gary's image. Don Sullivan, spokesman for the Gary Business Development Commission, tried to separate his idea of Gary from the national image. "You have to look at Gary with the correct idea, that Gary is an easel on which is to be painted one of the great success stories of the 20th century." In the late 1980s, the officials of Gary were desperately trying to reverse its image. However, very few were buying the validity of Gary's self-image.[32]

CONCLUSION: THE INHERITANCE
OF THE CHILDREN OF GARY

Hollywood films in the early 1990s developed two new trends. With pop culture phenomena such as *Pulp Fiction* (1994) and *Reservoir Dogs* (1992), Quentin Tarantino helped to lead a surge in nostalgia for 1970s cinema. At the same time, films such as *Boyz n the Hood* (1991) redefined the cinematic portrayal of the black inner city. The 1996 film *Original Gangstas* tried to combine these two. The film starred many of the icons of 1970s black cinema, including Fred Williamson (*Black Caesar*), Jim Brown (*Three the Hard Way*), Richard Roundtree (*Shaft*), Pam Grier (*Foxy Brown*), and Ron O'Neal (*Super Fly*). In the film they play the founders of a street gang called the Rebels. Now adults, these same folks try to wrest control of their neighborhood away from the current Rebels, who have transformed the gang into a roving band of violent thugs. Blaxploitation meets, and trumps, gritty urban drama.

Unlike the south central Los Angeles location of *Boyz n the Hood*, however, *Original Gangstas* was set in the city of Gary. This setting established the key juxtaposition. Williamson and company represent the Gary of the 1970s, the high point of Gary's black pride, while the younger Rebels come out of the deindustrialized and violent Gary of the 1990s. Against shots of urban decay, the film's opening voiceover established the city's tragic transformation.

> You're looking at Gary, Indiana, USA. A city with the highest murder rate in America, maybe the world; a factory town that somehow became a gang town. Back in the 50s, the community was supported by the U.S. Steel mill. It was damn hard work but people raised their families well. Then just twenty years later, without warning, U.S. Steel shut down 70 percent of the mill. First the workers thought it was temporary, but it wasn't. Their savings went, unemployment ran out, and slowly the former steelworkers lost the last two things they had left: their pride and their hope. And that has been the inheritance of the children of Gary.

Here was the pride in Gary's working past and the disillusionment of its present. It was particularly poignant for Williamson to be the chief protagonist of the film. Born and raised in the city, Williamson was a football star at Froebel High School before moving on to Northwestern University and the National Football League. Just as Karl Malden, Tony Zale, Tom Harmon, and Alex Karras became the heroes of white ethnic Gary, so too did Williamson, the Jacksons, and George Taliaferro become the icons of black Gary. *Original Gangstas* served as a sort of homecoming for Williamson. Given the transformations of the city, it is apropos that the climactic battle for Gary's streets at the end of *Original Gangstas* takes place in an abandoned steel mill.

"It is quite evident that there is a serious problem with violence in the city of Gary," remarked one resident in 1993. "People are being killed at alarming rates. . . . Gary is probably known all around the world for being its murder capital." United Steelworkers vice president Lorenzo Crowell tied crime directly to the loss of jobs. "In an environment where corporations are farming out our jobs to Mexico, where there is no real job retraining programs, where plants are closing and reducing our work forces," he concluded, "it's no wonder we're seeing an upsurge in violence." Others blamed the city's administration. "The city of Gary is so poorly run," lamented one former city employee. "I often wondered if I would be paid on time . . . at this rate Gary may just fall into Lake Michigan." Confronting the national image of the city, some politicians appealed to the federal government for assistance. Writing to U.S. Attorney General Janet Reno, U.S. Representative Peter J. Visclosky asked, "Now more than ever Gary and Northwest Indiana are in dire need of federal assistance to combat crime and reclaim our streets." U.S. Senator Dan Coates asked Reno for monetary assistance. Even the city's mayor asked for the nation's assistance during a CNN interview. "Gary, Indiana, is part of America," he stated. "We need help on the national level to end this insanity."[33]

"In Search of America"

In June 2009, the city of Cleveland celebrated the fortieth anniversary of perhaps its most infamous moment. In 1969, the Cuyahoga River, which had long served as an open sewer for the city, caught fire and burned. Although the fire was relatively small and caused little damage, the event became crystallized in the nation's imagery of the city and within the city's imagery of itself. "The fire turned Cleveland into 'The Mistake by the Lake,' a national punch line that would endure for decades," reported the *New York Times* in a 2009 piece. "Meanwhile, the city worked to reclaim its river." The reclamation of the river also meant a reclamation of the city and its image. "The Cuyahoga River fire was a spark plug for environmental reforms around the country," said Cameron Davis to the *Times*. "The Cuyahoga's progress is notable because of how infamous it was," Matthew Doss added. "This 40th anniversary gives us an opportunity to celebrate the progress we've made nationwide." From the ashes of an embarrassing fire, the city had fought hard to redeem itself. "This didn't happen because a bunch of wild-haired hippies protested down the street," said John Perrecone, a manager with the EPA. "This happened because a lot of citizens up and down the watershed worked hard for 40 years to improve the river."

Yet part of the irony of the *New York Times* piece, and the relevance of Cleveland's story to the cultural history of Gary, is that the fire in 1969 was not shocking because the river caught fire. Within an industrial society, such pollutants, dangers, and disasters were to be expected. The Cuyahoga had caught fire before. "In the 1930s, when most people in Cleveland worked in factories, a fire on the river was considered just a nuisance," commented Jonathan Adler, an environmental law professor at Case Western Reserve University. Instead, "the outrage caused by the fire was a symptom of a society starting to leave its industrial identity behind." Not only were there very real stakes involved in the balance between national imagery and community action (the fire gained much of its notoriety from an article in *Time* magazine), but as Americans' understanding of industrialism and post-industrialism changed over the century, their fascination with and acceptance of industrial spaces transformed as well.[1]

The story of Gary in the twentieth century is, in many ways, the story of industry and industrial mill towns. What began as a promise of industrial capitalism and urban planning became a wasteland of urban decay and capital disinvestment. Gary was an industrial space born out of capital mobility and automation, and ultimately it became the victim of these same global processes. It was automation that allowed for fewer workers needed for the Gary Works in the 1980s and the movement of other work to smaller finishing mills elsewhere in the country. At the same time, industrial cities such as Gary and indeed heavy industries such as U.S. Steel became marginalized by the slow rise of neoliberal economics from the late 1960s through the early 1980s. Free trade imports of steel, especially Japanese steel, undercut much of the American steel industry's markets and seemed to force, in the minds of U.S. Steel executives, rounds of wage cuts, automations, and plant closures. The relationship between U.S. Steel and the United Steel Workers, steeped as it was in suspicion and animosity, did little to help this situation.

Perhaps more important, however, was the fact that heavy industries such as steel were not beneficiaries of the new neoliberal economic order that rewarded global finance and foreign debt payments. Steel was not a finance industry; it was far more invested in the political and economic system that neoliberalism strove to replace. Despite its conflicts with the United Steel Workers and government regulation, U.S. Steel was heavily involved in Keynesian economic nationalism and, as Judith Stein has shown, a key corporate citizen within the twentieth-century New Deal compact. By the early 1980s, however, U.S. Steel responded to the steel crisis by not only closing many plants and automating others but also acquiring Marathon Oil and rebranding itself as the USX Corporation. Of course, none of this lessened the blows that deindustrialization brought to the city. One of the great paradoxes of deindustrialization is that its origins and causes often exist within the *longue durée* of economic and political transformations that are transnational in scope, yet its effects, especially plant closure and unemployment, are most deeply felt at the local level. Capital mobility may be a long process, but plant closure is an immediate and shocking transformation.[2]

Even more than a city such as Cleveland, Gary was deeply affected by deindustrialization. Not only did deindustrialization change the basic economics of the city (in other words, there were far fewer jobs), but it also changed the city's place within the American imagination. Gary was an artificial environment created by industry for a specific purpose. Gary existed as much as an imagined metaphor of industrialism as a physical space of industrial production. This was made possible, perhaps even necessary, because, while Gary was on Chicago's and the nation's physical periphery, it was central to the industrial economy and the culture of industrialism. Hence people paid attention, and the narrative tropes they applied mattered. In a postindustrial economy, this focus on Gary, and thus the meaning of Gary, changed.

"FLINT, MICHIGAN, IS NO GARY"

While outsider narratives of decline and decay did not represent the whole truth of Gary, in many ways they were never supposed to. These were not stories about Gary so much as stories about industrialism's complications and contradictions. Outsiders read onto the city their own fears and assumptions about industry, race, corruption, and crime. While Gary's struggle with deindustrialization and job loss mirrored the conditions of other industrial cities such as Youngstown, Ohio, or Flint, Michigan, the narrative applied to Gary often differed from these other communities.[3] In 1987, *Money* magazine published its first survey of the best (and worst) places to live in the United States. At the bottom of the list, dead last at number 300, was Flint, Michigan. In response, the people of Flint gathered to show their anger at the magazine and defend their city. From the stage at the protest, a local deejay yelled to the crowd, "Has *Money* been to Gary, Indiana? Let me tell you—Flint, Michigan, is no Gary!" Michael Moore, who filmed the protest and included parts of it in his film *Roger & Me*, could only agree: "That was true; Flint was *worse* than Gary. Flint's unemployment rate during the early '80s had risen to 27%, vs. 15.7% in Gary." "So it seemed odd to me," concluded Moore, "that the battered citizens of Flint decided to vent their rage at *Money*."[4] An equally important question may be: why did they vent their rage at Gary? Despite the similarities between the two cities—both had suffered severe job loss, capital flight, and urban decay—the residents of Flint took solace in the idea that they were, at least, not Gary. Within this version of the deindustrialized narrative, Gary remained within the American public imagination something outside of the American norm.

"THE OTHER AMERICA, IF YOU WILL"

The effect of such deindustrial narratives and constructed reputations continued to shape the possibilities for urban renewal in Gary. Like many deindustrialized American cities, most notably Detroit, Gary has an intimate relationship with its industrial past. While recognizing the hard work, dangerous conditions, and environmental pollution, this smokestack nostalgia saw in the industrial age a kind of broad-shouldered democracy of good wages and limitless opportunities. Certainly descriptions of Detroit in the twenty-first century often juxtapose the city against this nostalgic midcentury golden age. So too do many people in Gary see the 1940s and 1950s (or earlier or later, depending on the storyteller) as a kind of golden age for the steel city. Communities of steel labor, including the steel mills as well as local bars, bowling alleys, coffee shops, and other public spaces, created a firm foundation upon which a good life could be built. Yet these debates are nostalgic because they assume that, through a variety of transformations, the world has changed and the world of industrial labor and steel work communities no longer exists.[5]

People trying to revitalize and reinvent the city of Gary may distance themselves from this industrial past and embrace the cultures of post-industrialism and the new realities of a service economy. Mayor Hatcher tried to reinvent the city as a transportation hub built around Gary's airport and as a center of black politics and culture. His successor in 1987, Thomas V. Barnes, thought that Gary's future rested in increased regional cooperation with Chicago and a series of gambling casinos on Lake Michigan. The next mayor, Scott King, advocated the rebirth of downtown through minor-league professional sports and a new baseball stadium. Yet all of these options failed largely because of the presence of the U.S. Steel mill. It was both a physical presence blocking access to Lake Michigan and a cultural presence reminding visitors and outside observers of Gary's industrial past and its reputations. Thus when the city announced in 2000 that it would host the Miss USA pageant to help showcase the city's new developments and postindustrial potential, *U.S. News & World Report* responded by asking, "Where will the 51 contestants frolic during the parts of the TV broadcast devoted to their nights on the town, in gritty steel mills?" Likewise, CNN reported that "publicity has never been much good to Gary. Mostly it's been bad, about classic Rust Belt decay." In 2002 as part of their series *In Search of America*, Peter Jennings and ABC News came to Gary to tell its story. Despite residents' hopes for a new story of their city, the episode, entitled "The Great Divide," repeated many of the standard twentieth-century narratives about the city. It was a slum, the episode declared, racked by drug violence and poverty—problems that a beauty pageant could not solve.[6]

By the turn of the twenty-first century, industrial spaces such as Gary were no longer important within an industrial economy; they were seen as outdated relics of an industrial past. As the United States came to embrace neoliberal economics, the assumption became that finance, globalization, and capital mobility were leaving places such as Gary behind. "The strongest American economy maybe casts the greatest economic shadow," Housing and Urban Development Secretary Andrew Cuomo remarked in 1999:

> There are people and places in this country that are not enjoying that great American success. They say that the rising tide raises all boats. Well, this tide is rising so fast that it's drowning some. I have been to the other America, if you will. I have seen the dual reality of the time that we live in. And I can tell you that the poverty, the despair, is just as bad in some places as it has ever been. And the sense of hopelessness is just as bad in some places as it has ever been.

For Cuomo, Gary was the perfect example of a city left behind.

> Gary, Indiana, tells the story here; population loss of 27 percent. Gary was also in the steel business. The steel mill is still there; it's just smaller than it was. You now have computers where you had people. Median income, $43,000 to $30,000; unemployment, 8.2 percent. I saw that sign in Gary; it said it all. "You have a life. Get a future." How telling for Gary.

In conclusion, Cuomo argued "there are places that are left behind. Gary, Indiana, as a place cannot compete. Suburbs will beat Gary, Indiana, every day."[7] Unlike successfully postindustrial cities such as Pittsburgh, old industrial spaces, the narrative ran, could not survive in the new economy.

Just as they did throughout the twentieth century, Gary's residents saw their story and their city differently. Many were furious about the documentary's image of Gary. "Mayor King felt betrayed," writes historian James B. Lane. "'It was a predetermined hatchet job,' he concluded."

> One resident complained, "It portrays Gary as just another slum city with no prosperous, upright citizens." Why no mention of young people developing their talents at Emerson School for the Performing Arts, Lisa DeNeal wondered. Or the activities of block clubs and community centers. Nate Cain wrote: "To indicate that all the good people have left was extremely disrespectful to the hard-working, tax-paying, family-oriented citizens of the community. For every criminal you show me, I'll show you 100 solid citizens. For every boarded-up building, I'll show you a block of well-maintained, residential homes."[8]

This response, along with the numerous others compiled by Lane in extensive oral histories, reminds us that residents have long presented another version of Gary's history. People of Gary have understood their city's problems and possibilities, but they have also understood the ways in which their city was imagined and used by others. From Rabbi August in 1929 to the response to Peter Jennings in 2002, defenders of Gary have regularly offered the same explanation. For every accusation that Gary was, as Cuomo would claim, "the other America," residents offered a common response. "Gary is America." said August. "Every American city is Gary writ large and small." Gary, claimed others, was "a microcosm of all American cities" and the "most American of all American cities."

INTRODUCTION

1. Graham Romeyn Taylor, "Creating the Newest Steel City," *Survey* 22 (April 1909); Elliott Flower, "Gary, the Magic City," *Putnam's Magazine* (March 1909): 643; Charles Pierce Burton, "Gary—A Creation," *Independent,* February 16, 1911.

2. Stephen G. McShane and Gary Wilk, *Steel Giants: Historic Images from the Calumet Regional Archives* (Bloomington: Indiana University Press, 2009).

3. William Cronon, *Nature's Metropolis: Chicago and the Great West* (New York: W. W. Norton, 1991), 5.

4. "Gary May Act against Toll Road Unit," *Chicago Tribune,* May 4, 1954; "Indiana Stops Building Toll Road in Gary," *Chicago Tribune,* December 5, 1954; "Indiana Toll Body to Pay Gary $1,500,000 Damages," *Chicago Tribune,* April 27, 1955.

5. James O'Gara, "Big Steel, Little Town: The Recent Steel Settlement Has Not Settled Everything," *Commonwealth,* November 25, 1949.

6. Woodrow Wilson, "The Fear of Monopoly," *Annals of American History,* 1912. Theodore Roosevelt would also campaign in Gary during the 1912 election, but he did not critique the city in the same way as Wilson, and he challenged Wilson's interpretation of trusts. "The Political Campaign: A Double Misstatement of Fact," *Outlook,* October 19, 1912, 326.

7. As quoted in James B. Lane, *Gary's First Hundred Years: A Centennial History of Gary, Indiana* (Valparaiso, Ind.: Home Mountain Printing, 2006), 89.

8. Joel Weisman, "Every Major City Problem Seems More Acute in Gary," *Washington Post,* December 2, 1974.

9. Raymond A. Mohl and Neil Betten, *Steel City: Urban and Ethnic Patterns in Gary, Indiana, 1906–1950* (Teaneck: Holmes and Meier, 1986); James B. Lane, *City of the Century: A History of Gary, Indiana* (Bloomington: Indiana University Press, 1978).

10. For social histories of Gary, see Ronald D. Cohen, *Children of the Mill: Schooling and Society in Gary, Indiana, 1906–1960* (Bloomington: Indiana University Press, 1990); Ruth Hutchinson Crocker, *Social Work and Social Order: The Settlement Movement in Two Industrial Cities, 1889–1930* (Urbana: University of Illinois Press, 1992); James Lewis, *The Protestant Experience in Gary, Indiana, 1906–1975* (Knoxville: University of Tennessee Press, 1992); Andrew Hurley, *Environmental Inequalities: Class, Race, and Industrial Pollution in Gary, Indiana, 1945–1980* (Chapel Hill: University of North Carolina

Press, 1995). On Gary's racial politics, especially in the 1960s and 1970s, see Alex Poinsett, *Black Power: Gary Style; The Making of Mayor Richard Gordon Hatcher* (Chicago: Johnson, 1970); Robert Catlin, *Racial Politics and Urban Planning: Gary, Indiana, 1980–1989* (Lexington: University Press of Kentucky, 1993); Edward Greer, *Big Steel: Black Politics and Corporate Power in Gary, Indiana* (New York: Monthly Review Press, 1979).

11. Sam Bass Warner, *The Urban Wilderness: A History of the American City* (New York: Harper and Row, 1972), 105.

12. On Haussmann, see David P. Jordan, *Transforming Paris: The Life and Labors of Baron Haussmann* (Chicago: University of Chicago Press, 1996); Walter Benjamin, "Paris: Capital of the Nineteenth Century," in *Metropolis: Center and Symbol of Our Times*, ed. Philip Kasinitz (New York: New York University Press, 1994).

13. Natalie Zemon Davis, *Fiction in the Archives: Pardon Tales and Their Tellers in Sixteenth-Century France* (Stanford, Calif.: Stanford University Press, 1987); Hayden White, *Tropics of Discourse: Essays in Cultural Criticism* (Baltimore: Johns Hopkins University Press, 1978).

14. Judith Walkowitz, *City of Dreadful Delight: Narratives of Sexual Danger in Late Victorian London* (Chicago: University of Chicago Press, 1992); Peter Fritzsche, *Reading Berlin 1900* (Cambridge, Mass.: Harvard University Press, 1996).

15. Arlette Farge and Jacques Revel, *The Vanishing Children of Paris: Rumor and Politics before the French Revolution* (Cambridge: Harvard University Press, 1991); Amy Gilman Srebnick, *The Mysterious Death of Mary Rogers: Sex and Culture in Nineteenth-Century New York* (New York: Oxford University Press, 1995); Carl Smith, *Urban Disorder and the Shape of Belief: The Great Chicago Fire, the Haymarket Bomb, and the Model Town of Pullman* (Chicago: University of Chicago Press, 1993); Timothy B. Spears, *Chicago Dreaming: Midwesterners and the City, 1871–1919* (Chicago: University of Chicago Press, 2005).

16. The symbolic importance of the capital metropolis is central to Walter Benjamin's analysis of nineteenth-century Paris's urban culture and the role of the *flaneur*. Benjamin, "Paris: Capital of the Nineteenth Century."

17. See, for example, Mary P. Ryan, *Civic Wars: Democracy and Public Life in the American City during the Nineteenth Century* (Berkeley: University of California Press, 1997); Perry R. Duis, *The Saloon: Public Drinking in Chicago and Boston, 1880–1920* (Urbana: University of Illinois Press, 1983); Roy Rosenzweig, *Eight Hours for What We Will: Workers and Leisure in an Industrial City, 1870–1920* (New York: Cambridge University Press, 1983); James Barrett, *Work and Community in the Jungle: Chicago's Packinghouse Workers, 1894–1922* (Urbana: University of Illinois Press, 1987); Christine Stansell, *City of Women: Sex and Class in New York, 1789–1860* (New York: Knopf, 1986); Robert Orsi, *Madonna of 115th Street: Faith and Community in Italian Harlem, 1880–1950* (New Haven, Conn.: Yale University Press, 1985).

18. Maiken Umbach, "A Tale of Second Cities," *American Historical Review* 110, no. 3 (June 2005): 659–92; Smith, *Urban Disorder and the Shape of Belief*.

19. Mike Davis argues that Los Angeles is a city of "pure capitalism" that is founded entirely upon real estate values and civic image. Its foundation, development, and continued growth depend on its urban image, thus the imagined city of Los Angeles always precedes the lived realities of its streets. This new kind of global city, symbolized by Los Angeles, is a sprawling metropolis with many centers of population and political power. Despite their high population density, these centers are disparate from and unconnected

to each other. Mike Davis, *City of Quartz: Excavating the Future in Los Angeles* (New York: Verso, 1990); Edward Soja, *The City: Los Angeles and Urban Theory* (Berkeley: University of California Press, 1996); Norman Klein, *The History of Forgetting: Los Angeles and the Erasure of Memory* (New York: Verso, 1997).

20. On the process of industrialization and class formation in commercial cities and mill towns, see Gary Nash, *The Urban Crucible: The Northern Seaports and the Origins of the American Revolution,* abridged ed. (Cambridge: Harvard University Press, 1986); A. F. C. Wallace, *Rockdale: The Growth of an American Village in the Early Industrial Revolution* (New York: Knopf, 1978); Thomas Dublin, *Women at Work: Transformation of Work and Community in Lowell, Massachusetts, 1826–1860* (New York: Columbia University Press, 1979); Richard Stott, *Workers in the Metropolis: Class, Ethnicity, and Youth in Antebellum New York* (Ithaca, N.Y.: Cornell University Press, 1990).

21. David Harvey, *Urbanization of Capital* (Oxford: Blackwell, 1985); David Harvey, *Consciousness and the Urban Experience* (Oxford: Blackwell, 1985).

22. James R. Barrett, "Americanization from the Bottom Up: Immigration and the Remaking of the American Working Class, 1880–1930," *Journal of American History* 79, no. 3 (December 1992): 1000.

23. Michael McGerr offers an analysis of the Progressive movement as a culmination of middle-class identity and pragmatic, not utopian, reform. Michael McGerr, *A Fierce Discontent: The Rise and Fall of the Progressive Movement in America, 1870–1920* (New York: Free Press, 2003).

24. Lizabeth Cohen, *A Consumers' Republic: The Politics of Mass Consumption in Postwar America* (New York: Knopf, 2003).

25. Thomas Sugrue, *The Origins of the Urban Crisis: Race and Inequality in Postwar Detroit* (Princeton, N.J.: Princeton University Press, 1996); Robert O. Self, *American Babylon: Race and the Struggle for Postwar Oakland* (Princeton, N.J.: Princeton University Press, 2005).

26. Philip Roth, *I Married a Communist* (Boston: Houghton Mifflin, 1998), 225.

27. David R. Roediger, *The Wages of Whiteness: Race and the Making of the American Working Class* (New York: Verso, 1991).

28. This revision of labor history is part of their introduction to a collection of essays on deindustrialization. Jefferson Cowie and Joseph Heathcott, eds., *Beyond the Ruins: The Meanings of Deindustrialization* (Ithaca, N.Y.: ILR Press, 2003).

29. Steven High, "Capital and Community Reconsidered: The Politics and Meaning of Deindustrialization," *Labour/Le Travail* 55 (Spring 2005): 187–96.

30. Robert Shackleton, *The Book of Chicago* (Philadelphia: Penn, 1920).

1. "AN INDUSTRIAL UTOPIA"

1. "Gary: The Largest and Most Modern Steel Works in Existence," *Scientific American,* December 1909.

2. Ibid.

3. John Kasson argues that the builders of Lowell, Massachusetts, tried to accommodate industrialization with republican theory by creating a pastoral city where young women would work for only a few years. Instead of corrupting male citizens, mill work could create good wives and mothers. John Kasson, *Civilizing the Machine: Technology and Republican Virtues in America, 1776–1900* (Toronto: Penguin Books, 1976).

4. Lewis Mumford, "The Foundations of Eutopia," in *The Lewis Mumford Reader,* ed. Donald Miller (New York: Pantheon Books, 1986), 217–27; originally published as Lewis Mumford, *The Story of Utopias* (New York: Boni and Liveright, 1922).

5. "Modern Methods of Steel Making—Interior of the Illinois Steel Works, South Chicago," *Graphic,* April 7, 1894, 269; *Visits and Excursions at the American Meeting, October 23 to November 12, 1904* (London: Offices of the Institute, 1904), 73–74, reprint from the *Journal of the Iron and Steel Institute,* Chicago Historical Society (CHS).

6. Max Weber as quoted in Edward Shils, "The University, the City, and the World," in *The University and the City from Medieval Origins to the Present,* ed. Thomas Bender (New York: Oxford University Press, 1988), 219.

7. Spears, *Chicago Dreaming.*

8. Frank Norris, *The Pit: A Story of Chicago* (New York: Doubleday, 1903), 60.

9. Rudyard Kipling, *From Sea to Sea: Letters of Travel, Part II* (New York: Charles Scribner's Sons, 1906), 139, 140.

10. Hamlin Garland, *Son of the Middle Border* (New York: Macmillan, 1917); Hamlin Garland, *Rose of Dutcher's Coolly,* rev. ed. (New York: Macmillan, 1899); Charles Dudley Warner, *Studies in the South and West with Comments on Canada* (New York: Harper's, 1889), as cited in Cronon, *Nature's Metropolis,* 9–13.

11. Giuseppe Giacosa, "Chicago and Her Italian Colony," *Nuova Antologia* 28 (March 1893): 16–28.

12. *Industries of a Great City* (Chicago: Little Chronicle Co., 1912), 104.

13. Committee on Industrial Locations, *Chicago as an Industrial Center* (Chicago: Metcalf Stationery, 1901), 11–17, 41–48.

14. *Chicago Tribune,* July 24, 1877.

15. Shackleton, *The Book of Chicago,* 87.

16. Vilas Johnson, *History of the Commercial Club of Chicago* (Chicago: Commercial Club of Chicago, 1977), 98.

17. Z. S. Holbrook, "The Lessons of the Homestead Troubles," address before the Sunset Club, November 17, 1892 (Chicago: Knight, Leonard, 1892).

18. Ibid.

19. Charles W. Eliot, "The Ethics of Corporate Management," address before the Merchants Club of Chicago," March 10, 1906, 21, miscellaneous pamphlets, Merchants Club of Chicago, CHS.

20. *History of the Industrial Club of Chicago* (Chicago: Lakeside Press, 1934), 5–7, 51. Copy in CHS.

21. Miscellaneous pamphlets, 1897–1905, Merchants Club of Chicago, CHS.

22. Stanley Buder, *Pullman: An Experiment in Industrial Order and Community Planning, 1880–1930* (New York: Oxford University Press, 1967).

23. Richard T. Ely, "Pullman: A Social Study," *Harper's Magazine* (February 1885): 452–66.

24. Thomas Hines, *Burnham of Chicago: Architect and Planner* (New York: Oxford University Press, 1974); James Gilbert, *Perfect Cities: Chicago's Utopias of 1893* (Chicago: University of Chicago Press, 1993).

25. William Thomas Stead, *If Christ Came to Chicago: A Plea for the Union of All Who Love in the Service of All Who Suffer* (Chicago: Laird & Lee, 1894).

26. Tristram Hunt, *Building Jerusalem: The Rise and Fall of the Victorian City* (New York: Metropolitan Books/Henry Holt, 2005).

27. Judith Walkowitz shows how Stead's narrative about the sexual dangers in London gave readers of the *Pall Mall Gazette* a visual map of the city's ever-changing districts. Walkowitz, *City of Dreadful Delight*.

28. Daniel Burnham, *The Plan of Chicago, Prepared under the Direction of the Commercial Club during the Years 1906, 1907, 1908* (Cambridge: Da Capo Press, 1970); Carl Smith, *The Plan of Chicago: Daniel Burnham and the Remaking of the American City* (Chicago: University of Chicago Press, 2006).

29. Johnson, *History of the Commercial Club*, 95.

30. *Merchants Club of Chicago—1896–1907*, 8–9, CHS.

31. Archie H. Jones, *The Chicago Plan*, Merchants Club of Chicago, CHS.

32. In 1932, the Industrial Club of Chicago would also merge with the Commercial Club.

33. Commercial Club of Chicago, *Presentation of the Plan of Chicago*, 3, CHS.

34. Ibid., 25–33.

2. "MAKING A CITY TO ORDER"

1. Eugene J. Buffington, "Making Cities for Workmen," *Harper's Weekly* 53 (May 8, 1909).

2. Taylor, "Creating the Newest Steel City."

3. Ibid. On the building of company towns, see Margaret Crawford, *Building the Workingman's Paradise: The Design of American Company Towns* (New York: Verso, 1995).

4. On mapping and American culture, see John Short, *Representing the Republic: Mapping the United States, 1600–1900* (London: Reaktion, 2001); and Jerry Williams and Robert Lewis, eds., *Early Images of the Americas: Transfer and Invention* (Tucson: University of Arizona Press, 1993).

5. *Indianapolis News*, March 19, 1906; *Chicago Tribune*, March 19, 1906; "Gary: The Largest and Most Modern Steel Works in Existence," *Scientific American* (December 11, 1909); Taylor, "Creating the Newest Steel City."

6. "Gary, Pittsburg's Future Rival," *American Review of Reviews* 39 (February 1909); Daniel Vincent Casey, "The Sum of a Thousand Short Cuts," *System* 15 (January 1909).

7. "Sanitary Drainage and Sewerage," *Industrial Chicago*, 1891, vol. 2, CHS.

8. See Richard Schneirov, Shelton Stromquist, and Nick Salvatore, eds., *The Pullman Strike and the Crisis of the 1890s: Essays on Labor and Politics* (Urbana: University of Illinois Press, 1999), and Richard Schneirov, *Labor and Urban Politics: Class Conflict and the Origins of Modern Liberalism in Chicago, 1864–97* (Urbana: University of Illinois Press, 1998).

9. Jane Addams, "A Modern Lear," *Survey* 29 (November 2, 1912): 131–37. Addams wrote her piece in 1894 and first delivered it as an address. Graham Romeyn Taylor, "Satellite Cities: Pullman," *Survey* 29 (November 2, 1912): 117–31.

10. Henry Fuller, "An Industrial Utopia: Building Gary, Indiana, to Order," *Harper's Weekly* 51 (October 12, 1907); Graham Romeyn Taylor, "Satellite Cities: Gary," *Survey* 29 (March 1, 1913). On the militarization of space for the purpose of capital, see Davis, *City of Quartz*.

11. Buffington, "Making Cities for Workmen"; Fuller, "An Industrial Utopia." On Homestead, see Paul Krause, *The Battle for Homestead, 1880–1892: Politics, Culture, Steel*

(Pittsburgh: University of Pittsburgh Press, 1992). On the management of Homestead, see Kenneth Warren, *Triumphant Capitalism: Henry Clay Frick and the Industrial Transformation of America* (Pittsburgh: University of Pittsburgh Press, 2000).

12. Taylor, "Creating the Newest Steel City"; Buffington, "Making Cities for Workmen"; Fuller, "An Industrial Utopia"; *Indianapolis News*, March 19, 1906.

13. "Gary: The Largest and Most Modern Steel Works in Existence."

14. Casey, "Sum of a Thousand Short Cuts."

15. John Kimberley Mumford, "This Land of Opportunity: Gary, the City That Rose from a Sandy Waste," *Harper's Weekly* 52 (July 4, 1908); Burton, "Gary—A Creation."

16. Taylor, "Creating the Newest Steel City"; *Chicago Tribune*, March 19, 1906; Buffington, "Making Cities for Workmen"; Fuller, "An Industrial Utopia."

17. Graham Romeyn Taylor, *Satellite Cities: A Study of Industrial Suburbs* (New York: D. Appleton, 1915).

18. Shackleton, *The Book of Chicago*, 297.

19. Ibid., 298–300.

20. On Vandergrift, see Anne Mosher, *Capital's Utopia: Vandergrift, Pennsylvania, 1855–1916* (Baltimore: Johns Hopkins University Press, 2004).

3. "THE YOUNGEST CITY IN THE WORLD"

1. Woodrow Wilson, "The Fear of Monopoly," Library of Congress, Manuscript Division: Ray Stannard Baker Papers; Transcription, Swem Notes (as excerpted in Annals of American History).

2. On the crisis of masculinity at the turn of the century, see Kristin L. Hoganson, *Fighting for American Manhood: How Gender Politics Provoked the Spanish-American and Philippine-American Wars* (New Haven, Conn.: Yale University Press, 1998), and John Kasson, *Houdini, Tarzan, and the Perfect Man: The White Male Body and the Challenge of Modernity in America* (New York: Hill & Wang, 2001).

3. Richard Slotkin, *Gunfighter Nation: The Myth of the Frontier in Twentieth-Century America* (New York: HarperCollins, 1993). See also Richard Slotkin, *The Fatal Environment: The Myth of the Frontier in the Age of Industrialization, 1800–1890* (Norman: University of Oklahoma Press, 1998).

4. Lane, *City of the Century*, 34–37.

5. Cohen, *Children of the Mill*.

6. Another of these studies came from Randolph Bourne in a book entitled *The Gary Schools*. Reviews of these books lauded their authors' roles in creating a new and modern educational system. *Outlook* (August 11, 1915): 416; Dorothy Teall, "Bourne into Myth," *Bookman* (October 1932): 75; "The Wirt System," *Dial* (August 15, 1916): 108.

7. Elbert Gary, "Business To-Morrow," *Independent*, March 27, 1916, 447. See also Frank Chapin Bray, "Educational Summertime," *Independent*, August 24, 1914, 281; "The Gary System," *Youth's Companion*, August 13, 1914, 416.

8. "Religious Education," *Biblical World* (January 1916): 44; S. Turner Foster, "A Threefold Cord in Christian Training," *Herald of Gospel Liberty*, September 28, 1916, 1228; "The Religious World," *Independent*, May 4, 1914, 224.

9. "Both Sides, a Debate: The Gary School Plan," *Independent,* December 13, 1915, 452; Sidney Reid, "The Gary Plan in New York," *Independent,* December 16, 1915, 385; Mary Graham Bonner, "What Parents Think of the Gary Plan," *Outlook* (July 26, 1916); Bonner, "School Riots and the Gary System," *Outlook* (October 31, 1917): 334; "The New York Mayoralty Campaign," *Independent,* November 3, 1917, 214.

10. "Persons in the Foreground," *Current Opinion* (October 1915): 235; *Survey* (November 9, 1912): 180.

11. Crocker, *Social Work and Social Order.* See also Lewis, *The Protestant Experience.*

12. Slotkin, *Gunfighter Nation;* Lane, *City of the Century,* 44-62.

13. Lane, *City of the Century,* 37-43.

14. For instance, Armanis Knotts sold a lot at 11th and Broadway for $1,200 six months after buying it for $100.

15. Lane, *City of the Century,* 37-43.

16. Charles M. MacKay, "Reminisces," Charles MacKay Papers, CRA 409, Calumet Regional Archives.

17. Paul Dremeley, "memoir," Paul Dremeley Papers, folder 9, box 1, CRA 310, Calumet Regional Archives.

18. Michael Denning, *Mechanic Accents: Dime Novels and Working-Class Culture in America* (New York: Verso, 1987).

19. David Montgomery, *Workers' Control in America: Studies in the History of Work, Technology, and Labor Struggles* (New York: Cambridge University Press, 1979); Rosenzweig, *Eight Hours for What We Will.*

20. Barrett, *Work and Community in the Jungle;* Richard Oestreicher, *Solidarity and Fragmentation: Working People and Class Consciousness in Detroit, 1875-1900* (Urbana: University of Illinois Press, 1986).

21. "Interview of Helen Baxter Hansen by Andrew Phillips, August 30, 1989," in *Ellis Island Oral History Project,* Series DP, no. 046 (Alexandria, Va.: Alexander Street Press, 2004), 14.

22. "Interview of William B. Solyom by Willa Appel, February 11, 1986," in *Ellis Island Oral History Project,* Series AKRF, no. 146, p. 20.

23. John Bodnar, *The Transplanted: A History of Immigrants in Urban America* (Bloomington: Indiana University Press, 1985); David Emmons, *The Butte Irish: Class and Ethnicity in an American Mining Town, 1875-1925* (Urbana: University of Illinois Press, 1989).

24. Peter Gottlieb, *Making Their Own Way: Southern Blacks' Migration to Pittsburgh, 1916-30* (Urbana: University of Illinois Press, 1987); Joe William Trotter Jr., *Black Milwaukee: The Making of an Industrial Proletariat, 1915-45* (Urbana: University of Illinois Press, 1985); James R. Grossman, *Land of Hope: Chicago, Black Southerners, and the Great Migration* (Chicago: University of Chicago Press, 1989).

25. "In the Youngest City in the World," *Domestic Engineering,* December 23, 1922.

26. Ralph F. Warner, "Industrial Housing in War Time," *Bankers* 96, no. 6 (June 1918): 703. Richard Childs suggests that English garden cities will prevent just such land speculation and lack of planning. Ten years earlier, *Bankers Monthly* told its readers that Gary was a good place for real estate investment. Richard S. Childs, "The New Garden Cities of England," *Outlook* (March 6, 1918); "Investment News and Notes," *Bankers Monthly* 80, no. 2 (February 1910): 270.

27. David Brody, *Labor in Crisis: The Steel Strike of 1919* (Philadelphia: J. B. Lippincott, 1965), 17–27, 48.

28. Ibid., 48–60.

29. Edward Newell Collection, box 1, folder 1, CRA 64, Calumet Regional Archives.

30. Barrett, "Americanization from the Bottom Up," 1006; Bodnar, *The Transplanted*.

31. On the invention of nationalism, see Benedict Anderson, *Imagined Communities: Reflections on the Origin and Spread of Nationalism* (New York: Knopf, 1983). On Progressivism and the patriotism of war, see Alan Dawley, *Changing the World: American Progressives in War and Revolution* (Princeton, N.J.: Princeton University Press, 2003). On ethnicity war and citizenship, see John Bodnar, *Remaking America: Public Memory, Commemoration, and Patriotism in the Twentieth Century* (Princeton, N.J.: Princeton University Press, 1992), and John Bodnar, ed., *Bonds of Affection: Americans Define Their Patriotism* (Princeton, N.J.: Princeton University Press, 1996).

4. "THE GIBRALTAR OF THE STEEL CORPORATION"

1. Edward Johanningsmeier, *Forging American Communism: The Life of William Z. Foster* (Princeton, N.J.: Princeton University Press, 1998); James R. Barrett, *William Z. Foster and the Tragedy of American Radicalism* (Urbana: University of Illinois Press, 1999); Elliot Gorn, *Mother Jones: The Most Dangerous Woman in America* (New York: Hill and Wang, 2002).

2. Brody, *Labor in Crisis*, 69–100.

3. *Chicago Daily News,* September 10–21, 1919.

4. *Chicago Daily News,* September 25–30, 1919.

5. *Chicago Daily News,* October 1–5, 1919.

6. In his study of newspaper coverage in Berlin, Peter Fritzsche describes the modern industrial city as "distinctive as much for the everyday experience of unfamiliarity and flux as for the infiltration of smokestacks and proletarians." Fritzsche, *Reading Berlin 1900,* 17.

7. Farge and Revel, *Vanishing Children of Paris,* 18; Fritzsche, *Reading Berlin,* 3.

8. See William M. Tuttle Jr., *Race Riot: Chicago in the Red Summer of 1919* (New York: Atheneum, 1970), and Allan H. Spear, *Black Chicago: The Making of a Negro Ghetto, 1890–1920* (Chicago: University of Chicago Press, 1967).

9. *New York Times,* October 5, 1919; *Times* (London), October 5, 1919.

10. *Indiana Daily Times* (Indianapolis), October 6, 7, 1919; *Chicago Tribune,* October 5, 1919.

11. *Daily Calumet* (Chicago), October 5, 1919.

12. *Chicago American,* October 5, 1919.

13. Tuttle, *Race Riot.*

14. Richard Wright, *Native Son* (New York: Harper and Bros., 1940), 230–33.

15. Mohl and Betten, *Steel City.* On the use of language to create definitions of class, see Gareth Stedman Jones, *Languages of Class: Studies in English Working-Class History, 1832–1982* (New York: Cambridge University Press, 1984); Gareth Stedman Jones, *Outcast London: A Study in the Relationship between Classes in Victorian Society* (New York: Penguin, 1976); Dror Wahrman, *Imagining the Middle Class: The Political Representations of Class in Britain, 1780–1840* (New York: Cambridge University Press, 1995).

16. Roediger, *Wages of Whiteness.*

5. "YOU'RE A DAMNED LIAR—IT'S UTOPIA"

1. John Erskine, "A Shelf of Recent Books," *Bookman: A Review of Books and Life,* April 1922, 192.

2. Lewis Mumford, "The City," in *Civilization in the United States: An Inquiry by Thirty Americans,* ed. Harold E. Stearns (New York: Harcourt Brace, 1922), 3–20.3. Carl Sandburg, "Mayor of Gary," in *Smoke and Steel* (1920; reprint, New York: Harcourt Brace Jovanovich, 1970), 161.

4. *Indianapolis Daily Tribune,* October 11, 1919.

5. "Steel's Old Policy," *Time,* February 4, 1924.

6. Mary Harris Jones, *The Autobiography of Mother Jones* (Chicago: C. H. Kerr, 1925), 216–17.

7. Ibid., 226–27.

8. "Independent National Convention," *Independent,* June 5, 1920.

9. Evan J. David, "Leonard Wood on Labor Problems," *Outlook* (February 25, 1920).

10. "On Platforms and Candidates," *Outlook* (May 12, 1920).

11. Edward Earle Purinton, "Master Workshops of America," *Independent,* December 18, 1920.

12. Charles R. Flint, "Industrial Consolidation," *North American Review* (June 1921).

13. "Royalty Rambles," *Time,* November 22, 1926.

14. Virginia B. Lee, "Destiny," *Overland Monthly and Out West Magazine* 84, no. 11 (November 1926).

15. "Fiat City," *Time,* June 15, 1931.

16. Charles Longnecker, "Steel's Greatest Achievement," *Blast Furnace and Steel Plant,* August 1937.

17. "Steel Story," *Time,* July 2, 1934.

18. "Out of the Crucible," *Time,* November 12, 1951.

19. Ibid.

20. *Independent,* May 9, 1925.

21. Arthur Shumway, "Gary, Shrine of the Steel God: The City That Has Everything, and at the Same Time Has Nothing," *American Parade,* January 3, 1929, 23–32.

22. As quoted in Lane, *Gary's First Hundred Years,* 89.

23. Staughton Lynd's writings on Gary, which came out of labor and oral history workshops he ran in Gary in the early 1970s, show up in several versions. Staughton Lynd, "The Possibility of Radicalism in the Early 1930's: The Case for Steel," *Radical America* 6, no. 6 (November–December 1972): 37–64; "Personal Histories of the Early CIO," ed. Lynd, *Radical America* 5, no. 3 (May/June 1971): 49–76; Lynd, "Guerilla History in Gary," *Liberation* 14, no. 7 (October 1969); Federal Writers' Project, Indiana, *Calumet Region Historical Guide* (Gary, Ind.: German Printing Co., 1939); "Life in the Calumet Region during the 1930s," *Steel Shavings* 17 (1988); Alice and Staughton Lynd, eds., *Rank and File: Personal Histories by Working-Class Organizers* (Boston: Beacon Press, 1973).

24. Karl Malden, *When Do I Start?* (New York: Simon and Schuster, 1997), 15, 16 .

25. Ibid., 21.

26. Ibid., 22.

27. *Gary Works Circle,* February 1917.

28. Malden, *When Do I Start?* 22.

29. Ibid., 23, 48.

30. This storyline is repeated, although less often, with other people from Gary such as football player Alex Karras and actor Avery Brooks. While both men cite Gary as a shaping influence on who they became, both narratives fit the mold of Zale's, Taliaferro's, and Malden's stories more than create a narrative of their own.

31. On Tony Zale, see James B. Lane, "The Man of Steel with a Heart of Gold," *Traces of Indiana and Midwestern History* 19 (Spring 2007): 17–25.

32. Shirley Povich, "This Morning," *Washington Post,* September 25, 1946, June 7, 1948.

33. Howard Roberts, "Hard-Luck Champion," *Saturday Evening Post,* July 5, 1947.

34. When the book was made into a film in 1956, Zale was supposed to play himself; however, actor Paul Newman expressed some concern about sparring with someone who, on instinct, could hit him very hard.

35. On Taliaferro's memories of his childhood in Gary, see Dawn Knight, *Taliaferro: Breaking Barriers from the NFL Draft to the Ivory Tower* (Bloomington: Indiana University Press, 2007), 3–20.

36. It is worth noting, of course, that Malden's experience with steel work was during the Depression while Taliaferro's was during the Second World War. There can be little doubt that Taliaferro had different assumptions about the ever-present availability of work than Malden.

37. Lynd, "Possibility of Radicalism in the Early 1930's."

38. Lane, *City of the Century,* 74, 163.

39. "Sanitation Program Followed at Gary," *Engineering News Record,* April 9, 1923; "Operating Features of the Gary, Indiana, Water Works," *Municipal and County Engineering,* April 1924; Ruth Sutliffe, "Gary—An Industrial City with a Fine Recreation System and Exceptional Park Buildings," *American City,* March 1929.

40. Raymond Grow, "De King Is Daid!" *American Mercury,* October 1939.

41. *Chicago Herald Examiner,* January 27, 1922.

42. *Outlook,* April 18, 1923.

43. These articles were summarized in "Gary's Bootlegging Administration," *Literary Digest,* April 21, 1923.

44. "American Tragedies," *Time,* January 12, 1931.

45. "Grapefruit in the Garden State," *Time,* May 11, 1953.

46. "The New Pictures," *Time,* May 28, 1951.

6. "GARY IS A STEEL TOWN, YOUNG, LUSTY, BRAWLING"

1. "The House I Live In," music and lyrics by Earl Robinson and Lewis Allen (New York: Chappell, 1942).

2. "As the Twig Is Bent," *Time,* Oct. 8, 1945.

3. "No Gain," *Time,* September 15, 1947.

4. J. D. Ratcliff, "It's Murder," *Saturday Evening Post,* January 28, 1948.

5. "The Abandoned County," *Time,* April 29, 1966.

6. "Gary: A Game of Pin the Blame," *Newsweek,* January 26, 1970, 38–39.

7. Seth King, "In Gary, Clean Air Means No Job," *New York Times,* December 14, 1971.

8. *Fort Lauderdale News and Sun-Sentinel*, October 3, 1971.

9. "Shutdown in Gary," *Time*, January 20, 1975.

10. Hurley, *Environmental Inequalities*.

11. These oral histories have been collected and published in a series entitled *Steel Shavings*.

12. Joan Younger, "Time for Another Murder," *Ladies' Home Journal*, December 1953.

13. WCC Bulletin, January 1950, Women's Citizens Committee, CRA 30, box 3, Calumet Regional Archives, Gary, Indiana.

14. "Gary Cleanup," *Newsweek*, March 21, 1949.

15. *Cincinnati Enquirer*, June 11, 1949; *Chicago Daily News*, March 8, 1949; *Chicago Sun-Times*, March 15, 1949; "Who Killed Mary Cheever?" *Time*, March 21, 1949.

16. "What Women Did in Gary," *Ladies' Home Journal*, October 1951; A. B. Hendry, "The Angry Housewives of Gary," *Coronet*, June 1951.

17. Bernard Spong, "How We Cleaned Up Gary," *Male*, February 1953.

18. Joan Younger, "Time for Another Murder," *Ladies' Home Journal*, December 1953.

19. G. Gordon Liddy, *Will: The Autobiography of G. Gordon Liddy* (New York: St. Martin's Press, 1980), 74–75.

20. Harry Waters, "Gary: A Game of Pin the Blame," *Newsweek*, January 26, 1970.

21. James O'Gara, "Big Steel, Little Town: The Recent Steel Settlement Has Not Settled Everything," *Commonwealth*, November 25, 1949.

22. Philip Roth, *I Married a Communist* (New York: Vintage, 1999), 225–26.

23. Liddy, *Will*, 74.

24. Ibid., 82.

25. "Jim Crow, Jr.," *Time*, October 10, 1927.

26. Langston Hughes, "My Adventures as a Social Poet," in *The Collected Work of Langston Hughes*, vol. 9, ed. Christopher De Santis (Columbia: University of Missouri Press, 2002), 277.

27. "Discretion on De Facto," *Time*, October 30, 1964.

28. "Plea from Gary," *Time*, September 15, 1967.

29. On the 1967 election and the role of race in Gary's politics, see Poinsett, *Black Power: Gary Style*; "Social Trends and Racial Tensions during the Nineteen Sixties," *Steel Shavings* 25 (1996); Catlin, *Racial Politics and Urban Planning*; Greer, *Big Steel*.

30. "Vote Power," *Time*, May 12, 1967.

31. "Real Black Power," *Time*, November 17, 1967; "Black Power & Black Pride," *Time*, December 1, 1967.

32. Marshall Frady, "Gary, Indiana: For God's Sake Let's Get Ourselves Together," *Harper's*, August 1969.

33. Richard Mercer Dorson, *Land of the Millrats* (Cambridge, Mass.: Harvard University Press, 1981), 11, 18, 24; "Race Relations in the Calumet Region during the 1960s," *Steel Shavings* 6 (1980). On white flight and urban segregation, see Arnold Richard Hirsch, *Making the Second Ghetto: Race and Housing in Chicago, 1940–1960* (New York: Cambridge University Press, 1983), and Sugrue, *Origins of the Urban Crisis*.

34. "Godfather in Gary," *Time*, November 13, 1972.

35. *Newsweek*, January 10, 1983.

36. Michael Jackson, *Moonwalk* (New York: Doubleday, 1988), 8–59.

37. On the rise of postmodernist culture in the early 1970s, see Andreas Killen, *1973 Nervous Breakdown: Watergate, Warhol, and the Birth of the Post-Sixties America* (New York: Bloomsbury, 2006).

38. Michael Eric Dyson, "Michael Jackson's Postmodern Spirituality," in *The Michael Eric Dyson Reader* (New York: Basic Books, 2004), 442–60.

7. "EPITAPH FOR A MODEL CITY"

1. Austin Wehrwein, "Democrats Hail Welsh's Victory," *New York Times*, May 7, 1964; John Pomfret, "Gary, Ind.: Supposed Center of Backlash Appears to Be Heavily for Johnson," *New York Times*, September 9, 1964.

2. Rowland Evans and Robert Novak, "Failure to Heed Gary Racial Tensions Could Shift Indiana to Republicans," *Washington Post*, January 17, 1968; Joseph Kraft, "County Tests Kennedy's Skill to Wed Ghetto and Backlash," *Washington Post*, May 2, 1968.

3. Jack Newfield, *Robert Kennedy: A Memoir* (New York: E. P. Dutton, 1969), 260.

4. Godfrey Hodgson and George Crile, "Gary: Epitaph for a Model City," *Washington Post*, March 4, 1973.

5. Evelyn Brooks Higginbotham, "African-American Women's History and the Metalanguage of Race," *Signs* 17, no. 2 (1992): 255.

6. Wolf Von Eckardt, "Steel Mill Blends with Dunes Area," *Washington Post*, January 9, 1966.

7. Joel Weisman, "Gary Mayor Hits Layoffs by U.S. Steel," *Washington Post*, December 31, 1974.

8. Joel Weisman, "Every Major City Problem Seems More Acute in Gary," *Washington Post*, December 2, 1974.

9. James O. Gibson and Geno Baroni, "Gary: Another View," *Washington Post*, March 18, 1973; Godfrey Hodgson and George Crile, "More on 'Gary: Epitaph for a Model City,'" *Washington Post*, March 25, 1973.

10. Oral interview with Dr. John Peoples, July 11, 1997, tape and transcript, Center for Oral History and Cultural Heritage, University of Southern Mississippi.

11. "Gary Turns Her Back on Bias," *Ebony* 11, no. 9 (July 1956).

12. Robert Jackson, interview with Richard Dorson; Wilbert Harlan, interview with Dorson; Dorson, *Land of the Millrats*. For an example of black migration to and accommodation with industrial cities, see John Bodnar, Roger Simon, and Michael P. Weber, *Lives of Their Own: Blacks, Italians, and Poles in Pittsburgh, 1900–1960* (Urbana: University of Illinois Press, 1982).

13. H. Rap Brown, *Die Nigger Die: A Political Autobiography* (New York: Last Gasp, 1969), 130.

14. Dorson, *Land of the Millrats*; "Tie-Dyes and Color Lines: Life in the Calumet Region during the 1970s," *Steel Shavings* 29 (1999); "Work Experiences in the Calumet Region," *Steel Shavings* 7 (1981).

15. Imamu Amiri Baraka, "Toward the Creation of Political Institutions for All African Peoples," in *Black World* (Boulder: Johnson, 1972), 54–78; Lloyd Barbee, "Let's Stay Together," *Black Panther* 8, no. 4 (April 15, 1972): 54.

16. David Sibeko, "Unity in All Oppressed Communities," *Black Panther* 8, no. 1 (March 25, 1972).

17. "A State of Black Unity in Gary, Indiana," *Black Panther* 7, no. 30 (March 18, 1972).

18. Baraka, "Toward the Creation of Political Institutions for All African Peoples," 64, 66.

19. Imamu Amiri Baraka, *Eulogies* (New York: Marsilio, 1996), 13.

20. Herbert H. Denton, "Gary: Odd Place for a Convention," *Washington Post,* March 11, 1972.

21. "Gary: The Largest and Most Modern Steel Works in Existence," *Scientific American* (December 11, 1909); "Gary, Pittsburg's Future Rival," *American Review of Reviews* 39 (February 1909); Casey, "The Sum of a Thousand Short Cuts"; John P. Hoerr, *And the Wolf Finally Came: The Decline of the American Steel Industry* (Pittsburgh: University of Pittsburgh Press, 1988); *Gary Post-Tribune,* April 30, 1980.

22. On the concept and chronology of deindustrialization, see Barry Bluestone and Bennett Harrison, *The Deindustrialization of America: Plant Closings, Community Abandonment, and the Dismantling of Basic Industry* (New York: Basic Books, 1982), 6–7.

23. *Chicago Tribune,* March 6, 1988; *Gary Post-Tribune,* January 1, 1985. For studies that challenge the timing of "deindustrialization," see Jefferson Cowie, *Capital Moves: RCA's Seventy-Year Quest for Cheap Labor* (Ithaca, N.Y.: Cornell University Press, 1999), and Sugrue, *Origins of the Urban Crisis.*

24. Glastris, "Steel's Hollow Comeback"; Hoerr, *And the Wolf Finally Came,* 39–48.

25. *Gary Post-Tribune,* June 5, 1986; Paul Glastris, "Steel's Hollow Comeback," *U.S. News & World Report,* May 8, 1989, 49–51; William E. Schmidt, "A Steel City Still Needs Help Despite Big Steel's Comeback," *New York Times,* September 4, 1989.

26. Matt O'Connor, "U.S. Steel, Now USX, Regroups," *Chicago Tribune,* July 9, 1986.

27. Hoerr, *And the Wolf Finally Came,* 427–46. On the steel industry and labor negotiations, see Judith Stein, *Running Steel, Running America: Race, Economic Policy, and the Decline of Liberalism* (Chapel Hill: University of North Carolina Press, 1998), and Jonathan D. Rosenblum, *Copper Crucible: How the Arizona Miners' Strike of 1983 Recast Labor-Management Relations in America* (Ithaca, N.Y.: ILR Press, 1998).

28. *Gary Post-Tribune,* September 20, 21, 1987.

29. Ibid.; "Life in the Calumet Region during the 1980s," *Steel Shavings* 21 (1992).

30. Schmidt, "A Steel City Still Needs Help"; *Gary Post-Tribune,* September 30, 1985, September 21, 1987.

31. *Chicago Tribune,* August 4, 1985.

32. *Chicago Tribune,* April 17, 1988.

33. *Gary Post-Tribune,* January 2, 8, 9, 1994, February 2, 1994.

CONCLUSION

1. Christopher Maag, "From the Ashes of '69, a River Reborn," *New York Times,* June 20, 2009.

2. Stein, *Running Steel, Running America.* See also David Harvey, *A Brief History of Neoliberalism* (New York: Oxford University Press, 2005).

3. For two very different studies of this kind of memory and urban imagery, see Sherry Lee Linkon and John Russo, *Steeltown U.S.A.: Work and Memory in Youngstown* (Lawrence: University of Kansas Press, 2002), and Steven High and David W. Lewis,

Corporate Wasteland: The Landscape and Memory of Deindustrialization (Ithaca, N.Y.: IRL Press, 2007). For new interpretations and chronologies of deindustrialization, see Cowie and Heathcott, eds., *Beyond the Ruins*.

4. Michael Moore, "Flint and Me," *Money*, July 1996, 86.

5. There is a great tension within academic studies of deindustrialization between the impulse to deny nostalgic visions of industrialism and the danger in dismissing workers' lost relationship with industrial work and work sites as merely nostalgia. For a discussion of this debate, see High, *Corporate Wasteland*, 94.

6. Warren Cohen, "Gary's New Beauties: Hoping for a Makeover," *U.S. News & World Report* (March 13, 2000): 27; *CNN World Today*, March 10, 2000; *ABC News*, March 13, 2002.

7. Remarks by Secretary Andrew Cuomo, April 28, 1999, National Press Club, Washington, D.C., Housing and Urban Development press release; speech by Secretary Andrew Cuomo, April 12, 1999, University of Witswatersrand, Johannesburg, South Africa, Housing and Urban Development press release.

8. Lane, *Gary's First Hundred Years*, 269.

Anderson, Benedict. *Imagined Communities: Reflections on the Origin and Spread of Nationalism.* New York: Knopf, 1983.

August, Garry Joel. "Gary—An Interpretation." *Gary Post Tribune* (Indiana Room, Gary Public Library).

Barrett, James R. "Americanization from the Bottom Up: Immigration and the Remaking of the American Working Class, 1880–1930." *Journal of American History* 79, no. 3 (December 1992): 996–1020.

———. *William Z. Foster and the Tragedy of American Radicalism.* Urbana: University of Illinois Press, 1999.

———. *Work and Community in the Jungle: Chicago's Packinghouse Workers, 1894–1922.* Urbana: University of Illinois Press, 1987.

Bender, Thomas, ed. *The University and the City from Medieval Origins to the Present.* New York: Oxford University Press, 1988.

Benjamin, Walter. "Paris: Capital of the Nineteenth Century." In *Metropolis: Center and Symbol of Our Times,* ed. Philip Kasinitz. New York: New York University Press, 1994.

Bluestone, Barry, and Bennett Harrison. *The Deindustrialization of America: Plant Closings, Community Abandonment, and the Dismantling of Basic Industry.* New York: Basic Books, 1982.

Bodnar, John. *Remaking America: Public Memory, Commemoration, and Patriotism in the Twentieth Century.* Princeton, N.J.: Princeton University Press, 1992.

———. *The Transplanted: A History of Immigrants in Urban America.* Bloomington: Indiana University Press, 1985.

———, ed. *Bonds of Affection: Americans Define Their Patriotism.* Princeton, N.J.: Princeton University Press, 1996.

Bodnar, John, Roger Simon, and Michael P. Weber. *Lives of Their Own: Blacks, Italians, and Poles in Pittsburgh, 1900–1960.* Urbana: University of Illinois Press, 1982.

Brody, David. *Labor in Crisis: The Steel Strike of 1919.* Philadelphia: J. B. Lippincott, 1965.

Buder, Stanley. *Pullman: An Experiment in Industrial Order and Community Planning, 1880–1930.* New York: Oxford University Press, 1967.

Buffington, Eugene J. "Making Cities for Workmen." *Harper's Weekly* 53 (May 8, 1909).

Burton, Charles Pierce. "Gary—A Creation," *Independent* 70 (February 16, 1911).

Casey, Daniel Vincent. "The Sum of a Thousand Short Cuts," *System* 15 (January 1909).

Catlin, Robert A. *Racial Politics and Urban Planning: Gary, Indiana, 1980–1989.* Lexington: University Press of Kentucky, 1993.

Cohen, Lizabeth. *A Consumers' Republic: The Politics of Mass Consumption in Postwar America.* New York: Knopf, 2003.

Cohen, Ronald D. *Children of the Mill: Schooling and Society in Gary, Indiana, 1906–1960.* Bloomington: Indiana University Press, 1990.

Cowie, Jefferson. *Capital Moves: RCA's Seventy-Year Quest for Cheap Labor.* Ithaca, N.Y.: Cornell University Press, 1999.

Cowie, Jefferson, and Joseph Heathcott, eds. *Beyond the Ruins: The Meanings of Deindustrialization.* Ithaca, N.Y.: ILR Press, 2003.

Crawford, Margaret. *Building the Workingman's Paradise: The Design of American Company Towns.* New York: Verso, 1995.

Crocker, Ruth Hutchinson. *Social Work and Social Order: The Settlement Movement in Two Industrial Cities, 1889–1930.* Urbana: University of Illinois Press, 1992.

Cronon, William. *Nature's Metropolis: Chicago and the Great West.* New York: W. W. Norton, 1991.

Davis, Mike. *City of Quartz: Excavating the Future in Los Angeles.* New York: Verso, 1990.

———. *Ecology of Fear: Los Angeles and the Imagination of Disaster.* New York: Metropolitan Books, 1998.

Davis, Natalie Zemon. *Fiction in the Archives: Pardon Tales and Their Tellers in Sixteenth-Century France.* Stanford, Calif.: Stanford University Press, 1987.

Dawley, Alan. *Changing the World: American Progressivism in War and Revolution.* Princeton, N.J.: Princeton University Press, 2003.

Denning, Michael. *Mechanic Accents: Dime Novels and Working-Class Culture in America.* New York: Verso, 1987.

Dorson, Richard Mercer. *Land of the Millrats.* Cambridge, Mass.: Harvard University Press, 1981.

Dublin, Thomas. *Women at Work: Transformation of Work and Community in Lowell, Massachusetts, 1826–1860.* New York: Columbia University Press, 1979.

Duis, Perry R. *The Saloon: Public Drinking in Chicago and Boston, 1880–1920.* Urbana: University of Illinois Press, 1983.

Dyson, Michael Eric. "Michael Jackson's Postmodern Spirituality." In *The Michael Eric Dyson Reader,* 442–60. New York: Basic Books, 2004.

Emmons, David. *The Butte Irish: Class and Ethnicity in an American Mining Town, 1875–1925.* Urbana: University of Illinois Press, 1989.

Farge, Arlette, and Jacques Revel. *The Vanishing Children of Paris: Rumor and Politics before the French Revolution.* Cambridge, Mass.: Harvard University Press, 1991.

Fritzsche, Peter. *Reading Berlin 1900.* Cambridge, Mass.: Harvard University Press, 1996.

Fuller, Henry. "An Industrial Utopia: Building Gary, Indiana, to Order." *Harper's Weekly* 51 (October 12, 1907).

Gilbert, James. *Perfect Cities: Chicago's Utopias of 1893.* Chicago: University of Chicago Press, 1993.

Gorn, Elliot. *Mother Jones: The Most Dangerous Woman in America.* New York: Hill and Wang, 2002.

Gottlieb, Peter. *Making Their Own Way: Southern Blacks' Migration to Pittsburgh, 1916–30.* Urbana: University of Illinois Press, 1987.

Greer, Edward. *Big Steel: Black Politics and Corporate Power in Gary, Indiana.* New York: Monthly Review Press, 1979.

Grossman, James. *Land of Hope: Chicago, Black Southerners, and the Great Migration.* Chicago: University of Chicago Press, 1989.

Harvey, David. *A Brief History of Neo-Liberalism.* New York: Oxford University Press, 2007.

———. *Consciousness and the Urban Experience.* Oxford: Blackwell, 1985.

———. *Urbanization of Capital.* Oxford: Blackwell, 1985.

High, Steven. *Corporate Wasteland: The Landscape and Memory of Deindustrialization.* Ithaca, N.Y.: Cornell University Press, 2008.

Hines, Thomas. *Burnham of Chicago: Architect and Planner.* New York: Oxford University Press, 1974.

Hirsch, Arnold Richard. *Making the Second Ghetto: Race and Housing in Chicago, 1940–1960.* New York: Cambridge University Press, 1983.

Hoerr, John P. *And the Wolf Finally Came: The Decline of the American Steel Industry.* Pittsburgh: University of Pittsburgh Press, 1988.

Hoganson, Kristin L. *Fighting for American Manhood: How Gender Politics Provoked the Spanish-American and Philippine-American Wars.* New Haven, Conn.: Yale University Press, 1998.

Hunt, Tristram. *Building Jerusalem: The Rise and Fall of the Victorian City.* New York: Metropolitan Books, 2005.

Hurley, Andrew. *Environmental Inequalities: Class, Race, and Industrial Pollution in Gary, Indiana, 1945–80.* Chapel Hill: University of North Carolina Press, 1995.

Johanningsmeier, Edward. *Forging American Communism: The Life of William Z. Foster.* Princeton, N.J.: Princeton University Press, 1998.

Jones, Gareth Stedman. *Languages of Class: Studies in English Working-Class History, 1832–1982.* New York: Cambridge University Press, 1984.

———. *Outcast London: A Study in the Relationship between Classes in Victorian Society.* New York: Penguin, 1976.

Jones, Mary Harris. *The Autobiography of Mother Jones.* Chicago: C. H. Kerr, 1925.

Jordan, David P. *Transforming Paris: The Life and Labors of Baron Haussmann.* Chicago: University of Chicago Press, 1996.

Kasson, John. *Civilizing the Machine: Technology and Republican Virtues in America, 1776–1900.* Toronto: Penguin Books, 1976.

———. *Houdini, Tarzan, and the Perfect Man: The White Male Body and the Challenge of Modernity in America.* New York: Hill & Wang, 2001.

Killen, Andreas. *1973 Nervous Breakdown: Watergate, Warhol, and the Birth of the Post-Sixties America.* New York: Bloomsbury, 2006.

Klein, Norman. *The History of Forgetting: Los Angeles and the Erasure of Memory.* New York: Verso, 1997.

Knight, Dawn. *Taliaferro: Breaking Barriers from the NFL Draft to the Ivory Tower.* Bloomington: Indiana University Press, 2007.

Krause, Paul. *The Battle for Homestead, 1880–1892: Politics, Culture, Steel.* Pittsburgh: University of Pittsburgh Press, 1992.

Lane, James B. *City of the Century: A History of Gary, Indiana.* Bloomington: Indiana University Press, 1978.

———. *Gary's First Hundred Years: A Centennial History of Gary, Indiana.* Valparaiso, Ind.: Home Mountain Printing, 2006.

Lane, James B., and Edward J. Escobar, eds. *Forging a Community: The Latino Experience in Northwest Indiana, 1919–1975.* Bloomington: Indiana University Press, 1987.

Lewis, James. *The Protestant Experience in Gary, Indiana, 1906–1975.* Knoxville: University of Tennessee Press, 1992.

Liddy, G. Gordon. *Will: The Autobiography of G. Gordon Liddy.* New York: St. Martin's Press, 1980.

Linkon, Sherry Lee, and John Russo. *Steeltown U.S.A.: Work and Memory in Youngstown.* Lawrence: University of Kansas Press, 2008.

Lynd, Alice, and Staughton Lynd, eds. *Rank and File: Personal Histories by Working-Class Organizers.* Boston: Beacon Press, 1973.

Lynd, Staughton. "The Possibility of Radicalism in the Early 1930's: The Case for Steel." *Radical America* 6, no. 6 (November–December 1972): 37–64.

McGerr, Michael. *A Fierce Discontent: The Rise and Fall of the Progressive Movement in America, 1870–1920.* New York: Free Press, 2003.

McShane, Stephen G., and Gary Wilk. *Steel Giants: Historic Images from the Calumet Regional Archives.* Bloomington: Indiana University Press, 2009.

Miller, Perry. *The Responsibility of Mind in a Civilization of Machines.* Amherst: University of Massachusetts Press, 1979: 202.

Mohl, Raymond A., and Neil Betten. *Steel City: Urban and Ethnic Patterns in Gary, Indiana, 1906–1950.* Teaneck: Holmes and Meier, 1986.

Montgomery, David. *Workers' Control in America: Studies in the History of Work, Technology, and Labor Struggles.* New York: Cambridge University Press, 1979.

Moore, Michael. "Flint and Me," *Money,* July 1996, 86.

Moore, Powell A. *The Calumet Region: Indiana's Last Frontier.* Indianapolis: Indiana Historical Bureau, 1959.

Mosher, Anne. *Capital's Utopia: Vandergrift, Pennsylvania, 1855–1916.* Baltimore: Johns Hopkins University Press, 2004.

Mumford, Lewis. "The City." In *Civilization in the United States,* ed. Harold E. Stearns, 3–20. New York: Harcourt Brace, 1922.

Nash, Gary B. *The Urban Crucible: The Northern Seaports and the Origins of the American Revolution.* Abridged ed. Cambridge, Mass.: Harvard University Press, 1986.

Oestreicher, Richard. *Solidarity and Fragmentation: Working People and Class Consciousness in Detroit, 1875–1900.* Urbana: University of Illinois Press, 1986.

Orsi, Robert. *Madonna of 115th Street: Faith and Community in Italian Harlem, 1880–1950.* New Haven, Conn.: Yale University Press, 1985.

Poinsett, Alex. *Black Power: Gary Style; The Making of Mayor Richard Gordon Hatcher.* Chicago: Johnson, 1970.

Roediger, David R. *The Wages of Whiteness: Race and the Making of the American Working Class.* New York: Verso, 1991.

Rosenblum, Jonathan D. *Copper Crucible: How the Arizona Miners' Strike of 1983 Recast Labor-Management Relations in America.* Ithaca, N.Y.: ILR Press, 1998.

Rosenzweig, Roy. *Eight Hours for What We Will: Workers and Leisure in an Industrial City, 1870–1920.* New York: Cambridge University Press, 1983.

Roth, Philip. *I Married a Communist.* New York: Vintage, 1999.

Ryan, Mary P. *Civic Wars: Democracy and Public Life in the American City during the Nineteenth Century.* Berkeley: University of California Press, 1997.

Schneirov, Richard. *Labor and Urban Politics: Class Conflict and the Origins of Modern Liberalism in Chicago, 1864–97.* Urbana: University of Illinois Press, 1998.

Schneirov, Richard, Shelton Stromquist, and Nick Salvatore, eds. *The Pullman Strike and the Crisis of the 1890s: Essays on Labor and Politics.* Urbana: University of Illinois Press, 1999.

Self, Robert O. *American Babylon: Race and the Struggle for Postwar Oakland.* Princeton, N.J.: Princeton University Press, 2005.

Shackleton, Robert. *The Book of Chicago.* Philadelphia: Penn, 1920.

Short, John R. *Representing the Republic: Mapping the United States, 1600–1900.* London: Reaktion, 2001.

Slotkin, Richard. *The Fatal Environment: The Myth of the Frontier in the Age of Industrialization, 1800–1890.* Norman: University of Oklahoma Press, 1998.

———. *Gunfighter Nation: The Myth of the Frontier in Twentieth-Century America.* New York: HarperCollins, 1993.

Smith, Carl. *The Plan of Chicago: Daniel Burnham and the Remaking of the American City.* Chicago: University of Chicago Press, 2006.

———. *Urban Disorder and the Shape of Belief: The Great Chicago Fire, the Haymarket Bomb, and the Model Town of Pullman.* Chicago: University of Chicago Press, 1993.

Soja, Edward. *The City: Los Angeles and Urban Theory.* Berkeley: University of California Press, 1996.

Spear, Allan H. *Black Chicago: The Making of a Negro Ghetto, 1890–1920.* Chicago: University of Chicago Press, 1967.

Spears, Timothy B. *Chicago Dreaming: Midwesterners and the City, 1871–1919.* Chicago: University of Chicago Press, 2005.

Stansell, Christine. *City of Women: Sex and Class in New York, 1789–1860.* New York: Knopf, 1986.

Stein, Judith. *Running Steel, Running America: Race, Economic Policy, and the Decline of Liberalism.* Chapel Hill: University of North Carolina Press, 1998.

Stott, Richard. *Workers in the Metropolis: Class, Ethnicity, and Youth in Antebellum New York.* Ithaca, N.Y.: Cornell University Press, 1990.

Sugrue, Thomas. *The Origins of the Urban Crisis: Race and Inequality in Postwar Detroit.* Princeton, N.J.: Princeton University Press, 1996.

Srebnick, Amy Gilman. *The Mysterious Death of Mary Rogers: Sex and Culture in Nineteenth-Century New York.* New York: Oxford University Press, 1995.

Taylor, Graham Romeyn. "Creating the Newest Steel City," *Survey* 22 (April 1909).

———. *Satellite Cities: A Study of Industrial Suburbs.* New York: D. Appleton, 1915.

———. "Satellite Cities: Gary." *Survey* 29 (March 1, 1913).

———. "Satellite Cities: Pullman." *Survey* 29 (November 2, 1912): 117–31.

Trotter, Joe William, Jr. *Black Milwaukee: The Making of an Industrial Proletariat, 1915–45.* Urbana: University of Illinois Press, 1985.

Tuttle, William M., Jr. *Race Riot: Chicago in the Red Summer of 1919.* New York: Atheneum, 1970.

Wahrman, Dror. *Imagining the Middle Class: The Political Representations of Class in Britain, 1780–1840.* New York: Cambridge University Press, 1995.

Walkowitz, Judith. *City of Dreadful Delight: Narratives of Sexual Danger in Late Victorian London*. Chicago: University of Chicago Press, 1992.

Wallace, A. F. C. *Rockdale: The Growth of an American Village in the Early Industrial Revolution*. New York: Knopf, 1978.

Warner, Sam Bass. *The Urban Wilderness: A History of the American City*. New York: Harper and Row, 1972.

Warren, Kenneth. *Triumphant Capitalism: Henry Clay Frick and the Industrial Transformation of America*. Pittsburgh: University of Pittsburgh Press, 2000.

White, Hayden. *Tropics of Discourse: Essays in Cultural Criticism*. Baltimore: Johns Hopkins University Press, 1978.

Williams, Jerry, and Robert Lewis, eds. *Early Images of the Americas: Transfer and Invention*. Tucson: University of Arizona Press, 1993.

s. paul o'hara is Assistant Professor of History at Xavier University in Cincinnati, Ohio.